Dear Purnima and

with best wishes!

Swami Mukunda

Prema Rasa Siddhānta

(Philosophy of Divine Love)

Written by:

Śhrīmatpadavākyapramāṇapārāvārīṇa,

Vedamārgapratiṣhṭhāpanāchārya, Nikhiladarśhanasamanvayāchārya,

Sanātanavaidikadharmapratiṣhṭhāpanasatsampradāyaparamāchārya,

Bhaktiyogarasāvatāra, Bhagavadanantaśhrīvibhūṣhita

JAGADGURU 1008

SWAMI SHRI KRIPALU JI MAHARAJ

Translated by

Dr. Bageeshwari Devi

Jagadguru Kripalu Parishat

ISBN: 978-93-80661-69-8

First Edition: 1987
Fifth Edition: 15 July 2011

Published by:
Radha Govind Samiti
Golok Dham
H.A.F.(B) Part-1, Sector-10, Dwarka,
New Delhi-110075 • Phone 011-25081088
E-mail: rgs108del@yahoo.com

राधे

जगद्गुरु-आदेश

श्रीकृष्ण का माधुर्य-भाव युक्त निष्काम प्रेम प्राप्त कर, उन की नित्य सेवा ही तुम्हारा लक्ष्य है।

वह दिव्य निष्काम प्रेम, गुरुकृपा द्वारा अंतःकरण-शुद्धि होने पर ही प्राप्त होगा।

वह अंतःकरण शुद्धि, गुरु द्वारा निर्दिष्ट साधना द्वारा ही संभव है।

साधना - श्रीराधाकृष्ण का रूपध्यान करते हुये (स्वेच्छा से बनाये हुये रूप में दिव्य-भावना रखना है) रो कर उनके नाम गुण लीलादि का संकीर्तन करो।

सदा श्रीकृष्ण को अपने साथ ही मानो।

मोक्ष पर्यंत की कामना छोड़ कर, केवल दिव्य शुद्ध प्रेम की कामना से ही प्रेम करो।

"वे ही मेरे हैं" इस भावना को निरंतर दृढ़ करो, एवं श्यामिलन की परम व्याकुलता पैदा करो।

परदोष दर्शनादि कुसंगों से बचो।

मानव देह का प्रत्येक क्षण अमूल्य मानो।

— मैं सदा तुम्हारा सहायक हूँ —

तुम्हारा
कृपालु

राधे राधे गोविंद गोविंद राधे। राधे राधे गोविंद गोविंद राधे॥

Jagadguru Ādeśha

Your ultimate goal is the attainment of Divine Love of
Śhrī Kṛiṣhṇa and His Eternal Service.
This Divine Love can be attained only through the Grace of your Guru.
The Grace of your Guru will be attained upon complete purification of the heart.
The purification of the heart is only possible through devotional practice as instructed by your Guru.

Sādhanā

Shed tears of longing for the Divine Vision and Divine Love of Śhrī Rādhā Kṛiṣhṇa, singing the glories of their Names, Qualities, Pastimes, etc. along with rupadhyāna (mental visualization of the Divine Forms of Śhrī Rādhā Kṛiṣhṇa). You are free to choose any form but whatever form you meditate on you must feel that it is Divine.
Always feel the presence of Lord Kṛiṣhṇa with you.
Abandon all desires upto the desire for liberation. Practice devotion only with the desire of attaining Selfless Divine Love.
Develop a strong faith that Śhrī Kṛiṣhṇa alone is mine and intensify your yearning for Him.
Avoid spiritual transgressions such as fault finding, etc. Consider each moment of this human life as invaluable.

I will always be there to guide you.

Your's
Kripalu

राधे राधे गोविंद गोविंद राधे। राधे राधे गोविंद गोविंद राधे॥

Preface

Every living being desires and seeks happiness. What is true happiness and how can it be attained? Unless we have the right answers to these most vital questions, we will never attain true happiness. There have been many authorities on Hinduism who have written various books, based upon their experiences, which largely appear to contradict each other. Reading these texts, a reader cannot arrive at any decisive conclusion and in fact, can become even more confused than he was before. The remarkability of ***'Prema Rasa Siddhānta'*** *is that it reconciles all these contradictory philosophies with such simplicity, clarity and perfection that the profoundest spiritual wisdom becomes accessible even to a layman.*

Besides, quoting from the Vedas and other scriptures, Jagadguru Shri Kripalu Ji Maharaj has used practical everyday examples, in order to benefit people from all walks of life. The ease with which his directions are applicable to daily life is amazing.

Knowledge of the Divine science is limitless; yet, in this little book, Shri Maharaj Ji has revealed the subtlest aspects of subjects such as the Aim of Human Life, the Nature of God, the Soul and the World; Divine Grace; the Secret of Descension, etc., with such simplicity that even the most ordinary person can understand them. It easily dispels all doubts that could possibly arise in the minds of spiritual aspirants. His lucid exposition of the Impersonal and Personal aspects of God, and the Mystery of Descension is most unique, He has laid special emphasis upon the science of Karma Yoga, because every individual soul has to pursue his goal of attaining Divine Bliss whilst performing all his worldly duties.

In truth, I feel totally incompetent to give appropriate comments on the magnitude and profoundity of **'Prema Rasa Siddhānta'** *This book is like a vast ocean filled in a little pot.*

There was a great demand for a translation of **'Prema Rasa Siddhānta'** *in English. Translating any book on Hindu Philosophy into a foreign language is a demanding task. This translation is totally an outcome of Shri Maharaj Ji's Grace.*

I hope that it will serve as an unfailing source of inspiration, guidance and strength to spiritual aspirants all over the world.

Dr. Bageeshwari Devi

Priceless Treasure

1. *Śhrī Kṛiṣhṇa and Bliss are synonymous words. Every person in the world desires only Bliss. In other words he is a servant of Bliss and therefore unknowingly, a servant of Śhrī Kṛiṣhṇa.*

2. *Śhrī Kṛiṣhṇa (Divine Bliss) can be attained only through Bhaktiyoga, which is popularly known as Navadha Bhakti, the nine forms of devotional practice.*

3. *It is only by devotional practice that the heart becomes pure and then one can attain Divine Love of Śhrī Kṛiṣhṇa.*

4. *It is impossible to attain the divine qualities such as truth, non-violence, etc. without the purification of heart.*

5. *Every devotional practice is related only to the mind. Any spiritual discipline practised merely with the senses is not spiritual discipline at all.*

6. *The consequences of love and hatred in the material world are the same; therefore, true detachment can be attained only by being neutral.*

7. *The perfection of spiritual life is to perceive Śhrī Kṛiṣhṇa in all objects of the world - animate as well as inanimate.*

8. *Although human body is invaluable, yet it is transient. Therefore to procrastinate in devotional practice even for a moment is the greatest loss.*

9. *To see faults in others is the surest proof that we possess faults our -selves.*

10. *Spiritual practice is possible only under the guidance of a True Saint or Master.*

Guide to Hindi Pronounciation

अ	a	as *u* in b*u*t
आ	ā	as *a* in f*a*r
इ	i	as *i* in p*i*n
ई	ī	as *i* in mach*i*ne
उ	u	as *u* in p*u*sh
ऊ	ū	as *u* in *u*nion
ए	e	as *a* in *e*vade'
ऐ	ai	as *a* in mat; sometimes as *ai* in *ai*sle with the only difference that a should be pronounced as *u* in b*u*t, not as *a* in f*a*r.
ओ	o	as *o* in g*o*
औ	au	as o in pot, or as aw in saw
ऋ	ṛi	s *r* in Kṛishṇa
:	ḥ	which is a strong aspirate also lengthens the preceding vowel and occurs only at the end of a word. It is pronounced as a final *h* sound
.	ṁ	nasalizes and lengthens the preceding vowel and is prounounced as *n* in the French word bon.
क	ka	as *k* in kite
ख	kha	as *kha* in eckhart
ग	ga	as *g* in goat
घ	gha	as *gh* in dig hard
ङ	ṅa	as *n* in finger
च	cha	as *ch* in channel
छ	chha	as *chh* in staunch heart

ज	ja	as *j* in jar
झ	jha	as *dgeh* in hedgehog
ञ	ña	as *n* in lunch
ट	ṭa	as *t* in tub
ठ	ṭha	as *th* in hothead
ड	ḍa	as *d* in divine
ढ	ḍha	as *dh* in redhead
ण	ṇa	as *n* in burnt
त	ta	as *t* in French matron
थ	tha	as *th* in ether
द	da	as *th* in either
ध	dha	as *dh* in buddha
न	na	as *n* in no
प	pa	as *p* in pink
फ	pha	as *ph* in uphill
ब	ba	as *b* in boy
भ	bha	as *bh* in abhor
म	ma	as *m* in man
य	ya	as *y* in yes
र	ra	as *r* in remember
ल	la	as *l* in light
व	va	as *v* in vine, as w in swan
श	śha	as *sh* in shape
स	sa	as *s* in sin
ष	ṣha	as *sh* in show
ह	ha	as *h* in hut
क्ष	kṣha	as in freak show
ज्ञ	jña	as in big young
ड़	ṛa	
ढ़	ṛha	

There is no sign in English to represent the sounds ड़ and ढ़ they have been written as ṛa and ṛha, but the tip of the tongue quickly flaps down.

Contents

The Ultimate Goal of All Living Beings

It is a universally experienced and acknowledged fact that every action of every individual soul is performed with a definite aim. No action is performed without an aim. The *Darśhana Śhāstra* declares,

prayojanamanuddiśhya mando'pi na pravartate

"Even the most foolish person does not perform any action without an aim." Therefore, it seems natural to conclude that there would be various purposes behind different actions, but this is not so. Even though actions can be multifarious, the purpose behind all of them is one. This statement may appear to be strange and unbelievable, but given some thought, this is straightforward and obvious. However, some people claim that there are also actions which are performed without any aim,

khala binu svāratha para apakārī, je binu kāja dāhine bāṁye

(Rāmāyaṇa)

"The wicked cause harm to others without any valid reason." Similarly,

para upakāra vachana mana kāyā,
santa sahaja subhāva khagarāyā
bhūrja tarū sama santa kṛipālā,
parahita saha nita vipati visālā

(Rāmāyaṇa)

"The Saints do good to others without any personal motive." In the same way, the All-Powerful Supreme Lord is causelessly merciful to all. Thus it appears that all three - the wicked, the Saints and God, perform actions without any purpose. But, this is not so. There is definitely some purpose behind the actions of these three.

jo kāhū kī dekahiṁ vipatī, sukhī hohiṁ mānahu jaga nṛipatī

(Rāmāyaṇa)

"A wicked person is pleased when he sees others in distress." This is his hidden motive. In the same way, both God and the Saints grieve on perceiving the sufferings of others and rejoice on seeing others happy.

para dukha dukha, sukha sukha dekhe para

(Rāmāyaṇa)

So, God and the Saints perform actions for the welfare of others, because it makes them happy. So we see that causing distress to others makes an evil person happy and performing actions for the welfare of others makes God and Saints happy. This proves that the aim behind all actions is the attainment of happiness.

In brief, it could be said that a wicked person performs actions which cause harm to others for the momentary pleasure he derives from it, and the Saints and God, who are ever blissful, also derive pleasure by giving joy to others. Therefore, the ultimate aim of all three is happiness.

Let us now reflect upon other living beings, besides these three. Every living being in the universe performs actions only for the attainment of happiness. One might object, saying that practical experience shows that there are other goals like attaining wealth, having children, friends and so on, for which actions are performed. But, in fact only that unknown 'Bliss' is being sought through these goals. This fact is stated by Veda Vyāsa in the *Bhāgavatam*,

sarveṣhāmapi bhūtānām̐ nṛipasvātmaiva vallabhaḥ
itare' patyavittādyāstadvullabhatayaiva hi

(Bhāg. 10.14.50)

Some people claim that philosophers have accepted five aims of life - immortality, knowledge, independence, desire to control others and happiness. How then can it be proved that the attainment of happiness is the only aim of every living being? But here it should be noted that other goals such as eternal life, knowledge and so on are only for the sake of attaining happiness. We can thus conclude that every living being in the world - whether he be an ordinary person, a wicked man, a Saint or even God - is solely motivated by the aim of happiness in all his actions. However, if the path to attain happiness is right, one attains true happiness and if the path is wrong, one attains illusory happiness i.e. misery.

Now let us seriously reflect upon this goal of attainment of happiness. When there is so much diversity and variegatedness in the world, then why is it that everyone, from the ignorant to the all-knowing, is seeking only happiness even though nobody has been taught to do so? There must definitely be some secret science behind this. Yes, there is. The secret is,

ānando brahmeti vyajānāt, ānandāddhyeva khalvimāni bhūtāni jāyante, ānandena jātāni jīvanti, ānandaṁ prayantyabhisaṁviśhantīti

(Taitti. Up. 3.6)

According to this Vedic hymn, *Brahman*, God is Bliss Personified.

ānanda evādhastāt ānanda upariṣhṭāt, ānandaḥ purastāt ānandaḥ paśhchāt, ānanda uttarataḥ, ānando dakṣhiṇataḥ ānanda evedaṁ' sarvam

"There is nothing but Bliss below Him, above Him, to His East, to His West, to His North, to His South, outside of Him and within Him. Bliss and only Bliss overflows all around."

Now, this is with reference to the Supreme Personality, God. What about the aim of the individual soul that is being referred to here? According to the *Gītā*,

mamaivāṁśho jīvaloke jīvabhūtaḥ sanātanaḥ

(Gītā 15.7)

"Every individual soul is an eternal part of God."

God is Bliss Personified; therefore, being a part of Him, every individual soul naturally seeks Bliss. In fact, no living being can deviate from this goal of 'attainment of Bliss', even if he were to endeavour to do so for countless ages.

Some philosophers have interpreted this goal of 'attainment of Bliss' as complete freedom from suffering. For instance, the *Saṁkhya Darśhana* states,

duḥkhatrayābhighātāt jijñāsā tadabhighātake hetau

"Freedom from material afflictions is the ultimate aim of the individual soul." These afflictions are of three kinds,

1. *Ādhyatmika* or personal affliction is of two kinds. One is physical suffering, caused by illnesses such as fever, dysentery, etc. The second is mental suffering, caused by lust, anger, greed and so on.

2. *Ādhibhautika* are afflictions caused by other living beings such as humans, animals, trees, plants and so on.

3. *Ādhidaivika* are miseries caused by supernatural agencies such as heat, cold, rain and so on.

The *Sāṁkhya Darśhana* further states,

kutrāpi ko'pi sukhī tadapi duḥkhaśhabalamiti
duḥkha pakṣhe niḥkṣhipante vivechakāḥ

"There is no true happiness in the material world. If happiness is perceived anywhere, it is only an illusion, because worldly pleasures are momentary, limited and eventually result in sorrow."

In fact, this goal of freedom from suffering implies the attainment of Bliss. Besides this, every living being, without having been taught to do so, naturally loves divine qualities, such as truth, non-violence, peace, forgiveness, kindness and so on. You might object that there are just a handful of people - the Saints, who love these divine qualities; but this view is naive. Even the most foolish person, after innumerable lifetimes of effort will not be able to eradicate his innate nature to love and appreciate divine qualities and instead love falsehood, theft, immorality and so on.

You can understand this by a simple example. If a thief says that he approves of theft, then steal some precious possession of his and observe his reaction. Does he object to it or not? If he does object, why does he do so? If theft is truly approved of by him, why does he feel unhappy when he is robbed? Why does a liar feel upset when he is lied to? If you hurt someone who enjoys hurting others, why does he get upset? This proves that everyone loves divine qualities. The science behind this, is that every soul is a part of God and so has a natural love for divine qualities. Thus, besides the goal of happiness, every soul also aims to attain divine qualities.

Now let us consider whether there can possibly be a living being who desires neither happiness nor misery, and thus performs no actions. According to the *Gītā,* this is impossible,

na hi kaśhchit kṣhaṇamapi jātu tiṣhṭhatyakarmakṛit

(*Gītā* 3.5)

"No soul can remain inactive even for a moment." It is the inherent nature of every individual to constantly perform actions with the aim of attaining happiness. He will not cease to work until he attains Supreme Bliss.

From this we can conclude that every soul desires only Bliss and is constantly making an effort for its attainment. Now let us find out since when this endeavour has been going on.

According to the *Vedas,*

jñājñau dvāvajāvīśhanīśhāvajā hyekā bhoktṛibhogyārthayuktā
anantaśhchātmā viśhvarūpo hyakartā trayaṁ yadā vindate brahmametat

(*Śhvetā. Up.* 1.9)

"Every soul is eternal, without a beginning."

mamaivāṁśho jīvaloke jīvabhūtaḥ sanātanaḥ

(*Gīta* 15.7)

This verse of the *Gītā* also states that the soul is eternal. If someone asks you, "Since when have you existed?" the straightforward reply is, "Ever since God existed." And if you are asked, "How long has God existed?" the reply is, "Ever since I have." And if you are asked, "Since when have you and God existed?" the straightforward answer will be, "Since the time when even 'when' did not exist." This means that 'time' came into existence after God and us, and as such cannot be used as a frame of reference to determine our beginning. That is to say, we are all eternal.

There is one more point worth considering,

nāsato vidyate bhāvo nābhāvo vidyate sataḥ
ubhayorapi dṛiṣhṭo'ntastvanayostattvadarśhibhiḥ

(*Gītā* 2.16)

According to this verse of the *Gītā*, any existing entity cannot cease to be. In other words, if one exists today, one would have always existed. If one does not exist today, one could never have existed in the past.

na jāyate mriyate vā kadāchinnāyaṁ bhūtvā bhavitā vā na bhūyaḥ
ajo nityaḥ śhāśhvato'yaṁ purāṇo na hanyate hanyamāne śharīre

(*Gītā* 2.20)

"All individual souls are eternal, immortal and unborn."

So, it has been proved that we have been striving every moment since time immemorial to attain Bliss and will continue to do so. Now the astonishing fact is that, in spite of our continuous efforts of countless lifetimes, we have not as yet attained this Bliss. What is the reason for this? The fact is that we have not yet understood or made a firm decision as to what Bliss is, where it is to be found and how it is to be attained? Now let us reflect on what Bliss is. According to the *Vedas*,

yo vai bhūmā tatsukhaṁ nālpe sukhamasti bhūmā tveva vijijñāsitavyaḥ

(*Chhān. Up.* 7.23.1)

Bliss is always infinite in nature. It is never limited, because attainment of Bliss itself implies that it can never be overcome by suffering and there should be no other pleasure greater than it. Just as light can never be overpowered by darkness, the person who has attained Bliss can never be overcome by sorrow.

Let us now contemplate, where such everlasting and unlimited Bliss can be found. This question itself is a profound one. There have been innumerable contrary viewpoints on this subject since eternity. However, there is no reason to give up hope. It will be conclusively resolved right now.

We can divide all the prevalent theories for the attainment of Bliss into two categories. One is the materialistic viewpoint and the other, the spiritual one. If we thoroughly understand these two, then this controversy will be resolved indisputably.

Let us first consider materialism. The materialists hold the view that the creation, sustenance and destruction of the universe are all mechanical processes governed by natural laws. There is no entity named God. He is merely a product of a weak, degenerate mind. It is man who has fabricated a being called God. God has not made man. To bring God into the picture is an indication of insanity. The world has come into existence from the four elements: earth, water, fire and air.

These materialists further assert that every individual desires happiness. This happiness is attained only when the individual acquires the cherished objects of his every desire. Happiness will not be attained if these objects of desire are not acquired. This is a self-experienced fact.

However, the materialists are unable to prove whether these desires are fulfilled forever once we acquire the desired objects, or whether the desires recur. If the desires multiply, then striving to fulfil thẹm is as ridiculous as adding fuel to fire to extinguish it. If the materialists claim that fulfilment of desires leads to happiness, then I challenge their claim with my own experience of the truth. The happiness that is experienced upon the fulfilment of any desire is only transitory. It is immediately replaced by another stronger desire. Thus, there is no end to fulfilment of desires through acquisition of material things. Is there any individual in the history of materialists who has declared that such and such a person, after receiving a material thing, was completely satisfied forever? This is impossible, because desire is an ever-increasing disease.

A person suffering from scabies experiences temporary relief by scratching, but this scratching only makes it worse later. In the same way, the happiness which is experienced upon the attainment of desired objects is temporary and limited. Very soon the desire reappears in an even more formidable form. Whenever desires for material objects are fulfilled, the inevitable result is greed for more and if the desires are unfulfilled, the result is anger.

jyoṁ pratilābha lobha adhikāyī

(Rāmāyaṇa)

Thus misery follows with the advent of desire. No materialist can escape this inevitable consequence of material desire. Veda Vyāsa states,

yatpṛithivyāṁ vrīhi yavaṁ hiraṇyaṁ paśhavaḥ striyaḥ
na duhyanti manaḥ prītiṁ puṁsaḥ kāmahatasya te

(Bhāg. 9.19.13)

"If all the objects of the universe were available to one man, the disease of desire would nevertheless keep on increasing." Therefore, it is ridiculous to aim for satisfaction of desires through ordinary material things.

The materialists claim that they have made great progress in material science. "All routes by land, water and air are available to us now. We can go wherever we like by any route. We have created powerful hydrogen and atom bombs. Things that were considered impossible to attain, are now easily available. People were formerly barbaric, but are now civilized. Afflictions and diseases of the body have been controlled to a great extent as compared to the past." All these facts are absolutely true and we are willing to accept things even beyond this. But, can the materialist answer some simple questions - "Is there even a glimpse of inner peace and happiness to be found anywhere as a result of all this progress? Has there been any progress in values such as truth, non-violence and humanity? From the individual to the nation as a whole, can a glimpse of inner peace be found anywhere?" If not, then should not this so-called progress be labelled as mere deception? The decline of peace and happiness as a result of material progress can be seen everywhere. No expert is ready to guarantee that in future the world will not be a victim of the present materialistic progress. When materialistic progress can cause the destruction of the materialist himself, then the dream of attaining peace and happiness through materialism is an illusion.

It can be concluded from these facts that materialistic progress cannot purify the inner-self and without this, any hope of attaining peace and happiness is absolute madness.

Therefore, mere progress in materialism cannot bring about inner peace and happiness. If a madman is made to stay in a mansion having all the modern facilities, he will cause harm both to the building and to himself. Similarly, when the mind is not pure, materialism is bound to be used for destructive ends. Peace or happiness is experienced internally and cannot be attained by any external endeavour. Therefore, the goal of satisfying desires through material objects is totally wrong. However, material science is fully acceptable for the maintenance of the physical body.

Let us now consider the spiritual viewpoint. The *Vedas* declare,

raso vai saḥ, rasaṁ'hyevāyaṁ labdhvā''nandī bhavati

(Taitti. Up. 2.7)

"God alone is Bliss. It is only by attaining Him, that the individual soul can become blissful."

tameva viditvāti mṛityumeti nānyaḥ panthā vidyate'yanāya

(Śhvetā. Up. 3.8, 6.15)

"Only by knowing Him can the individual soul overcome material afflictions. There is no other way."

Now the question arises - Is there an entity called God, and should we accept that He exists merely because the scriptures say so, or is there any concrete proof of His existence? The empiricists do not accept anything unless it can be directly perceived. They say that they cannot accept anything on blind faith. Here, we come to a disagreement between the theist and the empiricist, which needs to be resolved.

Now, just ask the empiricist, "Have you seen your actual 'self'?" The answer will be, "No." This is because the soul is a subtle entity and can only be perceived by God-realized souls. In that case, what does the empiricist accept himself to be? Now ask him, "Have you seen your intellect and mind?" The answer again will be a definite, "No." It is impossible for ordinary men to see the mind and intellect, because they are subtle. "Okay, Mr. Empiricist, can you attain knowledge of just the letter 'A' through mere perception?" Even this is impossible, because we can neither recognize letters nor know their pronunciation unless we blindly accept the rules of the language they belong. This means that the empiricist cannot gain knowledge of even a single letter of the alphabet by direct perception. Again ask him, "Can you prove who your father is through direct perception?" The answer will be, "No." The reason is that, he was not even born at the time of his conception. "So if you can neither prove who you are, nor who your father is, or even directly perceive the existence of your mind or intellect, then what kind of empiricist are you?" Further ask him, "Can your senses perceive the subtle sensory powers of the sense organs?" "No!" "Then how do you wish to establish everything through perceptual evidence?" Again ask, "When you first saw a new country, you had no direct evidence about it prior to that. Then why did you make an effort to go there, believing that it existed? Do you scientifically examine the food you eat, the water you drink and the air you breathe, before using it? Can all the nations of the world be ruled simply by direct sensory evidence?[1] Do you disbelieve the existence of everything unless you directly perceive it? If so, then in my opinion you must first undergo mental treatment before you become an empiricist or the proponent of any other philosophy."

The second form of evidence is 'inferential' evidence. Although God is not a subject of inference, His existence can be established to a certain extent by this means of evidence. For instance,

1. Observing the orderly appearance of the universe, it can be inferred that such an order is possible only under some rule, and that ruler can only be God, because man has proven to be incapable of understanding even the mere organization of the universe.

2. The sun, moon and stars cannot be created even by the greatest scientists. Creation of a planet is a far cry from this,

---

[1] A president in governing a nation uses written reports that come to him. He simply believes the content of report that is submitted to him, since he cannot possibly have direct evidence of everything that is happening in the country.

when it has not been possible to acquire even preliminary knowledge about the surfaces of these celestial bodies!

3. The movements of the sun, moon, etc. are regulated by some definite laws whose controller must be some All-Powerful God.

4. The world is suspended in space. The effort involved in supporting the earth and other planets must be due to God.[2]

5. The laws existing in creation must have some lawmaker. That lawmaker must also be all-knowing in order to implement and enforce these laws.[3]

Any work in the world is possible only when the equipment, doer, knowledge, desire, effort and action are all combined. All these are also essential in the creation of such an extraordinary world, and this is possible only through God. If someone says, "I believe that all the above powers are present in nature," then this word 'nature' proves to be synonymous with God. In such a case, there is no controversy at all. Just as we say, *"Kṛiṣhṇāya namaḥ" Lord Kṛiṣhṇā, I bow to you, "Vāsudevāya namaḥ" Vāsudeva,*

---

[2] According to *Vaiśheṣhika Darśhana*, if a bird holds a piece of bread in its mouth, it does not fall. Subsequently, if the bird leaves it, the bread will fall down, for it cannot be upheld in the sky without a basis. Similarly, anything that is upheld must have a basis.

[3] This is an argument given in *Nyāya Darśhana* which states that in the world we see that one man puts in a lot of efforts and gets little results, while another man puts in little efforts and gets great results. This indicates that there is a law of *karmika* reaction that takes into account the activities of previous lives as well. Only someone who has full knowledge of all previous lives of all living entities can implement this law of *karma*.

I bow to you, in the same way we can say, *"Necharāya namaḥ" Nature I bow to you.* God has infinite names and forms. One name 'Nature' can be added to them. But, nature being an inanimate entity cannot have the power of creating the world. Therefore, we will have to accept the existence of a conscious entity for creating and sustaining the world.

In India, *Nyāya, Vaiśheṣhika* and other philosophies have used inference as evidence to prove the existence of God. They state that by observing creation, it can be inferred that its creator is certainly some competent and All-Powerful God. The logic used is that there are two types of actions: those that are performed by man and the others by God. Of these, we are familiar with actions performed by men, as we perform them every day. But those actions which cannot be performed by man are called divine, such as the creation of rivers, mountains, the sun, the moon and so on.

na prāṇibuddhibhyo'saṁbhavāt

The logical argument given is,

parvato vahnimān dhūmavatvāt

(Nyāya)

"When we perceive smoke rising from a mountain, it can be inferred that there must be fire on that mountain." Because it is a rule that wherever there is smoke, there must be fire.

Everyone accepts the fact that the accomplishment of any work requires certain conditions to be fulfilled. If someone enquires how an earthen pot is made, the simple answer could be that it is made of clay. But did the clay become a pot by itself? The next answer is that a number of means such as clay, pole, wheel, etc. are required. The potter who makes the earthen pot is also essential. Only then can a pot be made. The earthen pot cannot be made if the maker does not possess the skill of making pots. Therefore, the ability to make a pot is also essential. However, the pot need not necessarily come into being as yet, because even if the ability to do the work is present, if there is no desire or resolution to make it, or if an effort is not put, the pot will not be made. Thus, the making of a mere earthen pot requires a potter, clay, knowledge, desire, resolution, means, skill and effort. All these are essential, just to make a small pot. How then can we ignore these requirements for the creation of such an amazing and vast universe?

Even a mere drawing of the world requires an artist. If someone were to claim that a map of the world was made by itself without anyone drawing it, then such an individual would be considered insane by a sensible person. Then how can it be claimed that the universe came into existence by itself? To answer this, the scriptures make use of inference to prove the existence of God, and declare that the Creator of the universe is God alone.

Modern science has gone to the extent of declaring that atoms are energy forms and not gross material objects. These atoms are in fact vibratory functions of some unknown and unmanifest energy. It is easy to guess what that entity is, which science declares as 'unknown' and 'imperceptible'. The *Vedas* too declare that God is 'Unknowable' and 'Imperceptible'.

adṛiṣhṭa mavyavahārya magrāhya malakṣhaṇa machintya mavyapadeśhya mekātmapratyayasāraṁ prapañchopaśhamaṁ śhāntaṁ śhivamadvaitam

(*Māṇḍukya Up. 7*)

The renowned scientist Professor Eddington declared, "Some unknown, imperceptible power is working behind some unperceived action, but we do not know anything about it. We come across some such unknown element in our research, which is beyond explanation in material terms." You can now imagine how incomplete and hollow material science is! By merely naming that unperceived element as 'unknown', the search cannot be considered to have ended. Until this 'unknown element' is identified, science will remain incomplete. It will only be ignorant speculation.

Some material scientists state that atoms alone are responsible for creation; there is no need of God. They should seriously consider the law that only objects defined in space can combine. How can atoms with no definite location, combine with each other?[4] Even if we accept that contrary to the law, atoms do combine, a serious problem still confronts us. How do atoms

---

[4] According to Heisenberg's uncertainty principle and the quantum theory of modern science, the exact position of an electron can never be defined. It can only be said to have probabilities of existing at different places.

moving at the speed of one hundred thousand miles a second transfer knowledge to other atoms? Again, without such transfer of knowledge, how can living beings maintain continuity in their consciousness, because our experience reveals that even a man considered intelligent, forgets a thing he had read fifty years ago? Even if we accept that this is somehow possible, another serious problem still remains. What is the inherent nature of atoms? Is it creative, destructive[5] or both or neither? If we accept atoms to be inherently creative, then creation can be explained on the basis of atoms, but how will dissolution occur? According to the Entropy Theory of Clausius and other scientists, there will be dissolution one day - the earth will cool down and all living beings will be destroyed. If we accept the destructive nature of atoms, then dissolution can be explained, but how will the present creation be explained? If the nature of atoms is accepted to be both creative and destructive then, due to their opposing nature, neither creation nor dissolution can be explained. If we accept that atoms are neither creative nor destructive in nature, then the necessity of God is automatically established as the controller of those atoms.

Regarding atoms, we need to consider another universally accepted principle. This principle is that any object possessing

---

[5] If the atoms are inherently creative, then on their own they may combine to create objects. If atoms are inherently destructive, the objects created from them may slowly degenerate back into atoms with time.

form is created from a source material that is subtler and more permanent in comparison to it. Take cloth for example. It is created from thread; so cloth is less subtle and less permanent in comparison to thread. According to this rule, if atoms have a form, then they must be created from a source material that is subtler and more permanent. That can only be God!

There is another point which requires serious thought. We will have to accept that atoms possess properties of smell, taste, touch, etc. otherwise, from where will the earth derive these properties? The element 'space' contains the property of sound; air contains the property of touch in addition to sound; fire contains form, in addition to sound and touch; water contains taste, in addition to sound, touch and form; and earth contains smell, in addition to sound, touch, form and taste. Now if we accept that atoms possess only one property, then how will the others like smell, taste, etc. originate? Again, if we accept equality in all atoms, then water should also possess the property of smell along with its other properties, i.e. sound, taste, form and touch. In fact, even air will then possess the properties of smell, taste, etc. besides its accepted properties of sound and touch. Thus, it is absurd to accept the sole cause of creation to be the combination of atoms.

Some people use the example of the automatic functioning of a watch to argue that creation of the universe can also be automatic. There is no need of God. But these people must remember that the watch was not self-made. It was only when someone made it, that it started functioning. It will again stop functioning when damaged and will need to be repaired. Further, it is also worth considering that, although the watch-maker has made the watch, he cannot understand the mechanism of the metal atoms in the watch, in the sense that he cannot control them. Their controller is God. Therefore, God has to be omnipresent, otherwise those atoms will not function systematically.

Around 500 B.C. there were some philosophers in Greece who tried to explain the cause of creation. One of them, Thales, declared the first element and cause of creation to be water. Anaximander said that earth, water, etc. are not the primary cause of creation. There is some unknown substance from which earth, water, etc. are created. Anaximanes considered both these views to be incorrect. He claimed that the primary element of creation is air. It is from air that the world has evolved. Anexigorous rejected this belief and stated that the mingling of a number of elements and the desire of God are responsible for creation. Pythagoras said that some supreme number 'one' has created the variety of elements from void.

Now listen to another theory which might amuse you. The propagator of this theory is Charles Darwin (1809-1882). He declared that invertebrates came into being by gradual development from the amoeba. In time, they evolved into fish, then reptiles, dinosaurs, birds, terrestrial animals, primates such as monkeys and finally, into human beings. According to Darwin, the amoeba doubled itself to form the hydra. In this way, by gradual evolution, man came into being. In the

Museum of London, various skeletons are on display to illustrate this sequence of evolution.

Let us briefly examine this theory. We see that the sequence of the growth of a plant from a seed and a fruit from a flower exists today just as it existed in the past. Then why is the sequence of evolution not visible today? Why do we see only fish being born from fish and elephants from elephants? Why don't we see elephants being born from pigeons? Why has the process of evolution ceased? Today, we see that pigeons are born only from pigeons, and human beings from human beings.

Again, if evolutionists are asked to explain how creatures with bones came into existence from boneless creatures, they have no definite answer. They say that bones may have been formed as a result of mental stimulus. But bones do not have any connection with the mind. Teeth are also bones, but if they are poked with a needle, the mind experiences no pain.

The second explanation given in this context is that hard work resulted in formation of bones. This is another ridiculous theory. As far as our knowledge and experience go, hard work may result in external corns, or external hardness, but not in the formation of extra bones. Do the hands of an iron-smith have extra bones?

The third explanation is that bones were formed through a combination of arteries and veins. This explanation is even more ridiculous. If the arteries and veins were to combine together to form teeth, then how is it that teeth are formed again when milk teeth fall? If these evolutionists claim that there are countless arteries and veins, therefore teeth are formed again, then why do they not form again in old age when teeth fall for the second time? Are the arteries and veins of an old man destroyed?

Now listen to the last explanation of these evolutionists. They state that bones are a result of circumstantial necessity. But to consider circumstance as a cause, is naive. A brother and sister are born in the same circumstances, yet the sister has no beard and moustache. A male and female elephant are born in same circumstances, but the she-elephant does not have tusks. A peacock and peahen are born in the same circumstances, but a peacock has a long ornate tail, whereas a peahen does not. Cows and buffaloes do not have upper teeth, while horses have both upper and lower teeth. A dog's milk teeth do not fall. Horses have no breast nipples. Bulls have breast nipples close to their testicles. At the time of delivery, a mare's umbilical cord falls out. Observe, no logical sequence is perceivable anywhere!

Again, look at the hollow argument in the claimed steps of evolution. A mole has ten breasts. It evolved into a mouse, which has eight breasts. Next came the cat, which has six breasts. After that, came cows and buffaloes, which have four breasts. Finally, human beings evolved, having only two breasts. Is this development, or is it retardation?

Yet again, cows and buffaloes maintain the same colour of hair throughout their lives. On the other hand, the hair of human beings is black in youth, white in old age, and tinged yellow in very old age. Animals have inborn ability of swimming, etc. while human beings have to acquire it by learning. The bodies of animals are parallel to the ground when they stand, trees stand upside down, while human beings stand vertical. Trees are nourished by impure substances and polluted air, and produce pure air, good flowers and fruit. The direction of evolution appears to be reversed because we see that human beings are nourished by good food and pure air, and release polluted air and foul substances.

Look at the sequence of evolution of the life-span. A tortoise lives for a hundred and fifty years and a snake for a hundred and twenty years. The pigeon is supposed to have evolved from them, but its life-span is only eight years. Now listen to something amusing! The skeleton of a huge dinosaur is on display in the Museum of London. The skeleton weighs eight maunds or three thousand two hundred kilos. If the bones themselves weigh three thousand two hundred kilos, the dinosaurs must have been at least two hundred maunds or eight thousand kilos. When dinosaurs were so heavy, then human beings who are supposed to have evolved from them should weigh at least eight hundred maunds (thirty thousand kilos). Again, in Darwin's opinion, trees were so huge that the burning of jungles led to the formation of vast coal mines. In that case, human beings, who evolved later, should be even more gigantic than fifty-storied buildings!

Now listen to the views of various evolutionists regarding the age of the earth. Ernst Haeckel (1834-1919) and other supporters of Darwin maintain that the earth has been in existence for eight hundred and twenty thousand years. On the other hand, geologists estimate the age of the earth to be about a hundred million years. With the discovery of Radium, Professor Perry declared the age of the earth to be more than one hundred million years. Now, which of these estimates should we accept as correct? A few years back, Mr. John T. Reid found a shoe with excellent stitching in an excavation at Nevada. The shoe was estimated to be at least six million years old. This implies that man was fully advanced at that time. Now, if that shoe is accepted to be six million years old, then it must have taken at least four to five million years to arrive at that stage of advancement. From this, we can conclude the age of the earth to be not less than ten million years. According to evolutionists like Haeckel and others, man came into existence twenty-two links after the amoeba. If we assume the duration of one link to be ten million years, then accordingly, it must be two hundred and ten million years since the amoeba came into existence. The amoeba itself must have come into existence after millions of years. But Haeckel claimed the age of the earth to be only eight hundred and twenty thousand years. All these are only baseless presumptions. In reality, according to the *Vedas* and scriptures, the age of the earth is 197,961,610 years (at present). This calculation is based upon the beginning of the present day of the creator Brahmā. Each day of Brahmā is 4,320,000,000 years and Brahmā lives for hundred years of which fifty years have passed. If we throw a bullock cart, a motorcar and a rocket into a well today, what conclusions will archaeologists draw about the level of our progress in the 21st century when they dig this well in the future?

The modern scientific theories themselves make fun of Darwin, Haeckel, etc. stating that it was not man who evolved from the monkey, but on the other hand, monkeys originated from men. They sarcastically remark that in ancient times man made great progress in science, after which his brain became feeble and he was reduced to the level of a savage. This is certainly a warning for today's scientists, because scientific progress has again reached its peak, and they may have to suffer the same fate. It is significant to note that Darwin's son, George Darwin himself declared on 16th August 1905, that the mystery of life and creation is still as mysterious as it was before.

Psychologists are also declaring that they are unable to explain human activity based on material knowledge. Even the cause of tears cannot be explained. A few years back, in a meeting of scientists in England, the statement of Doctor Law was repeated. He had declared that the greatest discovery of modern science is that we have not been able to discover anything till now; that is, we have not been able to comprehend the primal cause as yet.

Darwin doubted the existence of God. His argument was that, if God did exist, and He was merciful and omnipotent, just as the theists claim Him to be, then He would not have created a world full of misery. Again, if God is accepted as the Creator of the world, then it will naturally be presumed that

He must have also created the individual souls. But accepting this would be contrary to what the scriptures say. The *Vedas* state that the individual souls are eternal, innumerable and unborn.

ajāmekāṁ lohitaśhuklakṛiṣhṇāṁ bahvīḥ prajāḥ sṛijamānāṁ sarūpāḥ
ajo hyeko juṣhamāṇo'nuśhete jahātyenāṁ bhuktabhogāmajo'nyaḥ

(Śhvetā. Up. 4.5)

jñājñau dvāvajāvīśhanīśhāvajā hyekā bhoktṛibhogyārthayuktā
anantaśhchātmā viśhvarūpo hyakartā
trayaṁ yadā vindate brahmametat

(Śhvetā. Up. 1.9)

The *Gītā* too supports this,

mamaivāṁśho jīvaloke jīvabhūtaḥ sanātanaḥ

(Gītā 15.7)

prakṛitiṁ puruṣhaṁ chaiva viddhyanādī ubhāvapi

(Gītā 13.19)

The *Rāmāyaṇa* also says,

īśhvara aṁśha jīva avināśhī, chetana amala sahaja sukharāśhī

(Rāmāyaṇa)

Now listen to the resolution of both of Darwin's doubts. God has not made this world at all. Hearing this, the atheist is bound to say, "That is exactly what I believe." But listen further, God did not create this world, He just manifested it. He has not created the individual souls. The individual souls are eternal, i.e. ever-existent, and the bondage of their countless past *karmas,* actions also accompanies them. God only manifests the souls, so that they can make an effort to liberate themselves. The *Vedas* declare,

sūryāchandramasau dhātā yathā pūrvamakalpayat divaṁ cha pṛithivīṁ chāntarikṣhamathosvaḥ

(Ṛig Veda)

It means that God desired the world to come into existence exactly as it was prior to dissolution.[6] It was simply by His desire that the world came into being. So, when the world was only manifested according to its pre-existing form, the question of God having created new souls does not arise. The word *'sṛiṣhṭi'* is derived from the Sanskrit root word *'sṛija visarge'*. It means 'to release', not 'to make'. The word *'janma'*, or birth, is derived from the root word, *'janī prādurbhāve'*, which means 'to be manifested'. In this way, *janma* and *sṛiṣhṭi* are not indicative of new creation. Just as energy already exists within water and scientists simply release it through their technology, similarly, the souls that were lying dormant in God during dissolution are manifested again with the same qualifications, merits and so on, that they possessed at the end of the previous creation. This can be compared to a five-day cricket match, where play

[6] The Vedas declare creation to be a cyclic process of *sṛiṣhṭi, stithi* and *pralaya* (creation, maintenance, dissolution). At the time of dissolution, creation unwinds into its primary form, *prakṛiti.* This *prakṛiti* then rests within God. At the time of creation, God releases *prakṛiti,* which again unfolds by reverse movement. This cycle has been going on since eternity.

is resumed on the following day, exactly at the position where it had ended the day before.

Spencer, Hamilton, etc. argued that if God exists and resides in the world, then He would be bound by material energy. He can be independent only if He is outside the world. But if He is outside the world, how will He acquire knowledge of the world? Actually, God is unlimited, inconceivable and all-powerful. It is naive to think that if He works within the world, He will be bound by material energy. Moreover, the main point is that systematic and intelligent development of inert material energy cannot take place unless God pervades it.

Some people suggest that this material world is created without an intelligent power, just as milk is produced from hay which is lifeless, and yogurt is produced from milk. However, this argument is also fallacious. If milk is produced merely from grass, then why don't bulls who also eat grass produce milk? In addition, the cow which eats grass and subsequently produces milk is a living being. Grass does not turn into milk on its own.

Some people say that *prakṛiti* or nature, and God together bring about creation. However, accepting this view would imply that God is incomplete and imperfect in Himself. Although this theory has been stated in the *Sāṁkhya Darśhana,* it is only with a view to prove that God does not engage directly in material activities; He uses His material energy to create, while He remains beyond matter.

Some people wonder how an insentient world was created from and by a sentient God. Such people should observe that insentient things like hair and nails originate from sentient human beings. Then why can't God, who is the controller of *Māyā*, create an insentient world?

Some suggest that a compromise should be made, i.e. the creator of the conscious should be accepted to be the Conscious Personality, God; and nature should be acknowledged as the cause of inert matter. But if this view is accepted, then God will again prove to be imperfect.

Others claim that 'time', *kāla* should be accepted as the creator; there is no necessity of God. This opinion is also very commonly held, but is wrong because 'time' itself originates from God.

akṣharāt saṁjāyate kālaḥ

(Veda)

The *Gītā* too states,

dvāvimau puruṣhau loke kṣharaśhchākṣhara eva cha
kṣharaḥ sarvāṇi bhūtāni kūṭastho'kṣhara uchyate

(Gītā 15.16)

Yet others claim that *karma* or fruits of actions, should be considered as the cause for creation. This again is impossible since *karma* is insentient and is itself dependent upon sentient beings.

Some people maintain that the individual soul, *jīva* should be accepted as the creator. This too is impossible since the individual soul is neither all-knowing nor independent. If the individual soul had been independent, why would he desire to suffer the fruits of his own actions?

Finally, some people state that according to the verse,

brahmavid brahmaiva bhavati

(Muṇḍaka Up. 3.2.9)

'Liberated souls who have attained *Brahman*, God are non-different from *Brahman*'.Such liberated souls should be accepted as the creators. However, the *Vedānta* very clearly declares,

jagadvyāpāravarjam

(Brahma Sūtra 4.4.17)

"Even liberated souls cannot create the material world." Their equality with *Brahman* is only from the standpoint of experiencing the same level of Divine Bliss.

bhogamātrasāmyaliṅgāchcha

(Brahma Sūtra 4.4.21)

Thus, we will have to accept God as the Creator. This view is not only declared by all the scriptures, but also proven by logical inference. However, the *Vedānta* declares that even though attempts are made to prove God's existence by means of logical reasoning, the existence of God is not a subject of logic. The surest proof of the existence of God is scriptural evidence. We must believe in Him because it is written in the *Vedas*, as they are divine in origin. If someone has doubts, he should engage in the spiritual practice or *sādhanā* prescribed in the *Vedas* and experience for himself whether God is a reality or not. Thereafter, if he does not attain God, he has the right to say that there is no such Personality. So, the existence of God is proved.

Here another question arises. If God is all-pervading, why don't we experience His presence? When we eat sugar or something sweet, we experience its sweetness. Then why don't we experience the Bliss of the All-Blissful God who pervades every particle of the universe? When we drink milk, we experience its taste. Similarly drinking poison, will have its effect as well. In the same way, we should experience God. People put forward this argument because they wish to believe only what they can directly experience. However, they should realize that evidence through direct perception is the feeblest kind of evidence. For example, a person suffering from jaundice sees everything as yellow. Obviously his experience is deceptive. A person bitten by a snake, finds the taste of the bitter neem leaf to be sweet. In the same way, the perceptual experience of the individual afflicted by the disease of *Māyā* is defective.

An ant returned after circling a mountain of sugar and was asked about its experience. It replied, "The mountain was made of salt." Great astonishment was expressed at this answer. But on investigation, it was found that there was a grain of salt in its mouth. Thus, even after roaming all around the mountain of sugar, the ant only experienced the taste of the salt in its mouth. In the same way, our senses, mind and intellect through which we experience the world, are material, imperfect and afflicted with the disease of the three *guṇas*. God on the other hand, is perfect, transcendental, divine and beyond the three modes of *Māyā*. Then, how can we perceive His divine form with our material senses? Until and unless the senses become divine, their experience can never be accurate.

sarvaṁ khalvidaṁ brahma *(Chhān. Up. 3.14.1)*

īśhā vāsyamidaṁ'sarvam *(Iśha. Up. 1)*

siyārāmamaya saba jaga jānī *(Rāmāyaṇa)*

prabhu vyāpaka sarvatra samānā *(Rāmāyaṇa)*

The above scriptural statements assert that God is in fact all-pervading, yet our senses cannot perceive Him because they are material and imperfect. Saints like Tulasīdāsa, Sūradāsa, Mīrābāī and so on, had been graced with divine vision, hence they experienced the blissful form of God everywhere. However, when they revealed their experience to us, we did not believe them and instead ridiculed them.

Besides this, God is an abode of innumerable contradictory attributes. Therefore, it is extremely difficult to comprehend Him. However, He can be attained by His Grace. It is through God's Grace alone that the material senses, mind and intellect attain the divine power by which He, the Divine Personality is realized.

However, every living being in the world is in fact a seeker of God. Even if one tries for countless ages, he cannot become an atheist. The reason is that even the so-called atheist is searching for Bliss. This 'Bliss' is synonymous with 'God', and so one who is searching for happiness, is searching knowingly or unknowingly for God. Besides, even the atheist loves divine qualities like truth, non-violence, kindness and so on. This again proves his love for God. In fact, his own existence is direct proof of the existence of God.

loke nahi sa vidyeta yo na rāmamanuvrataḥ

(Vālmīki Rāmāyaṇa)

The great Saint Vālmīki says, "There is not a single individual soul in the universe who is not a devotee of Lord Rāma." We may not know the path to attain Him, and could be endeavouring in the wrong direction. Yet, the fact remains that we do believe in God because we are seeking only Bliss.

If someone declares, "I am determined to oppose God," then he is definitely a staunch believer in God. In our history, there have been demons like Hiraṇyakaśhipu, etc. who vehemently opposed God. Such people should be considered staunch believers because only a being that exists can be opposed. If God did not exist, how could they oppose Him? It is also a historical fact that those demons who opposed God finally attained Him as their mind was totally absorbed in God with feelings of great enmity. Devotion means absorption of the mind in God with any emotion. It does not matter whether this absorption is through favourable emotions or unfavourable emotions.

kāmaṁ krodhaṁ bhayaṁ snehamaikyaṁ sauhṛidameva cha
nityaṁ harau vidadhato yānti tanmayatāṁ hi te

(Bhāg. 10.29.15)

Veda Vyāsa states that God can be attained by absorption of the mind in Him with any emotion, whether it be lust, anger, fear, affection, friendship or love. Therefore, one whose mind is totally absorbed in God, even through enmity, attains Him and is liberated from *Māyā*. To call such a person a non-believer only reveals one's own lack of faith in God.

Besides this, we have to accept the existence of God as the dispenser of the fruits of actions performed by individual souls, because actions are insentient. They cannot bear fruits on their own. The work of awarding the results of actions at the appropriate time can only be performed by an omniscient personality. Firstly, the individual soul is ignorant. He does not possess knowledge of the actions performed by him in countless past lives. Secondly, if he did have this knowledge, why would he desire to suffer the consequences of his own actions? Therefore, God has to be accepted as the dispenser of the fruits of actions. Even the *Nyāya* system of philosophy supports this view.

In reality, the existence of God cannot wholly be proved by either perceptual or inferential evidence. Hence, the *Vedānta* system of philosophy has proved the existence of God by means of scriptural testimony only. Generally, naive people claim that scriptural testimony is ordinary evidence. Only evidence through experience is acceptable as proof. But such people should bear in mind the fact that experience is gained only after spiritual practice and prior to spiritual practice, the words of the scriptures will have to be accepted. Further, if practical experience alone is accepted as proof, then all the actions of the world will be disproved. For example, a person suffering from jaundice sees the colour of a white object as yellow; a person bitten by a snake finds the taste of the bitter neem leaf to be sweet; an ant with a grain of salt in its mouth, wanders around a mountain of sugar, experiences it to be salty. The implication is that if the experience is imperfect or incomplete, it can be misleading. Therefore, it is only by means of scriptural evidence that the actual truth can be realized. If by practice of spiritual discipline as specified by the scriptures we fail to realize God, then and only then, we have the right to say that there is no God.

Now we may accept the existence of God, but he may question the purpose or necessity of worshipping Him. We could argue that just as we have a President in a country, God may be the President of the entire universe; but why do we need to worship Him? Such an argument is naive because our relations with the President of the country are limited and formal, whereas our relations with God are complete, loving and eternal. Further, we are selfish by nature. We are naturally attached to whoever or whatever fulfils our self-interest. This is an experienced fact. We all desire true, everlasting, unlimited happiness and that happiness is only in God. Therefore, our most intimate and only relationship is with God. If we could attain even an iota of happiness elsewhere, then our relations with God would have been the same as that with the President of the country.

However, you don't need to worry about attaining God. He is easily attainable. I can assure you that you do not have to engage in any spiritual discipline to realize Him. You may argue, "If we do not have to engage in spiritual discipline, how is it that we have not yet attained Divine Bliss?" Yes, this is a valid question. That is just what needs to be understood. Have a little patience and you will understand everything.

Let us reflect upon the essential nature of God, because the *Vedas* declare,

iha chedaśhakad boddhuṁ prāk śharīrasya visrasaḥ
tataḥ sargeṣhu lokeṣhu śharīratvāya kalpate

(Kaṭha Up. 2.3.4)

"Having acquired a human body if we do not realize God, we will have to suffer in the endless cycle of birth and death." This will be our greatest mistake. Therefore, realizing the importance of the human form, we must acquire knowledge of God so that we can attain our absolute, ultimate goal of Supreme Bliss.

राधे राधे गोविंद गोविंद राधे। राधे राधे गोविंद गोविंद राधे॥

The Nature of God

The scriptures clearly state,

nāvedavin manute taṁ bṛihantam

"One who does not know the *Vedas* cannot know God." Therefore, let us first find out what the *Vedas* have to say about God.

yasyāmataṁ tasya mataṁ mataṁ yasya na veda saḥ
avijñātaṁ vijānatāṁ vijñātamavijānatām

(Kena Up. 2.3)

"A person who thinks that God can be understood, does not understand Him. And one who thinks that God cannot be understood, has proper understanding." In other words, no one can understand God. But again, we have the *Vedas* emphasizing the need to know Him,

iha chedavedīdatha satyamasti
na chedihāvedīn mahatī vinaṣhṭiḥ

(Kena Up. 2.5)

"If God is not understood in this human life, it will be a terrible loss." This precious human life is unattainable even by the celestial gods.

The *Vedas* give us various reasons as to why God is incomprehensible. The first reason stated is,

indriyebhyaḥ parā hyarthā arthebhyaśh cha paraṁ manaḥ
manasastu parā buddhir buddherātmā mahān paraḥ

(Kaṭha Up. 1.3.10)

mahataḥ paramavyaktamavyaktāt puruṣhaḥ paraḥ
puruṣhān na paraṁ kiñchit sā kāṣhṭhā sā parā gatiḥ

(Kaṭha Up. 1.3.11)

"Beyond the senses are the sense objects, beyond the sense objects is the mind, beyond the mind is the intellect, beyond the intellect is the soul, beyond the soul is *Māyā* and beyond *Māyā* is *Brahman*, God." Thus, God is totally beyond the reach of the senses, mind and intellect, which are the only means the individual soul possesses. Therefore, He cannot be grasped and comprehended.

The second reason is,

divyohyamūrtaḥ puruṣhaḥ

(Veda)

"God is divine and the senses, mind and intellect are material." The material senses cannot grasp a Divine Personality.

The third reason is,

tameva bhāntamanubhāti sarvaṁ tasya bhāsā sarvamidaṁ vibhāti

(Kaṭha Up. 2.2.15; Muṇḍaka Up. 2.2.10; Śhvetā. Up. 6.14)

"He is the Supreme Illuminator, and the senses, mind and intellect are illumined by Him." The illumined cannot possibly illumine their illuminator. Hence, He is totally unknowable.

The fourth reason is,

yanmanasā na manute yenāhurmano matam
tadeva brahma tvaṁ viddhi nedaṁ yadidamupāsate

(Kena Up. 1.5)

"It is through inspiration from God, that the senses, mind and intellect perform their respective functions." Thus the inspired senses, mind and intellect are incapable of grasping their Inspirer, God.

Besides this, God is an abode of various, simultaneously existing contradictory qualities.

aṇoraṇīyān mahato mahīyān ātmā guhāyāṁ nihito'sya jantoḥ
tamakratuṁ paśhyati vītaśhoko dhātuḥ prasādān mahimānamīśham

(Śhveta. Up. 3.20)

He is smaller than the smallest atomic particle you could conceive and He is also bigger than the biggest space you could imagine. It is essential for Him to be smaller than the smallest, otherwise how could He permeate every particle of the universe and be omnipresent. Likewise, it is necessary for Him to be bigger than the biggest, so that everything remains established within Him and everything enters into Him at the time of dissolution, *mahāpralaya*. It may even be possible to understand that He is simultaneously both, but the *Vedas* further state,

neti netyasthūlamananuḥ

(Veda)

"He is neither big, nor small." Now how do we comprehend Him? It is further stated,

anyatra dharmādanyatrādharmādanyatrāsmāt kṛitākṛitāt
anyatra bhūtāchcha bhavyāchcha yattatpaśhyasi tadvada

(Kaṭha Up. 1.2.14)

He is beyond *dharma* and *adharma*, good and bad and also beyond cause and effect. Again it is stated,

sarvendriyaguṇābhāsaṁ sarvendriyavivarjitam
sarvasya prabhumīśhānaṁ sarvasya śharaṇaṁ bṛihat

(Śhvetā. Up. 3.17)

"God is without sense organs, yet He grasps the objects of all the senses." The same Upaniṣhad further says,

apāṇipādo javano grahītā paśhyatyachakṣhuḥ sa śhṛiṇotyakarṇaḥ
sa vetti vedyaṁ na cha tasyāsti vettā tamāhuragryaṁ puruṣhaṁ mahāntam

(Śhvetā. Up. 3.19)

"He has no feet, yet He runs. He has no hands, yet He holds. He has no eyes, yet He sees. He has no ears, yet He hears. He knows all that is to be known, but no one knows Him." Now listen to a totally contradictory definition.

sahasraśhīrṣhā puruṣhaḥ sahasrākṣhaḥ sahasrapāt
sa bhūmiṁ'sarvataspṛitvātyatiṣhṭhad daśhāṅgulam

(Puruṣha Sūkta)

"He has innumerable heads, innumerable eyes, innumerable legs and so on." If He did not have legs, we would presume Him to be lame. But it is said that He runs, so how can we possibly consider Him to be lame? The same is the case with the other sense organs.

tadejati tannaijati tad dūre tadvantike
tadantarasya sarvasya tadu sarvasyāsya bāhyataḥ

(Iśhā. Up. 5)

"He walks and at the same time He does not walk. He is farther than the farthest and at the same time, nearer than the nearest. He is both within all and outside all." Next, the *Vedas* state,

ajāyamāno bahudhā vijāyate, tasya yoniṁ paripaśhyanti dhīrāḥ

(Yajura Veda)

"He is unborn but He takes innumerable births." Again,

so'kāmayat bahu syāṁ prajāyeyeti sa tapo'tapyata sa tapastaptvā idaṁ'sarvamasṛijata, yadidaṁ kiñcha tatsṛiṣhṭvā tadevānu prāviśhat tadanupraviśhya sachcha tyachchābhavat niruktaṁ chāniruktaṁ cha nilayanaṁ chānilayanaṁ cha vijñānaṁ chā vijñānaṁ cha satyaṁ chānṛitaṁ cha satyamabhavat yadidaṁ kiñcha tat satyamityāchakṣhate tadapyeṣha śhloko bhavati.

(Taitti. Up. 2.6)

"He desired and performed austerities which resulted in creation." This implies that He is the Creator of this universe. But, it is also stated,

anantaśhchātmā viśhvarūpo hyakartā
trayaṁ yadā vindate brahmametat

(Śhvetā. Up. 1.9)

"He is a non-doer. He does nothing."

Describing the attributes of God, the *Gītā* states,

mattaḥ parataraṁ nānyat kiñchidasti dhanañjaya,
mayi sarvamidaṁ protaṁ sūtre maṇigaṇā iva.

(Gītā 7.7)

mayā tatamidaṁ sarvaṁ jagadavyaktamūrtinā

(Gītā 9.4)

gatir bhartā prabhuḥ sākṣhī nivāsaḥ śharaṇaṁ suhṛit
prabhavaḥ pralayaḥ sthānaṁ nidhānaṁ bījamavyayam

(Gītā 9.18)

ahaṁ sarvasya prabhavo mattaḥ sarvaṁ pravartate

(Gītā 10.8)

paraṁ brahma paraṁ dhāma pavitraṁ paramaṁ bhavān,
puruṣhaṁ śhāśhvataṁ divyamādidevamajaṁ vibhum

(Gītā 10.12)

athavā bahunaitena kiṁ jñātena tavārjuna,
viṣhṭabhyāhamidaṁ kṛitsnamekāṁśhena sthito jagat.

(Gītā 10.42)

Similarly, the *Bhāgavatam* states,

dravyaṁ karma cha kālaśhcha svabhāvo jīva eva cha
vāsudevātparo brahmanna chānyor'tho'sti tattvataḥ

(Bhāg. 2.5.14)

sarvaṁ puruṣha evedaṁ bhūtaṁ bhavyaṁ bhavachcha yat
tenedamāvṛitaṁ viśhvaṁ vitastimadhitiṣhṭhati

(Bhāg. 2.6.15)

pādeṣhu sarvabhūtāni puṁsaḥ sthitipado viduḥ
amṛitaṁ kṣhemamabhayaṁ trimūrdhno'dhāyi mūrdhasu

(Bhāg. 2.6.18)

Veda Vyāsa gives an extraordinary definition,

yatra yena yato yasya yasmai yad yad yathā yadā
syādidaṁ bhagavān sākṣhāt pradhānapuruṣheśhvaraḥ

(Bhāg. 10.85.4)

God is the one who has taken the form of the world; He is the one for whom all actions in the world are performed; He is the one who protects the world; He is the one for whom it exists; He is the one from whom it has manifested; in whom it is established and by whom it is maintained and He is the one who is the Lord of *Māyā* and of all living beings.

The *Rāmāyaṇa* too states the same,

rāma svarūpa tumhāra vachana agochara buddhi para,
avigata akatha apāra neti neti nita nigama vada.

jaga pekhana tuma dekhana hāre
vidhi hari śhaṁbhu nachāvana hāre

teu na jānahiṁ marama tumhārā,
aura tumahiṁ ko jānanahārā

rāma atarkya buddhi mana bānī,
mata hamāra asa sunahu sayānī

(Rāmāyaṇa)

All these verses establish that God is totally imperceptible, unapproachable and incomprehensible.

adṛishṭamavyavahāryam

(Māṇḍūkya Up. 6)

Veda Vyāsa goes to the extent of saying that even the governors of the universe like Brahmā and Śhaṅkara, do not know Him.

nahaṁ na yūyaṁ yadṛitām gatiṁ vidur
nuvūmudevaḥ kimutāpare surāḥ
tanmāyayā mohitabuddhayastvidaṁ
vinirmitaṁ chātmasamaṁ vichakṣhmahe

(Bhāg. 2.6.36)

The *Vedas* refer to *Brahman* or the Supreme Being as possessing three aspects,

etajjñeyaṁ nityamevātmasaṁsthaṁ nātaḥ paraṁ veditavyaṁ
hi kiñchit bhoktā bhogyaṁ preritāraṁ cha matvā
sarvaṁ proktaṁ trividhaṁ brahmametat

(Śhvetā. Up. 1.12)

If these three aspects are known, then one can be freed from *Māyā*. The first is *Bhoktā Brahman,* the enjoyer (all the individual souls); the second is *Bhogya Brahman,* the enjoyable *(Māyā),* and the third one is *Preraka Brahman,* the Inspirer (God). With regard to *Bhoktā Brahman,* Veda Vyāsa says,

ātmānaṁ' rathinaṁ viddhi śharīraṁ' rathameva tu
buddhiṁ tu sārathiṁ viddhi manaḥ pragrahameva cha

(Kaṭha Up. 1.3.3)

indriyāṇi hayānāhur viṣhayāṁ'steṣhu gocharān
ātmendriyamanoyuktaṁ bhoktetyāhurmanīṣhiṇaḥ

(Kaṭha Up. 1.3.4)

vijñānasārathiryastu manaḥ pragrahavān naraḥ
so'dhvanaḥ pāramāpnoti tadviṣhṇoḥ paramaṁ padam

(Kaṭha Up. 1.3.9)

"The body is the chariot and soul is the master of the chariot, the intellect is the charioteer, the mind is the reins and the senses are the horses." Such an entity, comprised of a soul, mind, intellect and senses is referred to as the 'enjoyer' or '*Bhoktā Brahman*'.

With regards to *Bhogya Brahman,* that which is enjoyable, the *Vedas* say,

ajāmekāṁ lohitaśhuklakṛiṣhṇāṁ bahvīḥ prajāḥ sṛijamānāṁ sarūpāḥ
ajo hyeko juṣhamāṇo'nuśhete jahātyenāṁ bhuktabhogāmajo'nyaḥ

(Śhvetā. Up. 4.5)

This entity is also eternal and it is referred to as *Māyā*. It is tri-coloured owing to its constituent *guṇas* or modes; *sattva* - the mode of goodness is symbolized as white, *rājasa* - the mode of passion is symbolised as red, and *tāmasa* - the mode of ignorance is symbolized as black.

All the three entities, God - Inspirer *Brahman,* soul - enjoyer *Brahman* and *Māyā* - enjoyable *Brahman* are beyond the comprehension of the intellect.

Now what we have to reflect upon is when God is beyond our understanding, how can we expect to know Him? And without knowing Him we cannot have faith, without faith we cannot attain Him and without attaining Him, there is no question of attaining Divine Bliss, which is the goal of every living being.

However, the *Vedas* declare,

tasya yonim̐ paripaśhyanti dhīrāḥ

(Puruṣha Sūkta)

vedāhametam̐ puruṣham̐ mahāntam ādityavarṇam̐ tamasaḥ parastāt
tameva viditvātimṛityumeti nānyaḥ panthā vidyate'yanāya

(Śhvetā. Up. 3.8)

There have been those who have known God. On the one hand the scriptures declare God to be unknowable and imperceptible and on the other hand they state that He is knowable and perceptible. How will this problem be resolved? We shall reflect upon this subject next.

राधे राधे गोविंद गोविंद राधे। राधे राधे गोविंद गोविंद राधे॥

The Grace of God

nāyamātma pravachanena labhyo
na medhayā na bahunā śhrutena
yamevaiṣha vṛiṇute tena labhyas
tasyaiṣha ātmā vivṛiṇute tanūṁ'svām

(*Kaṭha Up.* 1.2.23)

tamakratuḥ paśhyati vītaśhoko
dhātuḥ prasādān mahimānamātmanaḥ

(*Kaṭha Up.* 1.2.20)

Although the Supreme Personality, God, cannot be grasped by the greatest senses, mind and intellect, yet that unknowable and invisible God can be fully known and seen by that fortunate soul who is graced by Him, with His divine power.

tatprasādāt parāṁ śhāntiṁ sthānaṁ prāpsyasi śhāśhvatam

(*Gītā* 18.62)

"O Arjuna! It is only by the Grace of God that you can attain Supreme Peace and His eternally blissful divine abode." When Arjuna attained divine knowledge and the darkness of his ignorance was dispelled, he himself accepted this truth,

naṣhṭo mohaḥ smṛitir labdhā tvatprasādān mayāchyuta

(Gītā 18.73)

"By Your Grace alone, I have attained divine knowledge and my ignorance has been dispelled forever." It is important to understand that true knowledge can never be overpowered by ignorance, just as light cannot be eclipsed by darkness. Now let us see what the *Purāṇas* say in this regard. Veda Vyāsa states,

athāpi te deva padāmbujadvayaprasādaleśhānugṛihīta eva hi jānāti tattvaṁ bhagavanmahimno na chānya eko'pi chiraṁ vichinvan

(Bhāg. 10.14.29)

"No one can know God even if he endeavours to know Him for innumerable lifetimes, but when God imparts His Grace to a soul, he can know Him and attain Divine Bliss for eternity." The *Rāmāyaṇa* states the same,

soi jānai jehi dehu janāī
jānata tumahiṁ tumahiṁ hvai jāī

tumharihiṁ kṛipā tumahiṁ raghunandana,
jānata bhagata bhagata ura chandana

rāma kṛipā binu sunu khagarāī
jāni na jāi rāma prabhutāī

(Rāmāyaṇa)

In relation to freedom from *Māyā,* the *Rāmāyaṇa* says that it is only by His Grace that one can be freed from the bondage of *Māyā.*

so dāsī raghubīra kī samujhe mithyā sopi
chhuṭai na rāma kṛipā binu nātha kahauṁ pada ropi

(Rāmāyaṇa)

With regard to freedom from delusion, the *Rāmāyaṇa* declares that it is only by God's Grace that one can be freed from delusion.

rajata sīpa mahaṁ bhāsa jimi, yathā bhānu kara vāri
tadapi mṛiṣhā tihuṁ kāla mahaṁ, bhrama na sakai kou ṭāri

jāsu kṛipā asa bhrama miṭi jāī, girijā so kṛipālu raghurāī

(Rāmāyaṇa)

Regarding mental afflictions the *Rāmāyaṇa* again says,

rāma kṛipā nāsahiṃ saba rogā

(Rāmāyaṇa)

"It is only through the Grace of God that one can be eternally free from all mental afflictions." Even the association of genuine Saints is not possible without the Grace of God. The *Rāmāyaṇa* declares,

binu satsaṅga viveka na hoī
rāma kṛipā binu sulabha na soī.

aba mohiṁ bhā bharosa hanumantā,
binu hari kṛipā milahiṁ nahiṁ santā.

santa viśhuddha milahiṁ puni tehī
rāma kṛipā kari chitavahiṁ jehī.

(Rāmāyaṇa)

"It is only by the Grace of God, that one attains the association of a true Saint."

Thus all the scriptures, from the *Vedas* to the *Rāmāyaṇa*, have unanimously declared that we can neither be eternally free from sorrow and suffering nor can we attain Divine Bliss without God's Grace.

Now, it appears that if everything depends on the Grace of God, then we are freed of all responsibilities. When He graces us, then everything will automatically fall into place. What is the need to practise devotion or any other spiritual discipline? A majority of people use this excuse and say that nothing happens without God's will. Not a leaf can stir without His will. Whatever God wills, happens. In fact, some people even go to the extent of blaming God for all their sinful and immoral actions and plead that they themselves are innocent.

īśhvaraḥ sarvabhūtānāṁ hṛiddeśhe'rjuna tiṣhṭhati
bhrāmayan sarvabhūtāni yantrārūṛhāni māyayā

(Gītā 18.61)

umā dāru joṣhita kī nāīṁ sabahiṁ nachāvata rāma gusāīṁ

(Rāmāyaṇa)

The scriptures declare that all living beings are like mechanical instruments operated by God. It is He Who directs us, and we act according to His directions. This principle is extremely dangerous if improperly understood. It can result in bringing about absolute ruin. But on the other hand, it can also lead to great spiritual progress if properly understood. So we need to seriously reflect upon it.

1. Let us first consider whether God is all-knowing or ignorant,

yaḥ sarvajñaḥ sarvavidyasya jñānamayaṁ tapaḥ

(Muṇḍaka Up. 1.1.9)

He, the Supreme Lord is omniscient. Now, if God is omniscient and is our director, i.e. the doer of our every action, how can we possibly perform actions of ignorance?

2. If God is the doer, why do we experience ourselves as doers and suffer the subsequent unhappiness arising out of those actions?

3. If God is the doer of our every action, then He should suffer the consequences of these actions or pardon Himself. We should not be made to suffer the fruits of those actions. Even an ordinary human being would not be so unfair as to do something wrong himself and make another person suffer for it. Is it possible that if one man eats, the hunger of another is satisfied? Or that if one man overeats, another suffers the consequences of over-eating?

4. If God is the doer, then why has He laid down a code of conduct in the *Vedas*, a list of do's and don'ts? He should have said that the individual souls don't have to do anything as He will make them act according to His will.

5. God is said to be impartial. Now, if this impartial God is accepted as the doer of everyone's actions, then why does He grant eternal Bliss to some people, such as Prahlāda, Dhruva,

Nānaka, Mīrābāī and so on, while others are made to suffer as slaves in the bondage of desire, greed and anger? How can He be so unjust? What was the need of the cycle of 8.4 million species of life?

6. If it is stated that all this is a mere play of God, and no one actually experiences happiness or sorrow, then there would be no need of attaining God and divine knowledge

According to the above accusations, it is evident that if we accept God as the doer, He will prove to be a tyrannical Being. Along with that, our indiscipline will also increase. We will become more and more negligent, and our activities will become demonic. We are negligent enough to start with and by accepting God as the doer we will end up taking a course leading to our own downfall.

There are those who accept that God is not to be blamed, as he is not the doer, but it is our destiny which is to be blamed. God makes us do whatever is destined for us. So, we are also blameless. They quote verses to support this,

hariṇāpi hareṇāpi brahmaṇāpi surair api
lalāṭalikhitā rekhā parimārṣhṭuṁ na śhakyate

(Sūkti)

"Even great personalities like Brahmā, Viṣhṇu and so on, cannot change destiny." But such fatalists do not even know what fate is. The *Hitopadeśha* explains,

pūrvajanmakṛitaṁ karma taddaivamiti kathyate

(Hitopadeśha)

The consequences of actions performed with free will in past lives are called 'fate' in the present life. In this way, whatever action is performed with free will in the present life will be called fate in the future. This obviously implies that we had freedom to act in the past. Now, if we were free to act in the past, how is it that the laws of the spiritual government have changed in the present and we have lost that freedom of action? Is it not absurd to hold such a view? The past was the present once upon a time, and the present will be the past in the future. Thus, if we were free to act in the past, then we are free to act even in the present. And if we claim that we are not free to act today, that is, we are bound by fate, then we must not have acted freely in the past either. Even a person with little common sense can understand this logic. In other words, using 'fate' as an excuse for negligence in spiritual endeavour, is even greater foolishness. Neither the scriptures, nor worldly people advise you to do nothing on the grounds that 'fate' will take care of everything. When it comes to worldly matters, we neither consider God the doer and renounce work, nor do we become lazy and leave everything to fate. We work diligently for the sake of wealth, for our children, etc. all the time, but use this philosophy as an excuse to make no effort to attain God.

Some people blame 'time' and become negligent, saying time will take care of everything. Some people say 'circumstances' force a person to sin. They engage in various kinds of wicked deeds using this as an excuse. All this is the result of one's own ignorance. In fact, 'God', 'time' and 'circumstances' cannot be blamed for our actions. There are some atheistic nations which hold the view that 'circumstances' cause one to sin, and some theistic nations state that God's will is behind all actions. But the astonishing thing is that there is no evidence in the history of either the atheistic nations or the theistic nations of people not being punished for their crimes, even though they may hold the view that 'circumstances' are the cause, or 'God's will' is the cause. All this implies that people simply concoct philosophies or distort the truth just to justify their sinful ways. The fact is that every individual is personally responsible for his actions or inaction.

Tulasīdāsa says,

nara tanu bhava vāridhi kahaṁ bero
sanmukha maruta anugraha mero

karṇadhāra sadguru dṛiṛha nāvā
durlabha sāja sulabha kari pāvā

jo na tarai bhavasāgara, nara samāja asa pāi
so kṛita nindaka manda mati, ātama hana gati jāi

so paratra dukha pāvai, sira dhuni dhuni pachhitāya
kālahiṁ karmahim īśhvarahiṁ, mithyā doṣha lagāya

(Rāmāyaṇa)

"One who blames God, time and fate in order to act whimsically and sinfully is a murderer of his own soul." He does not attain happiness in this world and he cannot even dream of attaining happiness in the next world. Thus, it is evident that to use God's Grace as an excuse for spiritual inaction, is a road leading to total ruin. The truth is that God does not impart His Grace whimsically. God's Grace is based upon some condition, whatever it may be. Whosoever fulfils this condition, attains His Grace and becomes eternally blissful. Such a person is called a Saint or a Great Soul, *Mahātmā*. The condition to attain God's Grace will be discussed next.

राधे राधे गोविंद गोविंद राधे। राधे राधे गोविंद गोविंद राधे॥

Surrender

First, let us go to the *Vedas*. The *Vedas* state,

yo brahmāṇaṁ vidadhāti pūrvaṁ
yo vai vedāṁśh cha prahiṇoti tasmai
taṁ'ha devamātmabuddhiprakāśhaṁ
mumukṣhurvai śharaṇamahaṁ prapadye

(Śhvetā. Up. 6.18)

tapaḥ prabhāvād devaprasādāchcha

(Śhvetā. Up. 6.21)

"Surrender to the Supreme Lord, Who is the Creator of even Brahmā and other celestial gods and by Whose Grace, the soul and intellect are illumined." This implies that it is only through surrender, that we receive God's Grace. The *Gītā* says,

tameva śharaṇaṁ gachchha sarvabhāvena bhārata
tatprasādāt parāṁ śhāntiṁ sthānaṁ prāpsyasi śhāśhvatam

(Gītā 18.62)

"Arjuna! Surrender to the Supreme Lord alone with all your being, then you will receive His Grace by which you will attain the divine abode and everlasting peace." The reason for this is,

daivī hyeṣhā guṇamayī mama māyā duratyayā
māmeva ye prapadyante māyāmetāṁ taranti te

(Gītā 7.14)

"This external divine power of Mine called *Māyā*, consisting of the three modes, can only be crossed by one who surrenders to Me."

Veda Vyāsa states,

tasmāt tvamuddhavotsṛijya chodanāṁ pratichodanām
pravṛittaṁ cha nivṛittaṁ cha śhrotavyaṁ śhrutameva cha

(Bhāg. 11.12.14)

māmekameva śharaṇamātmānaṁ sarvadehinām
yāhi sarvātmabhāvena mayā syā hyakutobhayaḥ

(Bhāg. 11.12.15)

"O Uddhava! Abandon all actions governed by the three modes of *Māyā* and surrender completely to Me, because I am the Soul of all souls, the Supreme Soul. Only then can you become fearless and cross the ocean of *Māyā*."

mana krama vachana chhāṁṛi chaturāī
bhajatahiṁ kṛipā karahiṁ raghurāī

(Rāmāyaṇa)

The *Rāmāyaṇa* states, "It is only through complete surrender, that one can attain Grace and be liberated from the bondage of *Māyā*." All this scriptural evidence implies that we must surrender to God. God's Grace is dependent upon surrender. All those souls who surrendered to Him, attained their supreme ultimate goal of Divine Bliss, whereas those who chose not to, have remained deprived of His Grace and are revolving in the 8.4 million species of life governed by time, destiny, their own natures and the three modes of *Māyā*, the *guṇas*.

phirata sadā māyā kara prerā,
kāla karma svabhāva guna gherā

(Rāmāyaṇa)

Now a question likely to arise is that, the act of doing something in order to attain God's Grace, is like a worldly business transaction of give and take. But to hold such a view is naive, because surrender actually means coming to a state of doing nothing. As long as a newborn baby does nothing, the mother does everything for it. When the child starts doing something, the mother lessens her responsibilities to the same extent. When the child begins to do everything, then the mother does nothing. This example fully explains what surrender is. As long as we suffer from the ego of being doers, we will remain bound by the fruits of our actions because we will be considered the doers of our actions. The moment the feeling of doership ends, we will become 'non-doers' and God will personally take care of all our needs and protect whatever we have for eternity.

teṣhāṁ nityābhiyuktānāṁ yogakṣhemaṁ vahāmyaham

(Gītā 9.22)

Therefore, if by surrender i.e. doing nothing, one attains freedom from *Māyā*, freedom from its three modes, *guṇas*, the three types of consequences of actions, *trikarma,* the three afflictions, *tritāpa,* the five sheaths, *pañchakoṣha,* etc. and simultaneously attains Supreme Bliss and Everlasting Peace, what greater Grace could there possibly be?

If we had done something and received God's Grace in return, an objection could have been raised that we had to do something to receive His Grace. But since we attain everything just by doing nothing i.e. complete surrender, this is only His Causeless Mercy. What effort is required of us in letting go off everything?

Understand this with an example: As long as a bird has a piece of food in its beak, it is noisily pursued by other birds and does not get a moment's peace. The moment the bird lets go off the piece of food, it attains peace immediately because the other birds now leave it alone. However, even if one lets go off everything and surrenders to God, it cannot be the price for His Grace. This is because what God gives is divine, unlimited and perfect, and what we let go off is material, limited and defective. Besides, of what use are material things to God?

Let us look at an example from the *Mahābhārata*. Draupadi, the wife of the Pāṇḍavas was being insulted openly in court by being stripped off her clothing by Duḥśhāsana. Initially, Draupadi had faith that her mighty husbands would save her. When they did not respond to her entreaties, she turned to the elders in the assembly - Droṇāchārya, Kṛipāchārya, Vidura, Bhīṣhma, etc. who were authorities on religious principles. When she saw no help coming from them either, she tried to protect herself and clenched her *sārī* between her teeth. Lord Kṛiṣhṇa still did not come to her help. When Duḥśhāsana pulled her *sārī* with a jerk, she lost hold of it, and was totally helpless. Now, she surrendered herself completely to Lord Kṛiṣhṇa. In other words, she came to a state of doing nothing. It was only when she ceased to expect protection from elsewhere, that she was protected by Him. The Lord states in the *Gītā*,

sarvadharmān parityajya māmekaṁ śharaṇaṁ vraja

(Gītā 18.66)

"Abandon all kinds of righteous and unrighteous actions and surrender to Me, then I will forgive all your sins of uncountable past lifetimes." God who acts as a judge dispensing justice for all becomes merciful for those who surrender to Him. In the material world, if a criminal surrenders to the law, the court still punishes him for his past crimes. However, God is so merciful, the moment a soul surrenders to Him completely, He forgives him i.e. He liberates him from the bondage of countless lifetimes of good and bad deeds and also bestows the Ultimate Bliss upon that soul. In addition, He takes care of his needs and protects whatever he has for eternity. Is this not Causeless Grace? Even an ignorant person will agree to this. Now this should put an end to the question whether God requires 'something' as a price in return for His Grace.

If a cloth merchant supplies a dress free of cost for your daughter's wedding, he is being really kind. If a washerman were to clean your clothes and not charge you for it, we would say that he has done you a favour, even though the clothes could become dirty again. Whereas, when God purifies your mind, it never becomes impure again. When a woman marries, she automatically becomes an equal owner of her husband's property. Similarly, when you surrender to God, you automatically acquire His unlimited Knowledge, Bliss and Love.

tasya kāryaṁ na vidyate

(Gītā 3.17)

Now, let us find out what we have, to surrender to God. We possess body, senses, mind and intellect. The scriptures say,

mana eva manuṣhyāṇāṁ kāraṇaṁ bandhamokṣhayoḥ

(Pañchadaśhī)

"The mind alone is the cause of bondage and liberation." Veda Vyāsa declares,

chetaḥ khalvasya bandhāya muktaye chātmano matam
guṇeṣhu saktaṁ bandhāya rataṁ vā puṁsi muktaye

(Bhāg. 3.25.15)

It means that the factual cause for bondage and liberation is the mind. So, we must surrender the mind to God. By surrendering it, all else will automatically be surrendered. Usually people worship God physically, but keep their minds attached to the world. Such external worship only leads to worldly results. The unalterable law is that one's attainment will either be spiritual or material, according to the attachment of one's mind, and not according to one's physical actions. Thus, if we physically engage in worldly activities, but keep the mind attached to God, then we will not have to bear the fruits of our physical actions. Instead, we will only receive spiritual results because of the attachment of our mind to Him.

Thus, surrender of the mind is true surrender. Just as it is impossible to run with tied feet, or speak with a closed mouth, it is impossible to practise devotion to God with the mind attached elsewhere. In reality, it is only the attachment of the mind which is referred to as devotion in the spiritual realm. But this same attachment, if directed to the material world, is referred to as infatuation.

"duī ki hohiṁ ika saṅga bhuālū, haṁsaba ṭhaṭhāi phulāuba gālū"

"It is impossible to laugh loudly and puff up one's cheeks at the same time." In the same way it is impossible for the mind to be attached to God and the material world simultaneously. The mind can be attached to only one area at one time.

There is a story told of some Brahmins of Mathurā, who in a state of intoxication got into a boat that was chained to the shore. After a night of vigorous rowing, they found that they had not moved forward an inch. Exactly like that, devotion to God practised even for innumerable lifetimes with the mind chained by attachments to wealth, children, spouse and so on, will result merely in attainment of the material world, because devotion to God did not factually take place. There was only some external act of prayer, worship or ritual. The result one reaps depends on the attachment of the mind alone.

The *Gopīs* expressed their devotional state to Uddhava very beautifully in the following lines,

ūdho! mana na bhaye dasa bīsa
eka huto so gayo śhyāma saṅga ko avarādhe īsa

"O Uddhava! We have only one mind and that is with Śhyāmasundara (Kṛiṣhṇa). If we had many minds, then we could have used each one in different areas and managed both devotion to God and to the world." But God is aware of the fact that if each individual were to be given two minds, then no one would have been able to fulfil the condition of exclusive surrender to Him.

māmekaṁ śharaṇaṁ vraja

To conclude, surrender of the mind alone is true surrender to God, no matter what the physical actions may be. Now, we need to analyse the difficulties in bringing the mind to the state of complete surrender. The only difficulty is that the mind has been attached to the material world since time immemorial, and this attachment has become very firm. Had the mind been neither attached to the world nor to God, then surrender would have been very easy. Therefore, we need to understand the factual nature of the world, so that we can become detached from it. It is only then, that surrender to God will be possible.

The Soul, Material World and Detachment

Nature of the Soul

Let us reflect on the questions, "Who am I?" and, "Is it personal happiness that I seek or the happiness of others?" The answer will be "I do not know who I am, but I do know that I only desire my own happiness." Now if you were a material being, then you would have attained happiness from material objects. But being a part of God, you can be truly happy only after attaining Divine Bliss. This is logically acceptable and has been proved by our own experience since eternity. If, being divine souls, we could have attained true happiness through material objects, then we would have never been unhappy, dissatisfied or miserable because we have attained material happiness in varying degrees throughout our innumerable past lives. This is a definite proof of the fact that we are divine souls and not material beings, because material things have never really satisfied us. However, this fact requires more serious reflection.

There is a materialistic viewpoint, known as Empiricism, which states that the 'self', like the senses, is just an effect or product of the physical body. In other words, both the 'self' and the body are made of four elements - earth, water, fire and air. The goal of life is the attainment of wealth, *artha* and the fulfilment of material desires, *kāma* and nothing beyond that. Only that which is directly perceived, can be accepted as evidence. Even among these empiricists, some consider the body, some the senses and others, the vital air to be the 'self'. For them, heaven is the attainment of worldly sense pleasures and separation from them is hell. Chārvāk has stated,

yāvaj jīvet sukhaṁ jīvet ṛiṇaṁ kṛitvā ghṛitaṁ pibet

(Chārvāk)

"Be merry while you live, even if you have to borrow money to gratify the senses." He further states,

bhasmībhūtasya dehasya punarāgamanaṁ kutaḥ

(Chārvāk)

"After death, the 'self' also ends along with the physical body."

Even though in everyday conversation we say, "I am fat", "I am thin" and so on, it would be very naive to identify ourselves with the body. The reason is that even as the body goes through changes from childhood to youth and so on, the knowledge that it was 'I' who was the child, the youth, etc. always remains. There is no change in that. If it had not been so, then the knowledge that, "I who was a child earlier and a youth now," should not remain in youth and so on.

Consciousness cannot be perceived in the gross elements like earth, water, etc. so, it cannot be said to be a property of these elements. If it is still insisted upon that consciousness manifests when these elements combine to form a body, the validity of this statement can be challenged, because in a dead body the elements are still together in the form of a body, but there is no consciousness. If it is said that a combination of elements produces consciousness, then the destruction of any constituent, should result in the destruction of consciousness, because the combination has been tampered with, but this does not happen.

Now, if we consider each part of the body to be individually conscious, then there would constantly be opposition between the parts, since they are individually conscious, but we do not experience this.

As long as the body is alive, we experience knowledge, desire, etc. However, simply based on this visible phenomenon, it would be naive to conclude that the body itself is 'I'. If we do not see fire anywhere due to the absence of wood and coal, we cannot conclude that fire does not exist.

If the 'experience' of material elements is described as 'consciousness', then it can be argued that material elements are only the 'objects' of experience. They cannot experience themselves. Just as fire has the power to burn everything, but is incapable of burning itself. An acrobat is incapable of sitting on his own shoulders. If 'consciousness' were a quality of material objects, they would be incapable of making themselves the subject of their own experience. Just as a bulb will not give light in the absence of electricity because 'light' does not originate from the bulb. Similarly, consciousness is not an attribute of the body as it is absent when the soul is absent.

Now let us reflect on our own practical experience. In our waking state, we say, "I see, I hear, I smell and so on." Here, you are implying that you are the sense organs. However, in your dream state, when your gross senses are inactive, you continue to see, hear, smell, etc. This proves that you are not the senses. But what about the mind? In the state of deep sleep, *suṣhupti* you experience nothing. ***"na kiñchidahamavediṣham"*** "I was not aware of anything." This experience of the absence of unhappiness is described as 'happiness'. After waking up from deep sleep, you say, ***"sukhamahamasvāpsam"***. "I had a very restful sleep." In that state there is no experience of the ego or self, because the ego is always connected with desires and this state of deep sleep is free from desires. In this state of '*suṣhupti*' or deep sleep, it is consciousness linked with the *māyika* power of '*avidyā*' that experiences the absence of knowledge, and it is consciousness associated with the mind that remembers in the waking state. This implies that the mind is absent in the state of deep sleep, which means that we cannot be the mind either. And, in normal speech we say, "my mind", "my eyes", "my ears", "my body", and so on. Then, what is 'mine', cannot be 'I'. 'Me' and 'mine' are always distinctive entities. If one is asked to explain 'me' logically, then it can be said that, all that is not 'mine' is 'me'.

All this proves the fact that this 'me' or 'I' is not any material entity or object. The mind, intellect, senses, etc. are all material. According to the *Vedas*,

chinmātraṁ śhrīhareraṁśhaṁ sūkṣhmamakṣharamavyayam
kṛiṣhṇādhīnamiti prāhurjīvaṁ jñānaguṇāśhrayam

(Veda)

"The soul is an eternal part of God."

This is also stated in the *Gītā* and *Rāmāyaṇa*,

mamaivāṁśho jīvaloke jīvabhūtaḥ sanātanaḥ

(Gītā 15.7)

Lord Kṛiṣhṇa declares, "The soul is My eternal part."

īśhvara aṁśha jīva avināśhī

(Rāmāyaṇa)

So, it is established that the 'I' is not the senses, mind or intellect, but an eternal part of God. Therefore, we can only be satisfied when we attain Divine Bliss. Both logic and experience show us that there is no such happiness in the world. For this reason, in spite of the mind and intellect trying to deceive us with the constant hope of attaining happiness through sense objects, we have not yet attained it, though we have acquired those objects time and again. Had we, i.e. the 'I' been of the same category as the mind and intellect, we would have been deceived. But the 'I' is a divine entity, so, even though we may have attained the best of material objects, we are not truly happy.

Nature of the Material World

'saṁsaratīti saṁsāraḥ' ; 'gachchhatīti jagat'

"That which is in a state of constant flux and is ever-changing is referred to as the world." The world is made of *Māyā*, and this *Māyā* is an eternal power of God. The *Upaniṣhad* states,

māyāṁ tu prakṛitiṁ vidyānmāyinaṁ tu maheśhvaram
tasyāvayavabhūtaistu vyāptaṁ sarvamidaṁ jagat

(Śhvetā. Up. 4.10)

"*Māyā* is not an illusion or false notion. It is a power of God."

ajāmekāṁ lohitaśhuklakṛiṣhṇāṁ bahvīḥ prajāḥ sṛijamānāṁ sarūpāḥ
ajo hyeko juṣhamāṇo'nuśhete jahātyenāṁ bhuktabhogāmajo'nyaḥ

(Śhvetā. Up. 4.5)

daivī hyeṣhā guṇamayī mama māyā duratyayā

(Gītā 7.14)

so dāsī raghuvīra kī samujhe mithyā sopi

(Rāmāyaṇa)

According to the above scriptural statements, *Māyā* is a power of God from which this world is created. The mind is material and so is the world, therefore there is a natural inclination of the mind towards *Māyā*. On the other hand, as God is divine, there is no natural attraction of the mind towards Him.

So, we shall discuss the nature of the world in detail. The mind is attached to the world, because it is the firm decision of the intellect that there is definitely happiness in the material world. Therefore, we are constantly endeavouring for it.

There are in fact, two worlds: the external gross world and the internal world of desires. This inner world is within the mind of every living being. It consists of innumerable subtle impressions created in countless lifetimes by the desires for various gross material objects. The gross world consists of the objects desired by the subtle inner world. Of the two, it is the subtle world of desires which is stronger, because even if the gross world is absent, the subtle world of desires does its work through thinking. For example, a faithful wife suffers pangs of separation from her husband, who is in England. However, if the object of the gross world had been present, then the effect on the subtle world of desires would have been stronger. Sometimes, these desires appear even without the presence of a gross material object and disturb the mind. Occasionally, a desire of which we are unaware suddenly emerges upon contact with an external object. However, our experience proves that even in the absence of external material objects these desires can intensify and cause us suffering.

Now, if we somehow put an end to inner desires, then the external objects cannot disturb our mental peace. These external objects disturb us only when the desires for those objects are present in the mind. Desire is the main problem. If desire is conquered, then even if external material objects continue to be present, they will have no impact on us.

One thing is certain, if the intellect makes a firm decision that the objects of the external world cannot fulfil our goal of Supreme Bliss, then internal desires will automatically come to an end. So the first step is to make a firm decision, through constant reflection, that there is not a trace of true happiness in the material world.

Let us now reflect on whether there actually is happiness in any material object or not. You may say that you experience happiness from your wealth, spouse, children and so on. Then how can your intellect possibly accept the fact that there is no true happiness in the world? However, if you seriously reflect upon this, the intellect will definitely change its decision. Now, which object is a source of happiness to you? If any object contains happiness, then everyone should receive happiness from it. Also, that happiness should be permanent and not followed by misery. However, neither of these conditions is fulfilled by anything material. Take liquor for instance. A drunkard experiences happiness at the very mention of liquor and definitely becomes happier when he actually drinks it. But the same liquor is a source of displeasure to a teetotaller. So the question is does liquor contain the happiness that is experienced by the alcoholic, or does it contain the revulsion experienced by the non-drinker? You may object saying that the non-drinker has never experienced the taste of liquor. If he were to actually taste it, he would also experience the same happiness as that experienced by the alcoholic. However, such an objection is naive. Because if that staunch teetotaller were made to drink alcohol, he would probably feel sick and be miserable the rest of his life.

Let's take another example. There was a man named Umesh who had a wife, a son, a friend, a servant, a neighbour and an acquaintance who owed him money. One day, Umesh suddenly died in the hospital. On hearing this news, the wife fell unconscious, as the sorrow was too much for her to bear. His son heard the news and though he did not fall unconscious, he became extremely unhappy and cried bitterly. Umesh's friend was not as upset as his son, but he did shed a few tears. The servant did not cry, but he felt slightly sad. The neighbour also heard that Umesh had died but felt neither happiness nor distress. He told his wife who was cleaning the house, "Did you hear? You know our neighbour Umesh? He just died." She also felt neither sorrow nor happiness, but following the rules of etiquette said, "Oh God! That's terrible. His child is small and his wife is so young. Anyway, whatever God wills, happens!" After saying this she continued cleaning. The person who owed money to Umesh was dishonest, so he felt very happy when he heard the news. He thought, "Now I am free from the debt!"

Now suppose Umesh suddenly came back to life. Actually he was only acting! Hearing this news, the wife fainted again out of happiness. When his son heard the news, he shed tears of joy. When the friend heard the news he felt happy, but to a lesser degree than the son. When the servant heard the news, it was a great relief for him. The neighbour casually told his wife, "Did you hear? Our neighbour is still alive." While continuing to clean the floor his wife said, "Oh, that's good." The person who owed Umesh money, felt very upset because now his debt would still have to be paid.

Now the question arises: Is Umesh a source of happiness, a source of sorrow, or neither? If he is accepted as a source of happiness, then what is the degree of happiness? Would it be the level of happiness experienced by the wife, or the level of happiness experienced by the son, or a level less than this? Or would it be the level experienced by his friend or by the servant? Or it may be that Umesh is in fact a source of sorrow, as was experienced by the debtor. Or it may be that he isn't a source of either happiness or sorrow as the neighbour felt. Each individual's experience was different. From this we can conclude that Umesh is neither a source of happiness nor sorrow. The degree of happiness each person experienced through him was directly proportional to the fulfilment of that person's own self-interest. And that happiness was proportional to the extent of each one's expectations of happiness from their relationship with him. Thus people imagined Umesh to be a source of happiness to the extent their own desires were fulfilled by him. They naively thought that Umesh was the source of the happiness they were experiencing. The conclusion is that a person derives happiness from an object that he himself mentally ascribes to, but naively assumes that it is the object itself that contains happiness.

There is one important truth that requires understanding. If happiness isn't experienced from any object, then sorrow won't be experienced from that object, either. The experience of sorrow corresponds to the experience of happiness. Observe, when Umesh died, his wife experienced the greatest sorrow; less than her grief was her son's grief; less than the son's grief was the friend's grief, and the one who felt the least grief was the servant. The neighbour, on the other hand was indifferent, while the debtor experienced happiness. Now, it is evident that when a person experiences a certain degree of happiness from an object or person, he is bound to experience sorrow in the same proportion when separated from that object or person. In reality, there is no sorrow in any object. Whatever we experience is the result of our own beliefs.

The second truth with regard to worldly happiness is that the happiness we experience from any object constantly diminishes. For example, a mother has been crying for two days in the grief of separation from her lost son. She is desperate to find him so that she could run and embrace him to her heart's content. Now, suppose he is found. She runs to him crying, "My son, my son," and embraces him very tightly, experiencing great joy. When she hugs him for the second time, the joy is less than what she experienced the first time. The third time, it is much less than the second time and when she embraces him for the tenth time, she experiences neither joy nor sorrow. The eleventh time, she says to her son, "Go out and play." But her son wants to remain in her lap. Now the mother begins to experience unhappiness because of his stubborn insistence. She shouts at him in irritation, "Are you a special child that I should constantly keep you in my lap? Leave me alone now because I have plenty of other things to do."

You must have eaten chocolates. When you ate the first chocolate you experienced great pleasure, on eating the second, the pleasure was less, on the third, even lesser. On eating the tenth, you experienced neither pleasure nor displeasure and on the fifteenth you protested, "Please, I can't eat another one. I feel sick." Now, if there was pleasure in chocolates or in any other food or object, why is there this constant abatement in the pleasure experienced and then eventually displeasure? Obviously our experience is a deception. It is merely a result of our own imagination, a fabrication of the mind.

When you are thirsty you love water, but not when your thirst is quenched. A lustful man longs for a woman, but when that lustful craving is absent, that same woman becomes burdensome. This fact is experienced by everyone, but no one actually bothers to reflect upon it. No one bothers to analyze the delusive nature of material happiness. It is obvious that there is not a trace of happiness in any object in the world. Whatever we experience is the deceptive result of our own imagination. Observe, people think that there is happiness in beauty, but our own experience is contrary to this. Suppose a child who is very ugly gets lost in a fair. His mother files a report at the police station. There she is shown a number of children who were found wandering about alone at the fair. She looks at them one by one, but experiences no joy because her ugly, squint-eyed son is not among them. Now, the other children present at the police station were better-looking than her son, but she did not experience any happiness from them. However ugly her son was, he alone was her source of joy.

One man is ready to shoot a beautiful woman and another man stands between them ready to die for her. Why? On making an enquiry it is found that the woman is the wife of the man who is ready to shoot her, and the other man willing to die for her is her lover. If there were happiness in beauty, both of them would have experienced it equally.

Liquor smells disgusting to a teetotaller and is immensely pleasurable to an alcoholic. Onions and garlic smell disgusting to one man and aromatic to another. The worm that lives in garbage would be repulsed or even die if surrounded by fragrant perfume. In other words, beauty, fragrance, etc. do not contain happiness. However, if someone repeatedly thinks of a particular object to be a source of happiness, he becomes attached to it.

dhyāyato viṣhayān puṁsaḥ saṅgasteṣhūpajāyate

(Gītā 2.62)

Consequently, one experiences happiness from that object and sorrow when deprived of it.

The third truth is that attainment of any worldly object is always preceded, accompanied and followed by unhappiness. We are miserable when we are separated from it. In spite of this fact, each and everyone is constantly striving in the hope of attaining happiness through material objects. For example, a woman desires to have a child. To fulfil her desire, she gets married and loses her independence. Now after many years of marriage her desire for a child is not yet fulfilled. She is restless and resorts to various medicines and remedies. Now she eventually becomes pregnant. She will obviously be happy, but that happiness will only be momentary, as it is immediately followed by the problems experienced during the nine months of pregnancy. The severe austerity a mother has to go through during pregnancy and the birth of a child cannot be completely realized, even by the mother herself, because she simultaneously experiences the happiness of expectation. What happens after the child is born? The happiness she experiences is again momentary, because it is immediately followed by the concern for protecting and looking after the child, and also by the constant fear of losing him. These anxieties continue throughout her life. If the child becomes a problem-child, then the mother is always miserable. If he dies, then intense grief is natural. The conclusion is that the effort to attain any material possession involves trouble; and once attained, constant protection of it together with the fear of losing it involves stress; and when that possession is destroyed, there is nothing but suffering and pain.

One more point needs to be noted. There is definitely an experience of momentary happiness when a desire is fulfilled, but it is immediately followed by greed for more. One who acquires a million rupees is engaged in finding the ways and means to acquire two million. Thus the vicious cycle of planning and implementation of the plan follows. If the desire is not fulfilled, anger arises. Every desire is either fulfilled or unfulfilled, so either anger or greed is bound to follow the desire. Thus, pain inevitably follows the appearance of any desire. If you say that one should abstain from desires, it is not possible. The reason is that unless and until we attain Divine Bliss, the emergence of desires is natural. No one can put an end to them.

Another major delusion regarding material pleasures is that everyone feels that his present possessions are not sufficient to make him happy. He feels that he will definitely attain happiness if he reaches the next higher class. A person who is a millionaire thinks that if he could only become a billionaire, then everything would be perfect. However, this is mere deception. Let us suppose that a Prime Minister was touring his country and his car happened to break down in a village. He left his limousine by the roadside and went home in another car. A poor villager saw the limousine and was very impressed by its shape, sparkle, luxurious seats, radio and so on. He thought to himself, "If I could sit in this car for even a second, how much pleasure I would get!" It so happened that the villager fell into debt and went to Delhi to stay with his relative, who was a driver. He too learned driving and happened to get employed as the chauffeur of the Prime Minister. Now, the simple villager sat with the Prime Minister of the country, in the very car he had longed to sit in for just a few seconds! He was overjoyed in the beginning, but after only a few days of working for long hours, he came home and told his wife, "My duty is only for six hours, but I am made to work for eight hours. This is a dog's life. It is better to be a beggar than a driver." Now the very sight of the car disgusts him. What happened to the pleasure he imagined he would get from the car?

This is the experience of each and every person. Before an object is acquired, one experiences pleasure in the delusive hope of attaining happiness in the future if that object is acquired. But the moment we acquire it, the experience is quite the opposite. Instead of happiness, one begins to experience sorrow. Therefore, one should abandon this foolish expectation of attaining a higher level of happiness upon acquiring better material objects. The happiness experienced by a beggar in embracing her ugly, lame child is the same as that experienced by a queen in embracing her beautiful delicate prince. There is absolutely no difference in the happiness experienced, although it may externally appear to be totally different. The pleasure experienced by a cow eating green grass is the same as that experienced by a king who is served innumerable delicacies.

When people see things at an exhibition for the first time, they feel great pleasure. But they do not want to go to the exhibition a second time. They protest, "We have already been there. What are we going to do there a second time?" In other words, happiness comes to an end. A big crowd gathers to see a bride when she arrives at her in-laws for the first time, but no one comes afterwards even on being invited. Instead, they gossip about her, "She is too tall", "She is too short", "She is talkative", "She is dumb", "She is too conceited" and so on. This proves that it is only after something is attained that its true nature is revealed.

It is difficult to explain to the clerk of a High Court Judge that the pleasure he gets from his bicycle is the same as the pleasure the judge gets from his car. Let us assume that a clerk had been saving five rupees every day to buy a cycle. With great difficulty he has finally purchased a new bicycle with his savings and he is very happy. His boss had also been saving money and has purchased a new car today. He is equally happy as he proudly drives his car to his friends' houses. But after a few days, the boss comes back from a six-hour official trip and starts grumbling about how tiring driving a car is. The clerk comes back home after a long ride and complains to his wife about how exhausting riding a cycle is. But when he is told that his boss feels the same way about the car, he can't believe it. He thinks that his boss must be joking. Thus, we see that everyone believes their standard of living is unsatisfactory.

No one is willing to accept that those who are materially higher placed or better endowed are not happier than them. If we were to only understand the fact that after a person has enjoyed a certain standard of living for some time, it ceases to bring him pleasure, then the constant pursuit for a higher standard would come to an end. There would be peace, because cessation of desires itself implies freedom from sorrow.

If I elaborate upon the various levels of material happiness, you will be astonished. Let us look at what the *Vedas* state,

saiṣhā"nandasya mīmāṁsā bhavati, yuvā syāt sādhuyuvādhyāyaka, āśhiṣhṭho draḍhiṣhṭho baliṣhṭho tasyeyaṁ pṛithivī sarvā vittasya pūrṇāsyāt sa eko mānuṣha ānandaḥ

(Taitti. Up. 2.8)

If one person alone is given to rule the entire planet earth, and he is in the prime of youth, he is healthy, intelligent, his subjects are favourably inclined towards him and he enjoys all the material luxuries, he can be said to be enjoying the highest level of happiness on this earthly planet. But the *Vedas* say,

te ye śhataṁ mānuṣhā ānandāḥ
sa eko manuṣhyagandharvāṇām ānandaḥ

(Taitti. Up. 2.8)

This measure of happiness multiplied hundreds of times, is equal to one unit of happiness in the celestial abode of the *Mānava Gandharvas*. The *Vedas* further state,

te ye śhataṁ manuṣhyagandharvāṇāmānandāḥ sa eko devagandharvāṇāmānandaḥ

(Taitti. Up. 2.8)

The happiness of the *Mānava Gandharvas* multiplied hundreds of times is equal to a unit of pleasure of the *Deva Gandharvas*. Again,

te ye śhataṁ devagandharvāṇāmānandāḥ sa ekaḥ pitṛiṇāṁ chiralokalokānāmānandaḥ

(Taitti. Up. 2.8)

The pleasure of the *Deva Gandharvas* multiplied hundreds of times is equal to a unit of pleasure experienced in *Pitṛiloka,* the world of forefathers who have entered the celestial regions. Again,

te ye śhatam pitṛiṇāṁ chiralokalokānāmānandāḥ sa eka ājānajānām devānāmānandaḥ

(Taitti. Up. 2.8)

The pleasure of *Pitṛiloka* multiplied hundreds of times is equal to a unit of pleasure of the celestial *Ājānaja* gods. Again,

te ye śhatamājānajānām devānāmānandāḥ sa ekaḥ karmadevānam devānāmānandaḥ

(Taitti. Up. 2.8)

The pleasure of the *Ājānaja* gods multiplied hundreds of times is the pleasure experienced by the *Karma Devas*. The *Vedas* continue,

te ye śhatam karmadevānām devānāmānandāḥ
sa eko devānāmānandaḥ te ye śhatam devānāmānandāḥ
sa eka indrasyānandaḥ te ye śhatamindrasyānandāḥ
sa eko bṛihaspater ānandaḥ

(Taitti. Up. 2.8)

The pleasure of hundreds of *Karma Devas* together is equal to one measure of joy of a *Deva*. That pleasure, multiplied hundreds of times is the pleasure experienced by the king of the heavenly regions, *Indra*. The pleasure of *Indra* multiplied hundreds of times is equal to one measure of joy of his guru, *Bṛihaspati*.

te ye śhatam bṛihaspaterānandāḥ sa ekaḥ prajāpaterānandaḥ
te ye śhatam prajāpater ānandāḥ sa eko brahmaṇa ānandaḥ

(Taitti. Up. 2.8)

The pleasure of *Bṛihaspati* multiplied hundreds of times is the pleasure experienced by *Prajāpati*, one of the original progenitors of all created beings and the pleasure of a *Prajāpati* multiplied hundreds of times is the joy experienced by Brahmā, the creator of this material universe.

All the levels of happiness in the abodes referred to in these verses are within the realm of *Māyā*. Therefore, there is unhappiness, dissatisfaction and unfulfilment everywhere. Perfect or true happiness is countless miles away from the happiness attained in these abodes. It is only when we attain perfect happiness in the form of Divine Bliss, that we will be eternally satisfied, gratified, blissful and attain immortality. In the *Gītā*, the Lord says to Arjuna,

ābrahmabhuvanāllokāḥ punarāvartino'rjuna

(Gītā 8.16)

"O Arjuna! There is no trace of perfect happiness right up to the abode of Brahmā. Having attained even that abode, one continues to revolve in the endless cycle of birth and death."

māmupetya tu kaunteya punarjanma na vidyate

(Gītā 8.16)

Only by attaining Me and My abode can an individual soul become liberated and experience Divine Bliss." Now, when true happiness is not attainable even from the enjoyments of the abode of Brahmā, isn't it both surprising and foolish to expect true happiness by becoming millionaires and billionaires in this material world? The eminent Saint, Veda Vyāsa stated,

yat pṛithivyāṁ vrīhiyavaṁ hiraṇyaṁ paśhavaḥ striyaḥ
na duhyanti manaḥ prītiṁ puṁsaḥ kāmahatasya te

(Bhāg. 9.19.13)

"Even if a man is given all the possible material possessions anyone could ever want, his desire for more will be exactly the same as it was at the very beginning." In fact, Veda Vyāsa goes to the extent of saying,

girir mahān girerabdhir mahānabdher nabho mahat
nabhaso'pi paraṁ brahma tato'pyāśhā duratyayā

(Veda Vyāsa)

A mountain is said to be huge, but bigger than the mountain is the sea, bigger than the sea is the sky and bigger than the sky is God, Who is referred to as Infinite. But there is something that is even bigger than God and that is desire! In fact, it may be possible to know the unknowable God, to comprehend He Who is incomprehensible, see He Who is imperceptible but, from eternity till now, there never was nor will there ever be, an example of someone who has become completely contented by attaining material objects, even if they were of the highest pleasures of *Brahmloka*. You may have heard of the celestial abodes, *svarga* where there is a lot of happiness. But the *Vedas* deny the existence of true happiness even there!

avidyāyāṁ bahudhā vartamānā vayaṁ kṛitārthā ityabhimanyanti bālāḥ
yatkarmiṇo na pravedayanti rāgāt tenāturāḥ kṣhīṇalokāśhchyavante

(Muṇḍaka Up. 1.2.9)

There is ignorance, unhappiness and dissatisfaction even in those celestial abodes. Therefore, only the most foolish strive to attain them. There is no perfect happiness in those abodes. They are merely abodes where people are sent for a limited time as a reward for their virtuous actions. Thereafter, they are sent back to lower forms according to their past actions. Attainment of the celestial abodes has even been condemned by Veda Vyāsa,

ādyantavanta evaiṣhāṁ lokāḥ karmavinirmitāḥ
duḥkhodarkāstamoniṣhṭhāḥ kṣhudrānandāḥ śhuchārpitāḥ

(Bhāg. 11.14.11)

The *Gītā* also states,

te taṁ bhuktvā svargalokaṁ viśhālaṁ
kṣhīṇe puṇye martyalokaṁ viśhanti

(Gītā 9.21)

The *Rāmāyaṇa* supports this fact,

svargahu svalpa anta dukhadāyī

(Rāmāyaṇa)

The implication is that all these celestial abodes up to the abode of Brahmā, like this world, are material. It is impossible to attain our goal of Divine Bliss there as they are all within the realm of *Māyā*.

But astonishingly, even those who accept the *Vedas* and the scriptures do not believe this truth. That is why they are engaged in a never-ending hopeless search for happiness through the attainment of material objects. What a way to waste this precious human life!

This human life is unattainable even by the celestial gods. The rarity of this human form has been emphasized in all the scriptures,

nṛidehamādyaṁ sulabhaṁ sudurlabhaṁ
plavaṁ sukalpaṁ gurukarṇadhāram
mayānukūlena nabhasvateritaṁ
pumān bhavābdhiṁ na taret sa ātmahā

(Bhāg. 11.20.17)

The *Rāmāyaṇa* says,

sura durlabha sadgranthani gāvā

(Rāmāyaṇa)

Now isn't it absurd for men to aspire for the attainment of celestial joys, when the celestial gods themselves crave to attain the human form? Here a question naturally arises, "Why do people in *svarga* desire this human form when greater pleasures are to be found over there? The joys of this earthly planet are totally insignificant in comparison to celestial pleasures." However, you will no longer be perplexed when you understand the reason. The truth is that *svarga* is only an abode where people are sent temporarily as a reward for their virtuous deeds. They merely enjoy the rewards for their virtuous actions, but do not have the freedom to perform fruit-yielding actions. It is only in the human form where, though there is suffering for one's past actions, there is also a unique opportunity to work towards attaining freedom from the bondage of action. Man can attain freedom from material bondage through practice of spiritual discipline. However, those in heaven are deprived of this opportunity because their actions yield no results. Thus, to desire celestial joys and endeavour towards attaining them, is absolutely foolish. There is no true happiness right up to the abode of Brahmā and as this includes all the other celestial abodes, it is obvious that expecting or aspiring to attain happiness from the limited luxuries of this material world is absolute madness. We must seriously reflect upon the fact that there is not a trace of true happiness anywhere apart from God, as all the other abodes are dominated by *Māyā.* It is impossible for the soul to attain Bliss in any region where *Māyā* rules.

Now observe the constantly fluctuating and unusual nature of the world. There is a predominance of the three *guṇas,* the modes of *Māyā,* in the mind of each and every individual. These *guṇas* are *sattva, rājasa* and *tāmasa,* and they are constantly fluctuating. Sometimes *sattvaguṇa* predominates, sometimes *rajoguṇa* and sometimes *tamoguṇa* governs the mind. When the *sāttvika* mode governs the mind, a person is calm and serene. When the *rājasika* mode prevails, he becomes active, hopeful and ambitious for power, passion and profit. When the *tāmasika* mode predominates, he becomes lazy and violent. Now since these *guṇas* fluctuate constantly, every individual has varying temperaments throughout the day. Another fact about the *guṇas* is that there is no guarantee about which *guṇa* will predominate at any given time of the day. Normally, the atmosphere or environment that a person stays in most of the time, determines which *guṇa* will predominate and which two will become subordinate.

There is one more point to reflect upon. Due to a lack of *sāttvika* qualities and thoughts, it is only when a person is exposed to a *sāttvika* environment in abundance, that he is occasionally dominated by this mode. On the other hand, because there is an abundance of *rājasika* environment, a person is easily overpowered by this *guṇa* even with the slightest association. The *tāmasika guṇa* is the most powerful *guṇa* of all. For example, suppose you are praying. You are now in a *sāttvika* environment. At that moment, you are approached by your wife or son who addresses you lovingly. You see them, hear them and by receiving their loving touch, immediately enter into the *rājasika* mode. Just then, your neighbour also comes in and angrily says, "You are the biggest rogue I have ever met!" The moment you hear this you become angry and go from the *rājasika* to the *tāmasika* mode. This is an example of the constant play of the fluctuating *guṇas* in each and every individual.

With these constantly changing *guṇas*, how is it possible for anyone to have steady feelings and faith in God and the Saints? Sometimes we consider God to be merciful, sometimes we think of Him as an impartial judge who merely dispenses the fruits of our actions and at other times we blame Him for being cruel and even go to the extent of cursing Him, "What injustice there is, in the court of God! My neighbour was worried because he had twelve children. Now he has just had the thirteenth! And I had only one child and even that one child died today."

Although God and Saints are beyond the influence of the three *guṇas*, they appear to us to be endowed with these temperaments because our own perception is coloured by these *guṇas*. The astonishing fact is that the person who sees God with this defective vision is unable to judge whether it is God Who is dominated by the three *guṇas*, or whether it is his own thoughts that are projected upon whatever he perceives.

When each and everyone suffers from this disease, the wife, husband, father, son, friend and so on, then how can the relationship between two people remain constantly amicable?

Amity may be possible only by sheer coincidence, such as when two individuals are dominated by the same *guṇa,* at the same time. But even in this case, harmony may not necessarily result because, though the *guṇa* is the same, there is always a difference in the degree of intensity of the *guṇas* in each person. Take for example a husband and wife who were both dominated by *rajoguṇa.* They agreed to spend the evening at the movies. However, on the way to the theatre, they heard a spiritual discourse. Although both were exposed to the same spiritual environment, their reactions were entirely different. The husband was unaffected by the inspiring words of the preacher, because at that time *rajoguṇa* was very strong in him. In the wife, the *rajoguṇa* was less predominant, so the little that she heard of the discourse, stimulated the *sattvaguṇa* in her and she suggested to her husband that they should stay back to listen to the entire spiritual discourse. He became angry saying, "You suddenly appear to be very religious. You can attend the lecture if you wish. I am going to the movies." Saying that, he stomped off.

Such arguments are simply a result of a difference in the degree of the intensity of the *guṇas* in each individual. The astonishing fact is that you expect that the entire world will agree with you all the time and some of you actually believe that this is possible. If even one person opposes you, you are not only surprised, but also miserable. However, if you understood the continuous fluctuating situation of the *guṇas,* you would be surprised if even one person remained favourable to you for even a day. However, our understanding is the reverse. When a person is less favourable towards us, we are surprised. The fact is that no one in the world is favourable or unfavourable to anyone.

Where there is harmony in the *guṇas*, for that period there is friendship. When the *guṇas* are opposed to each other, then there is opposition. If this philosophy is understood, you will not feel distressed when people are unfavourable towards you, and the effort of trying to make everyone favourable towards you will automatically come to an end.

For example, if a madman were to abuse you and in return you also abused him, obviously people will think that you have also become mad, because you have taken offence at a madman's words. The same thing happens in the world. Each and every person is compulsively dominated by the constantly fluctuating *guṇas*, so why should you be hurt by another person's behaviour? Why don't you remember that he is afflicted by the disease of the three *guṇas*? He deserves pity. To be angry or upset by his behaviour certifies your own madness. Someone says you are 'bad' and it hurts you. The fact that you were hurt proves that you are bad. If you were good, i.e. sensible, then you would have ignored his words by thinking that his state is abnormal as he is afflicted by the three *guṇas*. On the other hand, if you are actually a bad person, there is no reason to feel hurt, because he is speaking the truth. By being disturbed by a mere sentence, you have fallen into the trap of anger and other related ailments of the mind.

Isn't it astonishing? Just tell someone that he is a little short-tempered and he will immediately deny it with an angry outburst, "How dare you make such a comment? When have you seen me angry?" Observe, he is already angry while asking you. When he has already given vent to anger, is there any need for a reply? This drama is a common part of each individual's life. A person who suffers from any imperfection is not aware of it because the knowing faculty, the intellect, is itself dominated by the three *guṇas*. So, it cannot give a judgment against itself. But why not accept the truth? In the world, when someone introduces a clerk, he says, "He is a clerk." Does this man object or become angry? Does he say, "Why didn't you introduce me as a manager?" A man who is blind is referred to as a blind man. He does not object or feel offended. Why then do you get upset without reason when someone calls you greedy, hot-tempered or boastful, although you give vent to these feelings several times a day? You are overpowered by feelings of resentment towards others day and night. You constantly think about and contemplate mere words they have said, and frequently resort to vindictive action. Isn't it an amazing drama!

Most worldly people suffer from a very great delusion. Each one expects everyone to love and favour them. However, it is my challenge that no woman in this material world loves her husband entirely for the sake of his happiness, no man loves his wife for the sake of her happiness. No worldly father loves his son only for the sake of the son's happiness. When husbands, wives, fathers, sons and so on, cannot love one another for the sake of the other's happiness, then to expect this from other casual acquaintances in the world signifies a greater madness than that of a lunatic in an asylum. But this is what we are striving for all the time.

You may object, saying, "My husband or my wife loves me for the sake of my happiness." This is exactly the delusion everyone suffers from. You never realize that each one deceives the other with mere talks about caring for the other's happiness, while the actual aim is one's own happiness. In spite of this constant deception, you call yourself wise. Until an individual attains true happiness, it is impossible for him to do anything for the sake of another person's happiness. And if it appears that someone is selfless, then you can be sure that there is definitely some great hidden selfishness behind that action, which will become apparent later.

If a wife claims that she loves her husband entirely for the sake of his happiness, a small test will easily reveal the reality. Simply write a fictitious letter on behalf of the husband to another woman. Use some shocking sentences like, "I love no one but you. I have been fooling my wife all these years and I am waiting for an opportunity to get rid of her so that I can live the rest of my life in peace with you." The moment the wife reads the letter, her love for her husband will immediately turn to hatred. There will be a storm of strong abusive words between the two. Now, even if the wife were told that the whole thing was a pretence, she will experience some difficulty in returning to a normal relationship with her husband. I am not suggesting that you actually test your loved ones in this manner. This example only reveals how quickly worldly love can come to an end, as each one desires only his or her own happiness. Had the wife desired her husband's happiness, she would not have been upset by the letter. On the contrary, she would have been pleased to share her husband's happiness, because her only desire would have been to see him happy. But there is no such selfless love in the world. A simple test of love can fool even the most intelligent person, so the question of a common man acting sensibly, just does not arise. The following verse from the *Vedas* reveals the selfish nature of worldly relations,

> ***na vā are patyuḥ kāmāya patiḥ priyo bhavatyātmanastu kāmāya patiḥ priyo bhavati na vā are jāyāyai kāmāya jāyā priyā bhavatyātmanastu kamāya jāyā priyā bhavati na vā are putrāṇāṁ kāmāya putrāḥ priyā bhavantyātmanastu kāmāya putrāḥ priyā bhavanti***
>
> *(Bṛihad. Up. 2.4.5 ; 4.5.6)*

"No worldly husband, wife, father, son, etc., can love another person for the sake of that person's happiness. Everyone loves for the sake of one's own happiness." The world is nothing but a stage where the selfish game of self-interest is being enacted. Each player plays his role according to his intellectual ability. But until we understand where our true self-interest lies, that is, until there is a firm decision that the material world is to be renounced, our ultimate purpose or aim will not be fulfilled. This means, one has to free oneself of love and hatred in the world and centre one's love exclusively in God.

vāri mathe baru hoi ghṛita sikatā te baru tela
binu hari bhajana na bhava tariya yaha siddhānta apela

(*Rāmāyaṇa*)

The *Rāmāyaṇa* refers to the futility of our efforts to realize our aim of Divine Bliss in the material world, and compares it with trying to extract butter from water or oil from sand. In fact, the result of our efforts in the world for happiness is even worse. Whatever actions we perform will result in bondage, because we will be bound forever by the fruits of our actions, which are endless.

Hence, the best remedy is not to consider anyone as either your friend or your enemy. In the world, everyone is wandering around for the fulfilment of their aim of perfect happiness. If an expert, a Saint tells us that the path to attain this goal is not here but in the opposite direction, then we will surrender to God and attain that Supreme Bliss. But those who don't surrender and continue to love the material world as they have done in countless past lives, remain bound. We waste our time and energy in an attempt to be called good, while it is totally impossible considering the truth stated above. We never make an effort to actually become good, we only want to be called good. All this results in a lifelong hypocrisy. We constantly remain concerned about acting, pretence and etiquette. There have always been and always will be two types of people in the world: good and bad. The people belonging to the spiritual realm are good and those dominated by the three *guṇas* are bad. Even among the bad, there are three categories; *tāmasa* being the worst, *rājasa* is better than *tāmasa* and *sattva* is better than *rājasa*.

Our aim should be to become truly good in the spiritual realm, after which there is no question of ever becoming bad again. Such a 'good' person will be opposed by three kinds of people, *tāmasika, rājasika* and *sāttvika*. So why do you expect that those dominated by *Māyā* will remain favourable to you? If you become *sāttvika,* then you will be criticized by *rājasika, tāmasika* and spiritual people. If you become *tāmasika,* then you will be criticized by *rājasika, sāttvika* and spiritual people. When three parties will always be in opposition, why don't you become good forever and become divinely blissful? The world will continue its work under the influence of *Māyā,* as is its nature. Why worry about it? Understand this point from a story.

Once Lord Śhaṅkara and his consort Pārvatī set out to tour the world along with their mount, the bull, Nandī. Every action of the divine couple was criticized by worldly people. When both walked alongside their mount Nandī, they were criticized for being foolish not to ride upon the bull. When they did mount it, they were again criticized for being cruel to animals. Both of them immediately got off the mount. This time they decided that Pārvatī alone would ride on the bull and Śhaṅkara would walk alongside. But people again criticized them, complaining that in the age of *Kali Yuga* men become slaves to women. Hearing these comments, Pārvatī got off and Lord Śhaṅkara mounted the animal. This time the criticism was against the strong, sturdy man who sat comfortably on the mount, without the least consideration for the lady walking alongside. Eventually, Lord Śhaṅkara and Pārvatī decided to carry the bull on their shoulders. This time criticism was inevitable. They were branded as crazy people, who needed to be sent to a lunatic asylum for treatment. Thus, it is obvious that there is no standard behaviour or action that will be approved of by everyone in the world. It is fruitless to waste our time and efforts to please the world. We cannot destroy the external world, so the only way out is to rectify the inner world by devoting ourselves to the right path.

Now, listen to an astonishing fact. Find the biggest fool in the world and lock him up in a room for seven days. Give him neither food nor water. Imagine how hungry he will be! On the eighth day, serve him the most delicious food on a golden plate. How delighted he will be to see the food. Now, just as he is about to put the first morsel in his mouth, have someone whom he trusts secretly whisper to him that the food has been poisoned. He will immediately leave the food. "Why aren't you eating when you are so hungry?" He will reply, "There is poison in the food, I don't want to die." Again ask him, "Have you experienced the taste of poison to confirm that there is poison in the food?" "Taste poison! Are you crazy? I would not have been alive here, had I experienced the taste of it." Ask him a third question, "Have you ever seen poison?" "I have never felt the need to, because I have never wanted to commit suicide." Now ask him a last question, "Did you actually see anyone mixing poison in the food?" "No, I didn't. But my friend told me and I believe him." Observe, this starving fool has complete trust in what his friend has said to him, even though he himself has neither experienced the taste of poison, nor seen it. But you, who claim to be intelligent, actually see and even experience the harmful consequences of material pleasures, yet you do not become detached. From this you can judge your own so-called intelligence and sensibility. Therefore, what you must do is thoroughly understand the nature and reality of the world. Even though this is not something that any text has advised, if you are honest with yourself, you will agree that your own daily experience proves that this is an absolute necessity. No one will have any hesitation or doubt in accepting this need.

Another astonishing fact is that people confidently assert that the world is an illusion and there is no happiness in it, yet they are speedily running towards it. There is a secret behind this which requires serious understanding. When a person is deprived of material wealth, spouse, children and so on, he says that the world is an illusion, just out of irritation. But the moment he acquires these possessions or if they are regained or replaced, he clings to them. This obviously means that he does not actually consider this world an illusion.

When any Hindu dies in India, the body is carried to the crematorium with loud chanting of the words, *"rāma nāma satya hai."* These words mean that the divine name of God alone is the true reality and everything else, all worldly relations are impermanent and perishable. Suppose someone's son dies. Accompanied by the chanting of *"rāma nāma satya hai,"* his body is being carried out of the house. The father, too, is chanting this supreme truth. All of a sudden, his son, whom the doctor has erroneously declared dead, sits up. The father immediately stops the chanting, because now his son alone is the truth for him and not the divine name of God. The reason he stops the chanting of this supreme truth is that chanting this slogan is considered inauspicious by people. They associate it with death. Had they believed that the name of Lord Rāma was auspicious, they would have happily chanted it on every occasion. But unfortunately, most people ignorantly believe that if the words *'rāma nāma satya hai'* are uttered, it may result in a death in the family. Isn't such a superstition ridiculous? The name of the Lord gives immortality, but these so-called believers have given this slogan a completely opposite connotation.

The reality is that we consider wealth, family and fame to be our sources of happiness and generally believe in God only for increasing and protecting these material possessions and relations. How then can we consider the loss of wealth, spouse, or child as good fortune? It is only when someone or something dear to us is destroyed, that we become philosophical and declare that everything is transient, an illusion, and that nothing actually belongs to anyone. This so called 'knowledge' is actually ignorance. It is only the absence of material things that forces us into this temporary realisation. When a son insults his father or when a wife insults her husband or vice-versa, the realisation that every worldly relation is selfish and untrustworthy enters the mind. You think, "No one can fool me now. I have realized the reality of worldly love. From now on, I am not going to love anyone." But two minutes later, if your son or wife apologizes to you saying, "Please forgive me. The harsh words I spoke were unintentional. You know you mean everything to me," your previous decision immediately changes. "Well, that is exactly what I was thinking. How could my son or wife possibly say such a thing to me?" Obviously, the knowledge that everyone is selfish is limited only to the time there is friction in worldly relations. But the moment worldly people show love, this knowledge changes immediately. This is our fluctuating state of mind everywhere and at every moment. The conclusion is that we hate or resent the absence of worldly things, we don't hate possessing them.

If we believe in God, then we must also accept His words. You might say, "Of course I will definitely believe in them." Then listen to what the Lord Himself declares in the *Bhāgavatam*,

taṁ bhraṁśhayāmi sampadbhyo yasya chechchhāmyanugraham

(Bhāg. 10.27.16)

yasyāhamanugṛihṇāmi hariṣhye taddhanaṁ śhanaiḥ

(Bhāg. 10.88.8)

"I deprive those whom I grace of their worldly wealth, relations, name, fame and so on." In other words, the absence of material possessions is a sign of God's Grace. How many people fully accept this truth? There are only a select few who do.

Most people would even go to the extent of considering the auspicious celebration of *Janmāṣhṭamī,* appearance day of the Supreme Lord Kṛiṣhṇa, as a bad omen because their son died on that day. So they don't celebrate this festival for generations even though the death was due to destiny and not anything to do with *Janmāṣhṭamī.* This is our so called knowledge. Therefore, true detachment means being detached even while possessing material wealth, spouse, children, status and so on. To be detached in their absence implies that we still love the world and become detached only when we lose it.

Some of you might ask whether it is possible to attain God while possessing all the opulences of the world. There are examples of great personalities like King Janaka, who had all the riches of the world but was completely devoted to God. Here it must be noted that they were God realized Saints to start with. In the beginning when we are engaged in spiritual practice, we need to keep ourselves away from the luxuries of the world, as this can bring about the downfall of even the greatest spiritual aspirants.

nahiṁ kou asa janamā jaga māhiṁ
prabhutā pāi jāhi mada nāhiṁ

(Rāmāyaṇa)

"There is no one in this world who attains worldly possessions and is not intoxicated."

We have the example of Kunti, the mother of the Pāṇḍavas, who begged for an extraordinary favour from God,

vipadaḥ santu naḥ śhaśhvat tatra tatra jagadguro
bhavato darśhanaṁ yatsyādapunarbhavadarśhanam

(*Bhāg.* 1.8.25)

"O Lord, let me be deprived of all material opulences and give me hardships instead. In the absence of material things, I will not be proud and my feelings of being destitute will grow. This will help me come closer to you."

Thus, in the initial stage of devotional practice, our contact with the world should be minimised to the extent that is absolutely necessary. Secondly, the mind should not get attached to any worldly object, only then can one attain perfection. Butter taken out from milk will retain its form even when put into water. But if milk is mixed with water before the making of butter, it will combine with the water, thus losing its pure form. In the same way, when we seclude ourselves from material objects, using only that which is necessary for our basic needs and absorb our mind in God through devotional practice, we will attain that supreme Divine Love. Once we attain that, we will remain unaffected even in the midst of the greatest material pleasures. Although seclusion does not mean the end of desires, yet there is no doubt that direct contact with material objects stimulates the desire for them. A child cries for sweets, even though they are not before him; but if he can see them, then he will do everything possible to get them. So, direct contact with material objects increases the desire for them. Therefore, the less you have of worldly luxuries, the better it is for you and whatever you do have, you should not be attached to. It is only then that you can practise devotion. Without this detachment, the state of both the pauper and the king will be the same. The person who does not have even one set of clothes to wear, is restless for one and the person who has fifty, is restless for the fifty-first one! There is no difference in the degree of restlessness.

There are four categories of people in the world,

1. Some people have all the worldly possessions that usually give rise to pride and yet remain devoted to God.

2. Some people do not have these worldly possessions, yet they yearn for them and work hard to acquire them.

3. A vast majority of people, intoxicated by their material possessions, run towards the world for more and more, and forget God.

4. Most people devoid of material possessions, lose hope in the world and surrender to God. Through spiritual association they understand the true reality of the world and become detached from the world.

There are very few who belong to the first category. To possess alluring material luxuries and have neither pride nor attachment to them, is possible only for a highly evolved spiritual person.

There are also very few people in the second category. Normally in the absence of worldly possessions one becomes humble and turns towards God. But there may be a few who, though poor, are not spiritually inclined owing to bad *saṁskāras* or bad company. Most people in the world belong to the third and fourth category. The *Rāmāyaṇa* refers to a universal law,

sukha ke māthe sila pare nāma hiye te jāya
balihārī vā duḥkha kī jo pala pala nāma raṭāya

(Rāmāyaṇa)

"Cursed be that happiness which leads to forgetfulness of God and blessed be that sorrow which leads to constant remembrance of Him." However, we are engaged in constant efforts to attain those cursed possessions that lead to forgetfulness of God! At the same time, we also momentarily think that it would be good to realize God.

In fact, we have a firm belief that there definitely is happiness in the world. If not today, we will surely attain it tomorrow. With this constant hope, we have wasted innumerable lives and who knows how long this delusive belief of ours will continue? We need to reflect on the real nature of worldly happiness. The following example will make us realize the futility of our belief.

Two boys were sitting together when they saw a pretty girl pass by them. One boy immediately resolved, "I definitely want to marry her." The other said, "Who knows where she is from or whose daughter she is or what kind of husband she wants. Why bother to get unnecessarily involved in this?" Saying this, the second boy went on with his studies without any distraction. The first boy started finding out everything he could about the girl. He then tried to establish a friendship with her. In this process, he failed his examination and was depressed for years. Eventually, his desire to marry the girl was fulfilled and he felt very happy.

Observe, he was happy even before seeing the girl. But, all the harm which he did to himself and the discontent which he felt during the intervening years were completely pointless. Now, the other boy passed his examinations and after some time he also got married to a beautiful girl without going through any tension or worry. So, we ourselves create desires, go through a long-drawn stressful process to fulfil them, and after fulfilling them, we reach the same point where we were when we started!

prakṣhālanāddhi paṅkasya dūrādasparśhanaṁ varam

(Sūkti)

It is like deliberately stepping into mud, then washing your feet and feeling clean again. But your feet were clean even before you stepped into the mud! In the same way, we make desires and then suffer. If the desire is fulfilled, we are happy. If it is not fulfilled, and that happens frequently, then not only is our time and efforts wasted, but we may possibly suffer from the disappointment of this failure throughout our life.

This is our imaginary worldly happiness. We can analyse our mental state before and after we make a desire from our own experience. Once we realize the reality of the world, detachment will follow. Now let us seriously reflect upon the meaning of 'detachment'.

The Nature of Detachment

Most often the word 'attachment' is associated with love. But this is not the complete meaning of the word. Attachment means absorption of the mind. This absorption of the mind can either be through love or even through hate. Thus, whether it be through feelings of love or feelings of hate, or in any other way, the absorption of the mind in all cases is referred to as attachment. When there is neither attachment through love nor attachment through hate, that state is referred to as detachment or non-attachment.

This fact can very easily be understood from our own experience. When you think of someone who is dear to you, your mind is occupied with thoughts of that person, "When will I meet her? How will I meet her? She is really a nice person. She loves me, she cares for me" and so on. In the same way, your mind occupies itself with thoughts of a person you dislike or hate, "Where will I meet her? When will I meet her? How will I meet her? She is my enemy. She is always trying to harm me. I must take revenge on her," and so on. Thus, the absorption of the mind is the same in the case of both love and hate. This is the main reason why it was not just the *Gopīs,* who united their minds with Lord Kṛishṇa through love, who attained Him, but also demons like Kaṁsa, Rāvaṇa and others, who united their minds with Him through feelings of animosity, also attained Him. Veda Vyāsa reveals this in the following lines,

kāmaṁ krodhaṁ bhayaṁ snehamaikyaṁ sauhṛidameva cha
nityaṁ harau vidadhato yānti tanmayatāṁ hi te

(Bhāg. 10.29.15)

"Whether the mind is attached to God through lust, anger, fear, love or through any other emotion, the result is attainment of God."

So, now you must have understood that to be detached from the world, it is necessary to free the mind of both love and hate. In other words, one has to reach a state of indifference towards the world. As Saint Kabira has expressed,

kabirā khaṛā bajāra meṁ, sabakī māṁge khaira
nā kāhū soṁ dostī, nā kāhū soṁ baira

(Kabīra)

Detachment is living in the hustle and bustle of the world without feelings of friendship or enmity towards anyone.

Suppose a mother happens to lose her child in a fair. She is desperately searching for him. Suddenly she spots a child at a distance whose dress, age and height resembles her son's. She rushes forward to embrace the child, crying, "My son! My son!" But when she comes face to face with him, she realizes her mistake. Although eager to embrace the child, she now becomes indifferent towards him. She doesn't think for a moment, "I can't find my son, so let me love this child instead", nor does she experience any feelings of hostility, "I thought you were my son, but now I see that you are not. Why did you deceive me?" It is this state of indifference, being devoid of love or hate, which is called detachment.

An alcoholic is on his way to a pub for a drink. He passes a number of shops selling various things. He sees all of them, but is indifferent. He does not stop at any store thinking, "Oh! Why not have some sweets instead of a drink?" Nor does he quarrel with any of the shopkeepers saying, "Why are you selling sweets when I want a drink?" He walks indifferently past every shop and heads straight towards his goal, the pub. This is detachment. Walking through the market-place of the world, we must neither love nor hate, but must make our way straight to the shop of God, which alone is the centre of Divine Bliss.

It is significant to note that as long as the mind is attached anywhere, to anything apart from God, be it through love or hate, it is impossible to totally surrender to Him. And detachment is also impossible until you have the firm conviction, that there is neither true happiness nor sorrow in the world.

To reach this conviction, constant reflection upon the reality of the world is absolutely necessary. It is only through repeated reflection that this conviction will come. Merely thinking about it once will be of no avail, because the opposite thought that there is happiness in the world is deeply embedded in every soul since eternity. These past impressions will have to be removed.

janma mṛityujarāvyādhiduḥkhadoṣhānudarśhanam

(Gītā 13.8)

Repeated reflection upon birth, death, pain, disease, sorrow, etc., will result in detaching the mind from the world. The most auspicious day for you will be the day your mind becomes free of all material attachments. It is this detached mind that has to be surrendered to God. The result of surrender is the attainment of God's Grace and this Grace in turn, results in attainment of Divine Knowledge and Bliss.

Now you might think that once the mind is freed of worldly love and hate, there is nothing left to be done, because in such a state, no desires will arise. Consequently, there will be neither greed nor anger, as fulfilment of any desire gives rise to greed and non-fulfilment of any desire causes anger. Thus the question of unhappiness or sorrow in this case will not arise at all. So why should one unnecessarily bother to waste efforts in surrendering to God? However, to hold such an opinion is naive.

Firstly even if the mind is perfectly detached, it is impossible to be desireless until you attain Divine Bliss, because it is the nature of the mind to desire.

The second reason is that the mind devoid of love and hate cannot remain inactive. How can it cease working? This is absolutely impossible. It has already been proved that the mind cannot remain inactive, even for a moment.

The third reason is that, due to *saṁskāras,* the impressions of innumerable past lives, it is natural that desire will arise. No one can escape or stop this.

The fourth reason is that as long as the individual remains under the control of *Māyā,* it will be his nature to have material desires.

The fifth reason is that fulfilment of desires or complete satisfaction is possible only after attaining God. It is impossible to attain complete fulfilment before that. A thirsty deer may realize the illusory nature of a mirage in the desert and become detached from it, but this does not make it free from thirst. This thirst can only be quenched when it actually drinks water. Thus detachment alone is not enough to attain Divine Bliss. Surrender to God is a must.

To put it simply, suppose you have lost your way home. A passer-by tells you that you are on the wrong road. You accept this fact, but will that acceptance enable you to reach home? No. In the same way, it is not enough to know that the path of fulfilment of desires through possession of worldly objects, is wrong. It may result in detachment, but we must also find out which path will lead us to the blissful abode of God. We must follow that path in order to attain our desired goal.

There are some who claim that it is futile to engage in efforts to detach ourselves. They state that if we directly devote ourselves to God, detachment will come by itself. But the question is why will anyone love God and with what will he love Him? The answer they give is that we will love with the mind. The reason for loving Him is that He is the Ocean of Bliss and attainment of Bliss is our desired goal. That Bliss can only be attained by loving Him. However, this view will immediately be opposed by the intellect. Because although people do accept that God is a source of happiness, yet at the same time they also believe that the world is a source of happiness too. Not only that, worldly happiness can actually be seen and experienced. Why then would anyone abandon it to grope in the dark? Taking this into consideration, how will the mind possibly love God? It is easy to talk about loving God, but very difficult to practise without detachment.

Seeing shimmering sand in a desert, a deer believes that there certainly must be water and pursuing this belief, dies of thirst in the process. In the same way, as long as the firm decision of the intellect that there is happiness in the world is not changed, true love for God will not be possible even after innumerable lives, because there will always be this constant hope of attaining happiness in the world some time or the other. Thus, if a person states that direct devotion to God will take care of everything, he is only deceiving himself. After all, it is the intellect that governs the mind.

manasastu parā buddhirbuddherātmā mahān paraḥ

(Kaṭha Up. 1.3.10)

According to this verse, the governor of the mind is the intellect. When the decision of the intellect is that there is happiness in the world, then who will let the mind be attached to God? Will the mind attach itself to God? That is absolutely impossible. If you claim that there were many examples of those who saw Śhrī Kṛishṇa and became engrossed in Him during the time of His descension, then perhaps you don't know who can see that all-attractive divine form of Lord Kṛishṇa.

chidānandamaya deha tumhārī vigata vikāra jāna adhikārī

(Rāmāyaṇa)

According to the *Rāmāyaṇa*, God's body is divine. A divine body cannot be seen with material eyes. Then, how will the mind become engrossed? You may have read in the *Bhāgavatam* that when Śhrī Kṛishṇa and Śhrī Balarāma were standing in the assembly hall of Kaṁsa, they were perceived differently by the citizens according to their individual feelings.

mallānāmaśhanirnṛiṇāṁ naravaraḥ strīṇāṁ smaro mūrtimān
gopānāṁ svajano'satāṁ kṣhitibhujāṁ śhāstā svapitroḥ śhishuḥ
mṛityurbhojapatervirāḍaviduṣhāṁ tattvaṁ paraṁ yogināṁ
vṛiṣhṇīnāṁ paradevateti vidito raṅga gataḥ sāgrajaḥ

(Bhāg. 10.43.17)

The same was the case when Lord Rāma stood in King Janaka's assembly hall. Each and everyone perceived Him differently, and not everyone was attracted to Him.

jākī rahī bhāvanā jaisī,
prabhu mūrati dekhī tina taisī
viduṣhana prabhu virāṭamaya dīsā,
bahu mukha kara paga lochana sīsā

(Rāmāyaṇa)

Some people saw His gigantic universal form and were terrified. How could everyone be overwhelmed with love on seeing Him? Only the devotees who were eligible to see His divine form, were overwhelmed with love.

haribhaktana dekhe doū bhrātā
ishṭadeva iva saba sukhadātā

(Rāmāyaṇa)

It is now apparent that if the mind is not attracted to God even during His descension, then the question of being attracted to Him at other times just does not arise. In fact, there is a greater possibility of someone turning into an atheist after seeing the divine personalities of Śhrī Rāma and Śhrī Krishṇa during their descensions, instead of being attracted to Them.

The reason is that until and unless you understand the secret that Their forms and actions are divine, your material vision will merely see material forms and actions. Then, where is the question of having divine sentiments towards Them? Therefore, guidance from a true Master or Guru is essential.

राधे राधे गोविंद गोविंद राधे। राधे राधे गोविंद गोविंद राधे॥

The Saint

After detaching the mind from the world and before surrendering to God, there is need of a divine entity, without whom one cannot attain the Supreme Goal. That entity is a God-realized Saint or Guru. It is the Guru, who decides which path is best for each devotee to enable his surrender to God. Again, it is he who dispels all doubts faced by the aspirant on the path. Mere detachment is not enough to attain God.

āchāryavān puruṣho hi veda

(Chhān. Up. 6.14.2)

parīkṣhya lokān karmachitān
brāhmaṇo nirvedamāyānnāstyakṛitaḥ kṛitena
tadvijñānārthaṁ sa gurumevābhigachchhet
samitpāṇiḥ śhrotriyaṁ brahmaniṣhṭham

(Muṇḍaka Up. 1.2.12)

"After performing ritualistic actions learned men have concluded that the mere performance of Vedic rituals cannot destroy the bondage of past actions. On the contrary, it only serves to increase that bondage. Thus, one needs the guidance of a Saint who has thorough knowledge of the scriptures and has practical experience of God." The *Gītā* states,

tadviddhi praṇipātena paripraśhnena sevayā
upadekṣhyanti te jñānaṁ jñāninastattvadarśhinaḥ

(*Gītā* 4.34)

"One who desires to know God, will have to surrender to a God-realized Saint and seek the supreme knowledge with the spirit of service and submission." Veda Vyāsa also states,

tasmād guruṁ prapadyeta jijñāsuḥ śhreya uttamam
śhābde pare cha niṣhṇātaṁ brahmaṇyupaśhamāśhrayam

(*Bhāg.* 11.3.21)

"The goal of attaining God can only be reached by surrendering to a genuine Spiritual Master." The *Rāmāyaṇa* also says,

"guru binu bhava nidhi tarai na koī"; "guru binu hoī ki jñāna"

(*Rāmāyaṇa*)

"Without the guidance of a Guru, one cannot cross the ocean of material existence." Again it says, "Without the guidance of a Guru, one cannot attain knowledge of God." Thus, the unanimous view of all the scriptures is that we must surrender to a Guru in order to know the unknown entity called God. So let us now reflect upon this entity known as the Guru or Spiritual Master.

It must be remembered that by a Saint or Guru we do not mean just a learned scholar of the scriptures, or just a man of practical experience of God. The scriptures stress the importance of both. My personal opinion however, is that even if a Saint is not a learned scholar of the various scriptures, if he has attained God, our goal will be achieved through him. This is because attaining God automatically results in the attainment of all knowledge.

In the various religious texts as well as in the world, we hear the terms - individual soul, *puruṣha,* great soul, *Mahā-puruṣha* and the Supreme Soul, *Parama Puruṣha*. Other terms for them are *jīvātmā, Mahātmā* and *Paramātmā*. This refers to the individual soul, Saints and God respectively. We have to reflect on the entity known as the great soul, or Saint. The intermediary between the soul and the Supreme Soul or God, is the great soul or Saint. He is one who knows God, has seen Him and is united with Him. In other words, the soul who has attained God is called a Saint.

However, it is very difficult for an ordinary person to determine whether or not a soul has attained God. A Saint can only be known by a Saint of the same level, because like God, his true identity cannot be grasped by the material senses, mind and intellect. Nevertheless, a Saint has to be recognized through perceptual, inferential and scriptural evidence, otherwise no one would have ever attained God since time immemorial.

Thus, although recognizing a Saint may require time and effort, it has to be done if we desire to attain God. Actually any effort of a preliminary aspirant to evaluate the divinity of a Saint, is as ridiculous as the effort of a child studying the alphabets, to evaluate the knowledge of a university professor. Yet, innumerable disciples have identified a genuine Guru, surrendered to him, followed the spiritual guidelines specified by him and through his guidance, have eventually attained God. So, in order to reach that same goal without losing hope, we too have to follow the same rules and tread the same path. When one person can accomplish a task, it implies that others can also do it.

In general, there are two categories of Saints and two categories of imposters. These four categories must clearly be understood, before the problem of recognizing a genuine Saint is resolved.

1. The first category of Saints include those who are saintly (divine) inwardly and whose external behaviour is also saintly. They have Divine Knowledge and Divine Bliss within, and also appear to be Saints externally. Their behaviour is not contrary to our notion of a Saint, so it is easy to recognize them. However, history bears witness to the fact that very few Saints belonged to this category.

2. The second category of Saints include those who are saintly inwardly, but appear to be worldly in their outward behaviour. We usually judge others by their external behaviour, so it becomes difficult to recognize such Saints. Most Saints belong to this category, because it is their nature to conceal themselves from the world.

gopanīyaṁ gopanīyaṁ gopanīyaṁ prayatnataḥ

The possible reason is the common notion that a good man does not declare his own greatness. So, if a Saint were to declare his own divinity, people would never accept him as a Saint. Whatever the reason, history bears witness to the fact that most Saints appeared outwardly worldly, but were divine within.

3. The first category of imposters include those who are worldly both inwardly and outwardly. In other words, they do not pretend to be Saints either in dress or behaviour and live like ordinary people. Therefore, they can be easily identified.

4. The second category of impostors include the so-called 'saints', who are inwardly worldly, but outwardly put on an act of being Saints. Not only do they give discourses based on the scriptures and dress in the garb of ascetics, but they even initiate disciples. It is extremely difficult to identify such impostors, because we normally judge a person according to his external behaviour.

Both, the second category of Saints and the second category of impostors require deeper reflection. How do we distinguish between those who are saintly internally but externally behave like ordinary worldly people, and those who are inwardly worldly, but outwardly behave like Saints? To properly identify both is a great problem. You may say that one who is inwardly saintly can never outwardly behave like a worldly man. Obviously, you have not studied the history of Saints very deeply. Therefore, let us get acquainted with some of them.

It is a well-known truth, that from the very moment a person attains perfect knowledge of God, he can never be overpowered by ignorance again. Once Divine Bliss is attained, the question of experiencing any sorrow just does not arise. The *Vedas* say,

sadā paśhyanti sūrayaḥ tadviṣhṇoḥ paramaṁ padam

(Veda)

A Saint always enjoys Divine Bliss. If that Bliss or Knowledge could be taken away, then no one would ever strive to attain it.

manuṣhyāṇāṁ sahastreṣhu kaśhchid yatati siddhaye
yatatāmapi siddhānāṁ kaśhchinmāṁ vetti tattvataḥ

(Gītā 7.3)

The *Gītā* states that it takes thousands of lifetimes to attain perfection. Why would anyone strive for so many lifetimes to attain Divine Bliss and Knowledge if that were temporary?

A grain of rice or wheat when roasted appears to be the same, but its germinating power is destroyed forever. No one can make that seed sprout now, by any means. Similarly, once a person attains God and is liberated from material bondage, then *Māyā* can never overpower or govern that person again. This is stated in the scriptures and is unanimously accepted as logical. On the basis of this, we have to understand how the divine personalities who were beyond *Māyā* happened to act like worldly people.

First, let us take Brahmā and Śhaṅkara, the personalities who create and destroy the universe. The *Rāmāyaṇa* says that even they became deluded by *Māyā*.

śhiva virañchi kahaṁ mohaī ko hai vapurā āna

(Rāmāyaṇa)

The *Rāmāyaṇa* again states this point more emphatically,

nārada bhava virañchi sanakādī je muni nāyaka ātamavādī
moha na andha kīnha kahu kehī ko jaga kāma nachāva na jehī

(Rāmāyaṇa)

"There is no one, not even Brahmā and Śhaṅkara, who can escape from being blinded by delusion."

It is important to understand here that Saints are of two kinds. The first are those who are eternally beyond *Māyā,* that is, they have never been under the bondage of *Māyā*. They are referred to as God's eternal associates, *nityasiddha*. The second kind, are those who were eternally bound by *Māyā,* but one day surrendered to a true Saint, followed the path specified by him, attained God and thereafter became Saints for eternity.

I will first refer to those divine personalities who were never under the influence of *Māyā*. Even those who have been Saints since eternity, have appeared to be blinded by delusion, desire, anger and so on. How and why this happened is a profound question that needs to be answered.

In *Satya Yuga,* we have the example of the four sons of Brahmā, Sanatakumāra, Sanātana, Sanaka and Sanandana. These four were *paramahaṁsas* who were eternally liberated souls and had realized the formless aspect of God, the Impersonal Brahman. The four of them were once going to Vaikuṇṭha, the abode of Lord Viṣhṇu. At the entrance, they were stopped by the gatekeepers of Vaikuṇṭha, Jaya and Vijaya. This infuriated them and they cursed Jaya and Vijaya to become demons. It is essential to note that a *paramahaṁsa* is one who is so absorbed in the Bliss of Impersonal Brahman that he neither sees, hears, smells, touches, thinks of, nor experiences anything other than the self. The *Vedas* state,

yatra hi dvaitamiva bhavati taditara itaraṁ jighrati taditara itaraṁ paśhyati taditara itaraṁ śhṛiṇoti taditara itaramabhivadati taditara itaraṁ manute taditara itaram vijānāti yatra vā asya sarvamātmaivābhūttatkena kaṁ jighrettatkena kaṁ paśhyettatkena śhṛiṇuyāttatkena kama-bhivadettatkena kaṁ manvīta tatkena kaṁ vijānīyāt yenedaṁ sarvaṁ vijānāti taṁ kena vijānīyādvijñātāramare kena vijānīyāditi

(Bṛihad. Up. 2.4.14)

How is it that such personalities, who had risen above all dualities and merged their minds in the Impersonal *Brahman*, again experienced duality? How did ignorance overpower them to the degree that they actually cursed someone?

You will be very much astonished to hear about Pārvatī, the divine power and consort of Lord Śhaṅkara. There is an episode in the *Rāmāyaṇa* where Śhrī Rāma was displaying anguish in separation from His Consort, the Divine Mother, Sītā. This was witnessed by both Pārvatī and Śhaṅkara. However Pārvatī was deluded by this and commented,

kabahūṁ yoga viyoga na jāke dekhā pragaṭa viraha duḥkha tāke

(Rāmāyaṇa)

"God is a personality, who experiences neither union nor separation but remains ever-blissful in His own identity. How can Rāma be God as He is experiencing anguish in separation from a woman?" At the same time she said,

śhaṅkara jagata vandya jagadīsā
sura nara muni saba nāvata sīsā
tina nṛipa sutahiṁ kīnha paranāmā
kahi sachchidānanda paradhāmā

(Rāmāyaṇa)

"Lord Śhaṅkara is the Lord of the universe and is worshipped by the entire world. He has addressed Śhrī Rāma as '*Sachchidānanda Brahman*' - the Supreme Lord and offered obeisance to Him." The word '*Jagadīśha*' that Pārvatī used for Lord Śhaṅkara is used in the *Vedas* for God, which means that she accepted Him to be God and yet she had doubts about the personality he offered obeisance to! She said,

brahma jo vyāpaka viraja aja akala anīha abheda
so ki deha dhari hoya nara jāhi na jānata veda

(Rāmāyaṇa)

"How is it possible for the formless Absolute to take a human form?" Just think. Even a simple, uneducated person would not have this kind of a doubt. The soul which is formless, revolves in the cycle of birth and death in 8.4 million forms. Surely God, Who is all-powerful and Who has manifested this universe merely by a smile, can assume a form!

Nevertheless, Pārvatī was besieged by doubt; firstly about the formless Absolute having a form and secondly about His being afflicted by feelings of union and separation. She concluded that Rāma could not be God. Again she thought,

śhaṁbhu girā puni mṛiṣhā na hoī śhiva sarvajña jāna saba koī

"Lord Śhaṅkara is all-knowing, his statements cannot be false." This word *'sarvajña'* or all-knowing is used in the scriptures only for God.

yaḥ sarvajñaḥ sarvavidyasya jñānamayaṁ tapaḥ
tasmādetadbrahma nāma rūpamannaṁ cha jāyate

(Muṇḍaka Up. 1.1.9)

In other words, accepting Lord Śhaṅkara as omniscient, Pārvatī still doubted his words. She assumed the form of Sītā through her divine power in order to test Lord Rāma. When Lord Rāma saw her sitting in the form of Sītā, the all-knowing Lord Rāma, the supreme actor, gave up His act of crying and asked, "O Mother, why are you sitting here alone? Where is My Father, Lord Śhaṅkara?" In His divine pastimes in this particular descension, Lord Rāma considered Śhaṅkara as His worshipable deity. It is from that point of view that Śhaṅkara is His Father, and Pārvatī is His Mother.

The test was over. Pārvatī returned to Lord Śhaṇkara, quite ashamed of her behaviour. But when Lord Śhaṅkara asked her whether she had tested Lord Rāma, she immediately lied in spite of accepting both him and Lord Rāma as all-knowing personalities,

kachhu na parīkṣhā līna gusāīṁ kīnha praṇāma tumhārihiṁ nāīṁ
(Rāmāyaṇa)

"I did not test Him, I only went to offer my respects to Him as you did." After this, Lord Śhaṅkara abandoned her, saying that he could not look upon her as a wife anymore, as she had taken the form of his mother, Sītā. It should be noted that before marriage, Sītā had worshipped Pārvatī as a mother and had been granted the boon of attaining Lord Rāma as Her husband.

mana jāhi rāṁchyo milai so vara sahaja sundara sāṁvaro

In this way, Pārvatī became the mother of Sītā-Rāma and yet Śhaṅkara said to Pārvatī, "You took the form of Sītā even though it was just for a few moments. Therefore, I am abandoning you." But in the past Śhaṅkara didn't renounce Pārvatī when she acted as the mother of Sītā and granted Her a boon. So why did he do it now? Moreover, Pārvatī's body with which she assumed the guise of Sītā, was a body created by *Yogamāyā*. She returned to Śhaṅkara in her own original form. Just think about it, Śhaṅkara's mother and father are Sītā-Rāma, and Rāma's father and mother are Śhaṅkara-Pārvatī, but Lord Rāma did not renounce Sītā by following this rule of Śhaṅkara. However, in this episode it appears that Pārvatī was deluded by *Māyā*. Thereafter, she gave up her body, took birth again and engaged in severe penance, after which she was accepted by Lord Śhaṅkara. This is all well-known.

Next, we come to Garuṛa, who is the eternal mount of Lord Vişhṇu. He is described in the *Rāmāyaṇa* as '*jñānī bhakta śhiromaṇi*', or the crest-jewel among both devotees and *jñānīs*.

jñānī bhakta śhiromaṇi tribhuvanapati kara yāna
tāhi moha māyā prabala pāmara karahiṁ gumāna

(Rāmāyaṇa)

Māyā deluded even such a great devotee as Garuṛa! Is that not amazing! Garuṛa is an eternally liberated divine personality who has existed ever since God has. You will be astonished to hear of his delusion.

bhava bandhana te chhūṭaī nara japi jākara nāma
kharva nisāchara bāṁdheu nāgapāsa soi rāma

(Rāmāyaṇa)

The *Rāmāyaṇa* states that Garuṛa saw Lord Rāma bound by the serpent darts of the demon Indrajīta. He was confused, "The very name of God has the power to destroy the bondage of the actions of endless lifetimes. Then how can God Himself be bound by a mere demon? This cannot be God."

In this bewildered state, Garuṛa went to the Sage Nārada and Lord Śhaṅkara to clear his doubts. They told him,

mahā moha upajā ura tore miṭai na vegi kahe khaga more

(Rāmāyaṇa)

"A great ignorance has overpowered you. We have no remedy for it." They advised him to go and associate for some time with the Saint, Kāgabhuśhuṇḍi. Garuṛa went and related his doubts to Kāgabhuśhuṇḍi, who said,

tuma nija moha kahī khaga sāīṁ
so nahiṁ kachhu ācharaja gusāīṁ

nārada bhava virañchi sanakādī
je muni nāyaka ātama vādī
moha na andha kīnha kahu kehī
ko jaga kāma nachāva na jehī

(Rāmāyaṇa)

"O Garuṛa! *Māyā* has bewildered you. This is not surprising, for it overpowers even great personalities like Brahmā and Śhaṅkara.

Next, let's come to the Sage Nārada. The scriptures describe how he too fell into ignorance. Once Nārada became proud that he had conquered lust and went to Lord Nārāyaṇa to boast about his victory. In order to crush Nārada's pride, Lord Nārāyaṇa humourously gave him the face of a monkey.

Now let us look at what happened during Lord Rāma's descension. The great devotee, Hanumāna, who is ever absorbed in the Bliss of Lord Rāma, failed to recognize Him on their first meeting! Assuming the guise of a Brahmin he went to Lord Rāma and asked,

kī tuma tīna deva mahaṁ koū nara nārāyaṇa kī tuma doū

(Rāmāyaṇa)

"Are you Brahmā, Viṣhṇu, Śhaṅkara or are You both *Nara* and *Nārāyaṇa*?" Enacting His role as an ordinary man, Śhrī Rāma said, "I am none of these. I am the son of Daśharatha and I am looking for My wife." Then Rāma questioned

Hanumāna, "And who are you?" This time, Hanumāna recognized Him and said in great astonishment,

mora nyāu maiṁ pūchhā sāīṁ
tuma kasa pūchhahu nara kī nāīṁ

tava māyāvaśha phirauṁ bhulānā
tāte nātha na maiṁ pahichānā

(Rāmāyaṇa)

"I failed to recognize You, being deluded by *Māyā*, but how is it that You, the governor of *Māyā*, failed to recognize me?"

Sugrīva, Rāma's intimate friend, after testing Lord Rāma and being assured of His divinity, forgot Him on gaining his kingdom. He remembered Him only upon being threatened by Lakṣhmaṇa. Sugrīva married his own sister-in-law, Tārā, whereas Lakṣhmaṇa established the ideal towards a brother's wife by only looking at Her feet and never beyond.

nūpure tvabhijānāmi nityaṁ pādābhivandanāt

Lakṣhmaṇa said, "I recognize only the anklets of Sītā, because I always bowed to Her lotus feet." Vibhīṣhaṇa also married his elder brother's wife, Mandodarī. However, when Vibhīṣhaṇa surrendered to Lord Rāma, Sugrīva and others objected strongly. But Lord Rāma said,

vibhīṣhaṇo vā sugrīva yadi vā rāvaṇaḥ svayam

"O Sugrīva! Vibhīṣhaṇa has surrendered to Me. Even if Rāvaṇa were to surrender to Me, I would have no objection. I would even accept him. I would willingly make Rāvaṇa the king of Ayodhyā. Since I have already given Vibhīṣhaṇa the title of the king of Lankā,"

All the residents of Ayodhyā harboured intense feelings of aversion towards Kaikeyī because of her role in Lord Rāma's exile, in spite of Lord Rāma Himself warning them that He would renounce anyone who had resentment towards Kaikeyī. This hostility in the people of Ayodhyā is surprising, because no one in Ayodhyā was under the control of *Māyā* at that time.

daīhika daivika bhautika tāpā
rāma rājya nahiṁ kāhuhiṁ vyāpā

"No one in Ayodhyā suffered from the three kinds of *mayika* afflictions."

jehi sukha lāgi purāri, asubha veṣha kṛita siva sukhada
avadhapurī naranāri, tehi sukha mahaṁ santata magana

"They were all beyond the bondage of *Māyā*."

The cruel words that Bharata, the brother of Śhrī Rāma, used for his own mother, would hardly be expected even from a worldly man, let alone a divine personality. He was ready to kill his mother Kaikeyī for her role in Śhrī Rāma's exile but was only concerned that Śhrī Rāma would abandon him for this act.

hanyāmahamimāṁ pāpāṁ kaikeyīṁ duṣhṭachāriṇīm

(Vālmīki Rāmāyaṇa)

Now let us consider the personal associates of Śhrī Kṛiṣhṇa during His descension. The creator Brahmā himself praises the cowherd boys who were the playmates of Śhrī Kṛiṣhṇa,

tadastu me nātha sa bhūribhāgo
bhave'tra vānyatra tu vā tiraśhchām
yenāhameko'pi bhavajjanānām̐
bhūtvā niṣheve tava pādapallavam

(Bhāg. 10.14.30)

aho bhāgyamahobhāgyam̐ nandagopavrajaukasām
yanmitram̐ paramānandam̐ pūrṇam̐brahma sanātanam

(Bhāg. 10.14.32)

tad bhūribhagyamiha janma kimapyaṭavyām̐
yad gokule'pi katamām̐ghrirajo'bhiṣhekam
yajjīvitam̐ tu nikhilam̐ bhagavān mukundas
tvadyāpi yatpadarajaḥ śhrutimṛigyameva

(Bhāg. 10.14.34)

"How fortunate are these cowherd boys who have the Supreme Lord Kṛiṣhṇa as their playmate and friend! I would consider it the greatest fortune if I could take birth even as a bird or any other lowly form in Vṛindāvana in order to attain their foot-dust." Similarly, for the *Gopīs* of Vṛindāvana, Brahmā says,

ṣhaṣhṭhivarṣhasahasrāṇi mayā taptam̐ tapaḥ purā
nandagopabrajastrīṇām̐ pādareṇūpalabdhaye
tathāpi na mayā prāptāstāsām̐ vai pādareṇavaḥ

(Vṛihad Vāmana Purāṇa)

"I performed penance for sixty thousand years to attain the dust of the feet of the *Gopīs*, but was unable to do so." However, those *Gopīs* and cowherd boys were all married, had children and led common household lives. Now, isn't it intriguing? They did not have even a trace of lust in them and yet they had families and children.

Arjuna, even after attaining the knowledge of the *Gītā* was infatuated by a woman from the nether world of Nāgaloka. He even had children with her. Not only Arjuna but all the Pāṇḍava brothers have an astonishing history. They were all born of different fathers. Yudhiṣhṭhira was the son of Yamarāja, Arjuna of Indra, Bhīma of Vāyu and Nakula and Sahadeva of the Aśhvini Kumāras. All five of them had a common wife - Draupadi. One of the Pāṇḍavas, Bhīma, married the demoness Hiḍimbā who bore him a son named Ghaṭotkacha!

Now let us again look at Arjuna's history as it is the most astonishing of all. Before the war of *Mahābhārata,* Arjuna and Duryodhana both approached Śhrī Kṛiṣhṇa for assistance. Śhrī Kṛiṣhṇa agreed to personally be with one side on the condition that He would not fight for them. He would give His entire army of eighteen divisions to the other side. Arjuna chose the weaponless Śhrī Kṛiṣhṇa. If Arjuna had not known that Śhrī Kṛiṣhṇa was God, how could he have made such a decision? Obviously, He knew that Śhrī Kṛiṣhṇa was the Supreme Lord. Nevertheless, he displayed ignorance on the battlefield by refusing to fight with his elders, although he already knew who he would be fighting against when he approached Śhrī

Kṛiṣhṇa for assistance. To dispel his ignorance Śhrī Kṛiṣhṇa enlightened him with the wisdom of the *Gītā*. All this happened, even though Arjuna had already been declared a divine personality in his previous life!

These examples from history prove that Saints externally behaved like worldly people, although they were, in fact, eternally liberated. An ordinary man can never understand how these Saints, who were beyond *Māyā*, performed actions of *Māyā* or ignorance. We can accept the fact that Saints can perform righteous deeds, but we find it difficult to understand that they can also perform unrighteous ones.

The truth is that, a Saint is a person who does no work whatsoever, either righteous or unrighteous. If he performs any kind of action, even for a fraction of a second, then he cannot be a Saint. This truth needs to be understood in detail. The *Gītā* clearly states,

yastvātmaratireva syādātmatṛiptaśhcha mānavaḥ
ātmanyeva cha santuṣhṭastasya kāryaṁ na vidyate

(Gītā 3.17)

"One who becomes a Saint ceases to work." Just as a seed is destroyed with the emergence of the sprout, and flowers wither with the growth of fruits, in the same way, after the attainment of God, a Saint becomes self-contented and eternally blissful. For what purpose would he perform any action thereafter? As an individual progresses towards God his accumulated fruit-yielding good and bad actions keep on decreasing and the moment he attains God, they come to an end forever. He reaches the stage of doing nothing. This can be understood by an example of a pregnant woman who reduces her activities with every successive month of pregnancy and stops all work at the time of delivery.

The purpose of the scriptures dealing with the philosophical schools of thought like *Mīmāṁsā* and others, is to direct the soul towards God. Thereafter, the various scriptures including the *Vedas* are not needed. After attaining God, the Saint does not need to follow the rules and regulations of the scriptures. The selfless activities prescribed in the *Mīmāṁsā* texts are first performed for the purification of the mind. Next, the spiritual aspirant listens to *Vedānta*, *śhravaṇa*. After that the *Nyāya* and *Vaiśheṣhika* teach one how to contemplate on those teachings, *manana*. Lastly one practices profound meditation, *nididhyāsana* as taught in *Sāṁkhya* and *Yoga* and thereby attains God. Once the goal is attained, the actions prescribed in the scriptures are no longer required. Some Saints appear to perform righteous acts to set an example for humanity while others appear to act in a totally undisciplined manner, violating the rules of the scriptures for reasons that will be clarified here.

Now, you must have understood that a Saint does not need to perform any action. When the ultimate aim behind the performance of any action, the attainment of Divine Bliss has been reached, the need for any further work ceases. The second point is that both good and bad actions cause bondage. Therefore, after attaining God and eternal Divine Bliss, how and why should a Saint engage in such actions again?

Thirdly, God is the controller of *Māyā*, *Māyā* is the controller of the soul, the soul is the controller of the intellect, the intellect is the controller of the mind, and the mind is the controller of the sense objects which control the senses. When the soul unites with God, the intervening power *Māyā* is removed forever and God directly controls the soul, the intellect, mind and senses. In other words, whatever a Saint is seen to be doing, is only the consequence of divine inspiration. The individual is selfishly motivated until he attains his goal, but once he attains Divine Bliss there is no reason to perform any action. Therefore, whatever actions the Saint performs are inspired by God and so are praiseworthy. It is only God who knows why He makes the Saints perform 'good' or 'bad' actions.

For example, if a car is involved in an accident, the car is not blamed, because the car cannot move by itself. It is an inanimate object. It is the driver that is to be blamed and punished. In the same way, as long as the individual soul does not surrender to God, he himself is the doer of every action. But once he surrenders completely to God, he no longer remains the doer. In fact, surrender itself means to become a non-doer that is, to reach a state of doing nothing. The Saint then becomes like an inanimate car. Just as a lifeless car is an instrument in the hands of a driver, so is a Saint in the hands of God. All his actions are performed by God alone.

ananyāśh chintayanto māṁ ye janāḥ paryupāsate
teṣhāṁ nityābhiyuktānāṁ yogakṣhemaṁ vahāmyaham

(Gītā 9.22)

God becomes the governor of the Saint and directs his every action. The Saint merely rests in His lap, free of all fears and totally absorbed in Divine Bliss.

Fourthly, every action is prompted by desire. Without desire, there is no basis for action. Once a person attains sainthood, he becomes totally fulfilled, hence desires naturally come to an end. Then, what reason does he have to perform any action thereafter? There is a saying,

jo karai so hari karai

(Kabīra)

So long as we are the doers, God does not perform our actions and we ourselves bear the consequences of these actions. Once we surrender, that is reach a state of doing nothing, then God does everything. When the individual is the doer, God performs the role of an impartial witness and takes note of his every action and rewards him accordingly. However, when the individual surrenders completely, God becomes merciful and resides within that soul as his governor eternally. From that very auspicious moment, the individual soul is liberated from material desires and their consequences. It is in this context that Lord Kṛiṣhṇa states in the *Gītā*,

samo'haṁ sarvabhūteṣhu na me dveṣhyo'sti na priyaḥ
ye bhajanti tu māṁ bhaktyā mayi te teṣhu chāpyahaṁ

(Gītā 9.29)

"I am the same to all beings, with no love or hate towards anyone. But those who worship Me with devotion, they are in

Me and I am in them." Further, since the Saint does nothing on his own, Lord Kṛiṣhṇa declares in the *Gītā,*

kaunteya pratijānīhi na me bhaktaḥ praṇaśhyati

(Gītā 9.31)

"Arjuna! It is My vow that My devotee will never fall from his path." The question of rising or falling can arise only if one personally performs actions. Since the Saint is free from the bondage of all actions, how can he suffer a downfall?

In addition to the above reasons, it should be borne in mind that a Saint also possesses divine powers, although he may not make use of them. By virtue of these powers, worldly actions appear to be performed by him even though he always remains beyond *Māyā*. An example will make this clear.

A person happened to see three people in a prison. He asked the first why he was there, and the man replied, "Don't you know that prison is a place where criminals are sent to suffer the appropriate punishment for their crimes? I am a criminal too." When the visitor heard this, he presumed that the other two people also belonged to the same category. But his presumption turned out to be totally wrong when he was told that the second person was the warden and the third was the ruler of the country. A warden is employed to look after the welfare and reformation of prisoners and a ruler too performs the same work. However, a ruler visits the prison only in cases of emergency, whereas the warden is always there.

The warden who always remains in the jail can be compared to the descended Saints who have attained eternal fulfilment. They stay in the prison of the world to help others attain God, in spite of being abused by the prisoners, the materially bound souls. The ruler can be compared to God, Who also descends to this world in different ages when circumstances are grave and require His direct intervention. These three types of personalities are seen in the prison of this world and though there is external similarity in their actions, there is a vast difference in their internal motives. One is a prisoner, bound by the shackles of *Māyā*, one is the liberated Saint, who is the servant of God, and one is the governor of *Māyā*, God Himself. The activities of the ordinary living beings take place under the control of *Māyā*. The Saint does nothing. It is God who performs actions through him by His personal power, called *Yogamāyā*. Similarly, God personally performs actions in His descension through the same power. These actions appear worldly, but their real nature is divine.

janma karma cha me divyamevaṁ yo vetti tattvataḥ
tyaktvā dehaṁ punarjanma naiti māmeti so'rjuna

(Gītā 4.9)

bhakta hetu bhagavāna prabhu rāma dhareu tana bhūpa
kiye charita pāvana parama prākṛita nara anurūpa

(Rāmāyaṇa)

Now you must have understood the difference between the actions of a Saint and those of worldly souls. Here, we must understand that the moment a soul attains God and becomes a Saint, God bestows His divine power upon him. Śhrī Kṛiṣhṇa says in the *Gītā,*

teṣhāṁ satatayuktānāṁ bhajatāṁ prītipūrvakam
dadāmi buddhiyogaṁ taṁ yena māmupayānti te

(Gītā 10.10)

Only the person who attains the divine power of God can perceive God. Not only this, if God did not bestow this divine power, no human being would be able to bear the unlimited Divine Bliss given to him. What to speak of unlimited Divine Bliss, even if a human being suddenly attained limited celestial pleasures it might cause him to die because of his inability to sustain them. How then can the material senses, mind and intellect with their limited capacity sustain the Divine Bliss which is infinite in nature? Therefore, the actions of a Saint who is endowed with divine power must also be divine. There is no question of doubt in this regard.

If anyone questions the actions of God and asks why He performs unrighteous actions, then this question itself is naive. This is because God has no selfish motive. Therefore, He has no attachment or aversion towards anyone. He is eternally blissful and all-knowing. So, the only motive behind His every action is the welfare of all living beings. It is another matter, that we may not understand the significance of these actions due to our limited, material intellect.

If anyone were to again question why the actions of God are beyond our comprehension, then the precise answer is that

He is all-knowing and we are ignorant. He is divine and we are material. He is unlimited and we are limited. He is all-powerful and we have very limited powers. He is the inspirer and we are inspired by Him. He is the illuminator and we are the illumined. He is the governor of *Māyā* and we are governed by *Māyā*. The implication is that God and His actions are totally beyond the comprehension of our material, defective and limited senses, mind and intellect. In the same way, the actions of Saints, who are united with God, are also beyond our comprehension. But at least we can understand the point that though they may be beyond our comprehension, all their actions are divine and solely performed for the welfare of others. Let alone the actions of God and the Saints, there are many actions that cannot be understood even in the material world.

For example, suppose an innocent six-year old child asks his parents, "Whose son am I?" Both the father and mother say, "You are my son." The child wonders how both are making the same claim. He concludes that one of them is telling a lie. So he goes and asks some other elders, whether he is the son of his father or of his mother. They also tell him that he is the son of both. He questions how that is possible. However, nobody is able to explain this to him, since he is still unacquainted with the facts of life. When the boy does not receive any definite answer, he has a meeting with his friends, "No one could answer my question properly. The excuse they made was that I cannot understand it at this age. Isn't that a lame excuse? What is it that we children don't understand? They just cannot explain it I think they are only fooling us. I am sure the truth is that I am the son of either only my father or only my mother." In other words, instead of realizing his own inability to understand, the little boy doubts his elders.

When explaining the subject of sex to a child who is unacquainted with the facts of life is impossible for even the greatest intellectual, then how is it possible for one who is afflicted with lust, greed, anger and so on, to understand the divinely empowered actions of God and Saints, Who are beyond *Māyā*? Like the innocent child, he will argue, "Why can't I understand? You just don't know how to explain it. This is all a deception. I will never accept this" and so on.

Now let us look at other religious traditions. Jalāluddina Rūmī, a famous Sufi Saint wrote in his book '*Masnavi*,' (Part I, Ch.12), that on the Day of Judgement, the good and bad actions of Saints will not be taken into account, because even though they appear to act, they have in fact not done anything. In the *Divāne-Śhamse-Tabrīza*, R.A. Nicholson, the author of 'The Islamic Mystics', writes that the actions of a Saint united with God are in fact performed by God and so the Saint is not responsible for them.

The conclusion is that Saints remain internally established in divinity, but sometimes externally they appear to be engaging in worldly actions. The examples previously given were mostly of descended Saints, who are eternal associates in God's divine pastimes. The scriptures that have described the episodes of their delusion, have also clarified that their delusion was only a pretence. In the *Rāmāyaṇa*, Garuṛa and Pārvatī put on an act of being deluded upon seeing the divine pastimes of Lord Rāma. This was only for teaching ordinary people the lesson that they should not apply their material intellect to understand the pastimes of God. In the case of Pārvatī, Lord Śhaṅkara clarifies this,

rāma kṛipā se pāravati, sapanehuṁ tava mana māhiṁ
śhoka moha sandeha bhrama, mama vichāra kachhu nāhiṁ

tadapi aśhaṅkā kīnheu joī,
kahatu sunata saba kara hita hoī

(*Rāmāyaṇa*)

"O Pārvatī! You have no doubts, nor can you ever come under the sway of *Māyā* or ignorance. You deliberately pretended to be deluded to warn others of the dire consequences of applying the material intellect to the divine pastimes of God."

Even the episode of Garura's delusion is clarified by Kāgabhuśhuṇḍi,

tumhahiṁ na saṁśhaya moha na māyā
mopara nātha kīnha tuma dāyā

(*Rāmāyaṇa*)

"O Garuṛa! You have no ignorance, doubts or delusion. You pretended to be deluded in order to come and grace me." The same is true of all the other episodes.

Just as several actors and actresses get together in order to make a movie, similarly, when God descends and enacts a *līlā*, His eternal associates descend with Him. They themselves present doubts and also dispel them for the welfare of all living beings. This is something that can be understood only by souls who have received Divine Grace.

Now let us leave aside the realm of the Saints, and look at the world. Suppose a girl has just gotten married and is leaving her father's house. Bidding her farewell, the father embraces her affectionately, but lust does not even enter his mind. The husband embraces the same girl and is immediately overcome by lust. The action of embracing was the same, but the internal effect was different. When even a worldly person can accomplish this through the power of thought, then what is impossible for Saints, who are divinely empowered?

Let us look at spiritual aspirants. A person practising *karma yoga*, which was recommended to Arjuna in the *Gītā*, incurs no bondage because his actions are devoid of any attachment. Arjuna, though responsible for the killing of so many, was not punished. A more gross example would be that of an executioner. A hangman does his job without any attachment or animosity and feels no disturbance, anger or sadness upon hanging someone. Thus, the detached actions of a *karma yogī*, one who performs his duties in the world in a detached spirit, but whose mind remains attached to God alone, do not result in *māyika* bondage. A *karma yogī* is actually a non-doer. Then how can a Saint, who is eternally fulfilled and whose actions are performed by God Himself, be considered the performer of his actions?

A police officer who kills a wanted criminal on the orders of the government is rewarded instead of punished, because it is considered part of his job and his intention was merely to do what he was instructed. He had no personal motive. Similarly, the actions of the eternally blissful Saints are inspired by God, and cannot be considered as their own, because they are devoid of any personal motive.

One thing has to be understood, that is as long as one is under the control of lust, anger and greed, one cannot play-act actions based on those negative emotions. Even if one could do it, it would only be up to a certain limit. However, the play-acting of Saints is completely by divine power and so they are totally untouched by those emotions.

If a Saint were to remain engrossed in his divine state and do nothing, then how could he show you the path and how would you be benefited? Therefore, while remaining eternally blissful and united with God internally, Saints write books and give instructions for the welfare of the entire world. Prahlāda and other Saints even ruled over the entire earth planet for thousands of years, but their actions were divine, because they were inspired by God.

Some people may object saying, "God and the Saints should refrain from so-called unrighteous actions. We accept that they can remain in their divine state even while performing such impious actions, but people will try to imitate them and will be doomed." The scriptures state,

mahājano yena gataḥ sa panthāḥ

(Mahābhārata)

"Whatever path is taken by great men, should be followed by others." So the common people will imitate the impious actions of God and Saints and will perish. Such an objection is naive. A similar doubt was voiced by King Parikṣhita when he heard that Śhrī Kṛiṣhṇa had performed His amorous pastimes with other men's wives.

At this point, we need to reflect on whether the actions of great personalities should be imitated or not. If they are not to be imitated, then why not? The *Vedas* answer this question,

yānyasmākaṁ' sucharitāni tāni tvayopāsyāni

(Taitti. Up. 1.11)

"Only the exemplary actions of divine personalities should be imitated." Again, the *Vedas* say, ***"no itarāṇi"***, implying that their other actions should not be imitated. Śhukadeva explains the reason for this to King Parikṣhita,

dharmavyatikramo driṣhṭa īśhvarāṇāṁ cha sāhasam
tejīyasāṁ na doṣhāya vahneḥ sarvabhujo yathā

(Bhāg. 10.33.30)

"Saints have often been seen as violating religious principles, but because they are perfect and their actions are divine, their acts are not transgressions. Just as fire consumes everything, both pure and impure, and yet remains unaffected by any kind of impurity, the Saints too are unaffected by good or bad, because they are beyond the realm of material bondage."

naitat samācharejjātu manasāpi hyanīśhvaraḥ
vinaśhyatyācharan mauḍhyād yathā rudro'bdhijaṁ viṣham

(*Bhāg.* 10.33.31)

"If anyone were to imitate the so-called 'unrighteous' actions of Saints even in his thoughts, he would bring destruction upon himself. Lord Śhaṅkara drank the most dreadful poison, *Halāhala*, but it merely enhanced his beauty and earned him the title of '*Nīlakaṇṭha*', the blue throated; but if anyone were to imitate this action of his by taking even a pinch of ordinary poison, it will cost him his life!"

īśhvarāṇāṁ vachaḥ satyaṁ tathaivācharitaṁ kvachit
teṣhāṁ yat svavachoyuktaṁ buddhimāṁs tat samācharet

(*Bhāg.* 10.33.32)

"The instructions of Saints are worthy of acceptance. But as far as their actions are concerned, only those actions are to be imitated which are appropriate to our own spiritual level. If we imitate actions that are of a higher spiritual class, we will only bring about our own downfall."

kuśhalācharitenaiṣhāmiha svārtho na vidyate
viparyayeṇa vānartho nirahaṅkāriṇāṁ prabho

(*Bhāg.* 10.33.33)

"The Saints have no selfish motive behind their good actions because they have attained eternal fulfilment and they will not be harmed even by their seemingly improper actions, because they have no desires at all. Whatever actions they perform are exclusively for the welfare of others."

yat pādapaṅkajaparāganiṣhevatṛiptā
yogaprabhāva vidhutākhilakarmabandhāḥ
svairaṁ charanti munayo'pi na nahyamānās
tasyechchhayā''tta vapuṣhaḥ kuta eva bandhaḥ

(Bhāg. 10.33.35)

"Devotees attain the dust of the lotus feet of the Supreme Lord and feel completely fulfilled in their hearts. *Yogīs* attain union with the Supreme Lord and cut asunder all bonds of *karma. Jñānīs* meditate on the Impersonal *Brahman* and become one with Him. It is at the request of His devotees that God manifests His eternally blissful divine form. Then how can we think that God Himself can be bound by His actions?" When even devotees and *yogīs* can perform detached actions that do not bind them, then any questioning about God Who is all-powerful, is absolutely futile. Even in this world, the consequences of one's actions are related to the intention, rather than the action itself. If one man intentionally murders someone, he can be executed. But if the man had no intention to kill and it is proved that the death was accidental, he will not be punished. Now, where is the question of the Saint being punished for his actions when the doer is God Himself?

Thus, it is obviously wrong to imitate the actions of divine personalities. Both God and Saints perform actions for all classes of spiritual aspirants. We are expected to imitate only those actions that relate to our class. There are separate guidelines for those who are seekers and for those who have attained perfection. Even within the category of seekers, there are various levels or spiritual classes. So the imitation of Saints should be in accordance with one's own spiritual level,

mahājano yena gataḥ sa panthāḥ

It is clearly stated that we should follow the path taken by great souls. We should not directly imitate the actions they perform at the level they have attained. In fact imitation of a higher level is not possible even in the material world. Suppose a student tries imitating his teacher by sitting in his chair. He scolds his own teacher upon his late arrival in the classroom. The teacher goes along with his act. So far, the student has managed to imitate his teacher. But if the teacher were to ask him a difficult question, the student would obviously have to give up his act, because he does not possess his teacher's knowledge.

A circus acrobat walks on a rope tied a hundred feet above the ground. A robust wrestler, seeing this thin, wiry man on the rope, thinks that being more athletic, he can perform the same act better. So he ties a rope one hundred feet above the ground and climbs a ladder to reach it. But you can imagine the disastrous result the moment he takes his first step on the rope. The circus acrobat only demonstrated his skill; he did not ask anyone to imitate him. If anyone desires to perform the act of this acrobat, he should find out from him how was he trained, where he began and how long it took him and then practise accordingly. This is the correct way of imitating someone.

From this it is obvious that imitation of a higher class is not possible even in the material world. If someone tries to do so, he will have to suffer the dreadful consequences. When imitation in the material world is so dangerous, you can well imagine what the consequences of imitating God and the Saints would be, taking into consideration the fact that they possess unimaginable divine powers!

Now let us come to the important subject of recognizing a Saint. Firstly, we should not accept anyone as a Saint on the basis of someone else's words. It is best to observe Him and rely on our own personal experience. The danger of accepting anyone as a Saint on the basis of someone else's words, is that our own faith in that Saint will waver as and when the other person's faith wavers. This may result in our being deprived of the association of a true Saint if we are told that he is actually an imposter and we believe it.

You must be aware of the fact that 90% of the world accepts a person to be a Saint for the fulfilment of worldly desires like getting a son, wealth and so on. If a Saint visits a worldly person's home and that person coincidently gains material benefit due to his own destiny, he ignorantly attributes this gain to the Saint's visit. He loudly proclaims, "He is a descended divine personality. I accept him to be God Himself" and others who hear him, also accept this statement. If on the Saint's next visit, the same man suffers some material loss due to his own destiny, he immediately loses his faith, and considers the Saint less than an ordinary human being. Now, this material loss he suffered was in no way connected with the Saint, but he unnecessarily criticizes and defames the Saint saying, "He calls himself God." Factually Saints never say things like this due to their innate humility. Look at what the Saint, Tulasīdāsa openly declares, ***"mo sama kauna kuṭila khala kāmī,"*** *Who could be as vile, wicked or depraved as myself?*

Nevertheless, people defame Saints and make false allegations against them just because of some loss to their worldly self-interest. By doing so, they commit the gravest spiritual transgression called *'nāmāparādha'* and cause others to do the same. Far from gaining anything, this causes them an irreparable loss. The nature of worldly people is so astonishing that they are immediately ready to accept something bad said about someone and extremely reluctant to believe anything good!

Therefore, we should not accept someone as a Saint merely because of someone else's opinion, even if it takes us a whole lifetime to recognize and accept someone as a Saint on our own. As per the maxim, 'better late than never', it is better to delay the process and do it right, than quickly make a false judgment and commit a serious spiritual transgression. It is an extremely astonishing fact that in the matter of Saints, people are immediately ready to believe the opinion of a man or woman who they know lies day and night for their personal gain.

How to recognize a Saint ?

Generally three types of nature are seen in Saints. A Saint can be,

(i) Simple and innocent as a child;

(ii) Intoxicated, with the appearance of a madman;

(iii) 'Uncivilised', rejecting all social norms of behaviour;

A Saint has a simple and innocent heart like that of a child. He is pleased with straightforward talk and behaviour. He remains unaffected by both praise and abuse. A man verbally abused Lord Buddha for an entire day. Instead of being annoyed or hurt, Buddha said, "This man must be really tired. Give him something to eat and drink, so that he can regain energy to continue abusing me." The man was shocked to hear this. Lord Buddha said to him, "O friend! Just answer my question. If you give a gift to someone and he does not accept it, with whom will the gift remain?" The man replied, "Obviously, it will remain with the giver." Lord Buddha smiled and said, "You showered abuses upon me, and I did not accept them. Now with whom will those abuses remain? And who is it that will be harmed by them?" The man understood the message and begged for forgiveness. Abuse is a kind of seed which germinates very quickly, but a Saint is like barren land where this seed remains fruitless. Tulasīdāsa suggests,

nindaka niyare rākhiye āṁgana kuṭī chhavāya
nita sābuna pānī binā ujjvala kare subhāya

(Tulasīdāsa)

"The person who hurls abuse should be given a place in the courtyard of the house, because his constant abuse will be the best test of our vanity."

Most people go to a temple and recite prayers to God shedding tears, ***"mo sama kauna kuṭila khala kāmī,"*** *Who can be a greater sinner than me?* But if someone were to call them a hypocrite even in jest, the moment they come out of the temple, they are ready to beat that person. On being asked why they are objecting, after having used the very same words to describe themselves in the temple, they angrily respond, "I was saying that to God, not to you!" This implies that the only person they found to deceive is God, Who is all-knowing, all-powerful, the witness of all, the well-wisher of all and the Lord of all. What a complete sham our humility is, even before God!

tulyanindāstutirmaunī santuṣhṭo yena kenachit

(Gītā 12.19)

nindā stuti ubhaya sama

(Rāmāyaṇa)

"A Saint remains tranquil in both praise and condemnation."

Next, a Saint should never be judged from his external appearance, such as dress, style of living and so on. You may find a Saint in coat and trousers and a demon in an ascetic's garb. We have historical evidence that ninety percent of Saints were family men and did not wear the saffron robes of a renunciate. In this *Kali Yuga*, people believe that unless a person wears saffron clothes he cannot be a Saint. So, imposters have found an opportunity to take full advantage of this misconception. Observe, the Saint Prahlāda ruled as a monarch for thousands of years. Even Dhruva, Vibhīṣhaṇa, Sugrīva, Janaka, Ambarīṣha and others ruled as kings. The *Gopīs*, whose foot-dust is sought after by the creator Brahmā, led ordinary household lives, had husbands and children and were illiterate village women. Kabīra, Tukārāma and others belonged to the same category. In addition, there has been no standard garb for renunciates. Some wore saffron, some yellow, some white and so on. Even within these different colours there have been variations in the shades. Therefore, using the colour of dress as a criterion for deciding the saintliness of a person is completely wrong.

Further, one should not make any wrong assessments about a Saint simply by reading his philosophy. All Masters have their own methods of explaining which can be very different. One may say *prāṇāyāma* is essential because he attained his goal on that path. Others, like Śhaṅkarāchārya, might ridicule it ***('ajñānāṁ prāṇapīḍanam')*** but both Masters are correct. Until one understands the subject in great depth, there is every possibility of committing spiritual transgressions by merely reading their teachings and drawing wrong conclusions.

One point to be carefully noted is that a genuine Saint never grants material boons to people. Nowadays, imposters have adopted this technique of granting boons to attract followers. They know that people in family life have many worldly desires and these desires are often fulfilled due to their own destiny.

So, these imposters involve themselves in a game of chance and offer false blessings to people. If the desire is fulfilled, people think that it was due to the blessing they received. In this way, cheats in the guise of Saints dupe people for their own self-interest. Just consider, a Saint is a person who has realized the transitory nature of the world and has renounced it to attain God. Why will he bless with these very material things that he himself has renounced? Such a person should actually be classified as a demon. It is unfortunate enough that we have forgotten God being intoxicated by material things. To make things worse, these imposters in the garb of Saints pretend to be capable of granting material boons and mislead us even more.

Let alone the Saints, even God does not grant worldly things to someone, against what is destined for him. There are rules laid down by God governing the granting of fruits of actions. What is the need for God or Saints to act contrary to these rules? And if they do so for some, won't they have to do it for everyone? Even if they do it for everyone, how can they be considered causelessly merciful if they are causing harm to worldly people by granting material things?

Let us look at the story of Abhimanyu in the *Mahābhārata*. He was the nephew of the Supreme Lord, Śhrī Kṛiṣhṇa. His father was the great Warrior-Saint, Arjuna and the person who had conducted his marriage was Veda Vyāsa, the descension of God, who wrote so many authoritative scriptural texts. Even these three great divine personalities could not prevent him from getting killed in the battle of *Mahābhārata* at the age of sixteen!

Then how do we, who are averse to God and commit transgressions day and night, and are totally engrossed in family life and worldly possessions, hope that our destiny can be changed by some so-called 'saint'? It is extremely unfortunate that we do not read our scriptures and keep making such foolish mistakes. Every year in India, we hear the tale of some so-called 'saint' who has made the impossible possible and who is attracting followers in thousands. If God and Saints had this kind of competence or authority, why would the world be existing in its present form, given the fact that innumerable descensions of God and Saints have taken place? All that the Saints receive from the world, is abuse and condemnation for their untiring efforts. What would they lose by just saying, "May all souls be liberated from *Māyā*." If they had the power to achieve this, we would have attained our goal just by their saying so. Impostors roam around fearlessly in our country fooling gullible people and surprisingly, most of you seek out these imposters. This is a matter of great shame for a religious country.

nābhuktaṁ kṣhīyate karma kalpakoṭi śhatairapi

(*Mahābhārata*)

"Even *paramahaṁsas*, whose minds are merged in the Bliss of *Brahman* cannot avoid their destiny." Therefore, it is completely futile for an ordinary materialistic person to hope that some so-called 'saint' can change his destiny.

para upakāra vachana mana kāyā

You might say that Saints, by their very nature, desire the welfare of others. So why can't they fulfil our material desires? The first point is that neither God nor Saints have the authority to do so and the second point is that even if they did fulfil our material desires, how will that lead to our ultimate welfare?

Next, you might object saying that there have been examples in history of devotees who have desired worldly pleasures from God. In these cases, two points are to be noted. The first is that these devotees were completely detached from the material world and were fully surrendered to God. It was for just a few that this rule of not granting material boons was broken. Secondly, when God or the Saints grant someone worldly favour with a special intention, they also empower that soul not to be attached, otherwise they would not be acting as his genuine well-wishers as they would be putting him in a dangerous situation. Therefore, these two conditions apply to all the well known instances in history where God and the Saints have granted some worldly boon to a devotee.

The next important point or danger signal to be cautious about is that, a genuine Saint never indulges in the performance of miracles or revelation of supernatural powers, *siddhis*. Most people fall into the trap of so-called 'saints' who perform miracles of a material nature. There is a common worldly adage, ***"chamatkāra ko namaskāra hai"***, which means *stay away from miracle-mongers.* Even though these miracles lead to hell or some abominable condition, we are very impressed by them.

For example, a *sādhu* presents raisins, dates, almonds and so on through *tāmasa siddhi*. You eat them without knowing what *siddhi* was used to manifest them, or what punishment this person will have to face after his death for exercising such *siddhis*.

There are five main types of *siddhis*. The lowest of all is *tāmasa siddhi*, this is also called *bhūta siddhi* in which the help of evil or demonic spirits is taken. The vilest kind of people exhibit these powers. The consequence of exercising *tāmasa siddhis*, is hell.

The second *siddhi* is *rājasa siddhi*. It is used for protection of people. It is better than *tāmasa siddhi*, but it still keeps you in the *māyika* world. Therefore, a wise person rejects them as well.

The third *siddhi* is *sāttvika* or *yogika siddhi*. There are several classes of these *siddhis*. The highest of them are the eight primary *siddhis* such as, *aṇimā, laghimā, garimā* and others. With these *sāttvika siddhis*, a person can make himself smaller than the smallest, lighter than cotton, he can become invisible, he can read the thoughts of others, he can create a subtle body that can fly, or walk on water or enter fire without being burnt and so on. When you meet a person with *sāttvika siddhis*, you might consider him to be no less than God Himself. However, all these attainments are just material. Their consequence is also disastrous. These supernatural powers get exhausted eventually with their repeated display. And even if they do not end, they are used to deceive people, because those who possess these powers, are still completely dominated by *Māyā*.

So how can they put them to proper use? Such attainments are extremely dangerous and one should stay thousands of miles away from them.

The fourth *siddhi* is divine and is called *mukti* or liberation. People who acquire this *siddhi* are liberated from material bondage and attain union with Impersonal *Brahman*, but they do not experience the Bliss of Divine Love. Just as a river which flows into the sea loses its identity, those who attain liberation merge into *Brahman*. Beware of this *siddhi* also. It has been referred to as a 'witch' by our Spiritual Preceptors,

bhukti mukti spṛihā yāvat piśhāchī hṛidi vartate
tāvad bhakti sukhasyātra kathamabhyudayo bhavet

(Bhakti Rasāmṛita Sindhu)

"As long as the two witches, first that of worldly desires right up to the attainment of *Brahmaloka*, named *bhukti* and the second, the desire for liberation, named *mukti*, reside in the heart, the Goddess named 'Devotion' cannot enter the heart. Therefore, those who are wise, remain aloof from this *'siddhi'* too.

asa vichāri je parama sayāne mukti nirādari bhakti lubhāne

The fifth *'siddhi'* is Divine Love which is the supreme attainment. One not only attains freedom from material bondage, but in addition, enjoys the Ultimate Bliss of Divine Love, for eternity.

Now you must have understood that you have to be extremely cautious about the first four attainments or *siddhis*.

One loses sight of one's goal completely if one gets involved with all these different types of 'miracle-mongers'.

The next point to bear in mind is that, a genuine Saint neither pretends to give blessings nor does he curse anyone. Often people hold the notion that Saints or ascetics are people who regularly get angry with others and curse them. However, this is a very wrong belief. If Saints start behaving like shallow streams, which keep flooding and drowning people, then what will happen to their ocean-like gravity? Actually they adhere to the principle, ***"nindā stuti ubhayasama"*** which means *they treat criticism and praise alike*, so the question of cursing anyone does not arise. Then again, they know that worldly people are veiled by ignorance and are bound to commit transgressions. The scriptures say,

na kaśhchinnāparādhyati

"Who will not commit transgressions as long as he is under the influence of *Māyā*?" The Saint knows this fact, so how can he possibly become angry with anyone? We have the example of the compassion of Saint Haridāsa who was an associate of Chaitanya Mahāprabhu. He was so severely beaten by ruffians, that his clothes were soaked in blood. When his assaulters thought him to be dead, they threw him into a river. However, upon regaining consciousness, Haridāsa prayed to God, "O Lord! It is not their fault, for they are ignorant. If you love me, then please accept my prayer and purify their hearts." Imagine, how kind-hearted the Saints are even towards their adversaries! Then how can they possibly curse anyone? If someone says that there is evidence in history of Saints cursing people, then we need to know that these instances were very rare and were solely for the benefit of the person. There is no question of Saints wishing harm to anyone.

A genuine Saint does not pretend to give blessings either. In the world it is often seen that when people bow to pseudo-saints, those 'saints' put their hands on people's heads and recite some long phrases of worldly blessings. Such blessings are just a stunt and have absolutely no value. You might think there is no harm in doing this, but it is all ignorance and such pseudo-saints should be totally avoided. One should know that a true Saint is the well-wisher of the entire universe, but will not give verbal 'blessings' merely to enhance a person's worldly life!

The most evident proof for recognising a Saint is that, by seeing and associating with him, the mind begins to get naturally attached to God. Of course, the degree of attachment of the mind will vary from person to person. A magnet definitely attracts iron, but if there is a mixture of other metals in the iron it will be attracted slowly. The greater the percentage of other metals, the lesser the attraction. It is not the fault of the magnet, but the fault of the other constituents mixed with the iron. In the same way, the spiritual aspirant gets attracted to a Saint according to the purity of his heart. The purer the heart, the greater will be degree of attraction. Therefore, we see that some people are immediately attracted towards a Saint, some get attracted after a while, whereas some remain more or less indifferent to them and yet others have nothing but abuse and ridicule for the Saint! However, even the person who abuses a Saint can benefit because he somehow hears about God from him. This knowledge remains with him and at the proper time when there is detachment from the world, those words will bear fruit and give him proper direction.

The second direct benefit of meeting a true Saint is that, he can practically resolve the difficulties and remove the confusions that arise on the spiritual path. Only he gives a right understanding of spiritual practice. Mere verbal knowledge without practical experience is of no use in the matter of guidance in the spiritual realm. Actually, it is mere verbal knowledge without practical experience which is the primary cause of confusion and doubt, and leaves an aspirant uncertain of what to do. He is not sure of what the correct path is and his spiritual practice comes to an end. At this stage, the aspirant tries to gain respect and prestige in the eyes of others by constantly voicing one doubt after another, and not only does he destroy himself in this process, but harms others as well.

ajñaśhchāśhraddadhānaśh cha saṁśhayātmā vinaśhyati
nāyaṁ loko'sti na paro na sukhaṁ saṁśhayātmanaḥ

(Gītā 4.40)

Only the Saint who has attained God and is well-versed in all the scriptures, can remove the doubts of a devotee, *sādhaka* and guide him on the right path of spiritual practice which is the biggest problem for an aspirant to solve. We hear and read so many things, but until our doubts are resolved, we are not able to practise devotion and only waste our time.

The third direct evidence of the genuineness of a Saint is that when devotees see the manifestation of Divine Love emotions, *sāttvika bhāvas* in the Saint from time to time, their enthusiasm and dedication naturally increases. By personally seeing these divine states, the spiritual aspirant develops firm faith in his path and progresses very quickly. He feels confident that he can also attain those divine qualities one day.

Inference supported by scriptural evidence is an important method in recognizing a Saint. A Saint has the wealth of Divine Love, which is the supreme among all attainments. It is a power by which a devotee binds God. This Divine Love sometimes manifests externally in the body of a Saint. Even though it is his nature to hide this Love, given the right environment and circumstances, it becomes impossible for him to suppress. How long can the swelling waves in the ocean of Divine Love, which is brimming in his heart, be controlled? This state is described by Veda Vyasa in the *Bhāgavatam*,

evaṁvrataḥ svapriyanāmakīrtyā jātānurāgo drutachitta uchchaiḥ
hasatyatho roditi rauti gāyatyunmādavan nṛityati lokabāhyaḥ

(Bhāg. 11.2.40)

"A Saint sings, dances like madman, laughs loudly and weeps, ignoring all social conventions". In other words, remembrance of the name, form and pastimes of the Beloved Lord, causes a Saint's Love to manifest externally in the form of various states of ecstatic divine emotions, known as *'sāttvika bhāvas'*. These *'sāttvika bhāvas'* mentioned in the scriptures are eight in number.

stambhaḥ svedo'tha romāñchaḥ svarabhedo'tha vepathuḥ
vaivarṇyamaśhrupralaya ityaṣhṭau sāttvikāḥ smṛitāḥ

(Bhakti Rasāmṛita Sindhu)

"Becoming motionless as a tree, perspiring profusely, having the hair on one's body stand erect (horripilation), choking of the voice, trembling of the body, changing of the skin colour, unceasing flow of tears and loss of consciousness, are the eight symptoms of divine ecstasy. Seeing their external manifestation, an estimation can be made of the unfathomable depth of Divine Love within the Saint. Observing these a true Saint, the devotee who has attained God, can be recognized,

yatra yatra dhūmas tatra tatrāgniḥ

"Where there is smoke, there must be fire." Similarly, the love which blazes forth externally in the form of '*sāttvika bhāva*' in a Saint, can give us some idea of the intense, unlimited Divine Love within him. In a fully devotional environment in which his Beloved Kṛiṣhṇa's name, virtues and *līlās* are remembered with love, the Saints inner Divine Love may manifest. This is the surest way to recognize a genuine Saint. He has the treasure of Divine Love, unattained even by *paramahaṁsa,* and in the right environment this inner state is revealed. Let us try and understand this by an example of ordinary worldly love. Let us say that you suspect your daughter of being infatuated with some boy. To verify it, speak to your wife in hushed tones within earshot of your daughter about her 'marriage' and mention the name of the boy as the eligible husband. Then call your daughter and ask her to bring you a glass of water. You will see her literally dancing when she brings you the water. Now two days later, again bring up in the conversation within her hearing, that the same boy met with an accident, and mark the sad look on her face. All this proves that internal attachment or love manifests through external symptoms and through these it can be identified.

Let us take another example of ordinary worldly love. Just talk to a faithful wife about her husband who died recently. Immediately you will find tears flowing down her cheeks. When selfish worldly love, which is a mere show, cannot be concealed for long, how then, and for how long, can the Saint conceal that surging unfathomable Love which permeates every fibre of his entire being. Associate with him for some time and you will have a glimpse of it.

One point to be noted here is that a Saint cannot be recognized right away. It takes time. Stay with him for some time and try to observe his internal state every moment. Only then you will be able to make a decision. Just a meeting of an hour or two can be very deceptive because of the Saint's playfulness and childlike nature!

In this way, a Saint can be identified by associating with him for some time. However, this is not something everyone can confidently claim to be able to do. The scriptures mention faith as a basic prerequisite in identifying a Saint. It is totally impossible to recognize a Saint merely on the basis of intellectual ability. Remember, Saints can put on an act if approached with pride and this will cause one to commit spiritual transgressions leading to one's downfall.

However, it is only upon attaining some degree of detachment from the world, that faith can develop and it is only then that meeting a Saint will bear fruit. Otherwise Tulasīdāsa's statement will apply,

mūrakha hṛidaya na cheta jo guru milahiṁ virañchi sama

(Rāmāyaṇa)

This means that, even a Guru of the stature of the creator Brahmā will be of no avail to a faithless person full of doubts and false arguments. For someone to benefit from a doctor and accept him as such, he has first to admit to being a patient. You might say that everyone knows that he is the victim of the diseases of lust, anger, greed and so on. Everyone does know but no one admits it. Tulasīdāsa states,

haiṁ sabake lakhi biralanhi pāye

(Rāmāyaṇa)

"Although the diseases of lust, anger, etc. are always present in everyone's mind, yet only a few people are aware of them." The few people that are aware of their diseased condition, feel the need to cure themselves. They accept the Saint as a doctor for their mental diseases and take his medicine in the form of *sādhanā* or spiritual practice. The rest of the people who half-heartedly accept the Saint as a doctor, are careless in taking the medicine which is practising the prescribed spiritual discipline. Therefore, they are deprived of the real benefit of a Saint's association. So we need to have genuine faith and we also need to surrender to a genuine Saint. Only then will we attain our goal. Thus, Tulasīdāsa declares,

śhaṭha sudharahiṁ sata saṅgati pāī

(Rāmāyaṇa)

Just as a touchstone can convert iron into gold, even the most wicked person can be reformed if he follows the instructions of a Saint with complete faith. The touchstone converts the iron into mere gold but the association of a Saint makes his faithful disciple a touchstone itself i.e. a Saint like himself. However, if the touchstone and iron have not properly come into contact with each other or if the iron is impure or if the touchstone is not genuine, then the transformation does not take place.

Now let us review the sequence once again. The goal of every living being is the attainment of unlimited Divine Bliss. This Bliss is found only in God and therefore God has to be attained. God is beyond our senses, mind and intellect, but if He graces someone, that person can attain Him. His Grace is attained upon surrender. By surrender it is meant 'surrender of the mind'. However, the mind has been attached to the world since eternity, accepting it to be a source of perfect happiness. Thus we need to understand the true nature of the world in order to detach the mind. Detachment means being devoid of love and hate. Repeated reflection upon the reality of the world results in detachment. The next step is to identify a Saint. Once we meet a true Saint, then we need to find out, from him, which path to follow to surrender to God? In other words, we need to know the various paths to attain God.

राधे राधे गोविंद गोविंद राधे। राधे राधे गोविंद गोविंद राधे॥

राधे गोविंद गोविंद राधे । राधे राधे गोविंद गोविंद राधे ॥
राधे गोविंद गोविंद राधे । राधे राधे गोविंद गोविंद राधे ॥
राधे गोविंद गोविंद राधे । राधे राधे गोविंद गोविंद राधे ॥
राधे गोविंद गोविंद राधे । राधे राधे गोविंद गोविंद राधे ॥
राधे गोविंद गोविंद राधे । राधे राधे गोविंद गोविंद राधे ॥
राधे गोविंद गोविंद राधे । राधे राधे गोविंद गोविंद राधे ॥

Paths to Attain God

राधे गोविंद गोविंद राधे । राधे राधे गोविंद गोविंद राधे ॥
राधे गोविंद गोविंद राधे । राधे राधे गोविंद गोविंद राधे ॥
राधे गोविंद गोविंद राधे । राधे राधे गोविंद गोविंद राधे ॥
राधे गोविंद गोविंद राधे । राधे राधे गोविंद गोविंद राधे ॥
राधे गोविंद गोविंद राधे । राधे राधे गोविंद गोविंद राधे ॥
राधे गोविंद गोविंद राधे । राधे राधे गोविंद गोविंद राधे ॥

There are only three paths or means to attain God. Some questions arise - Why are there only three paths, when materialism has made so much progress in different fields? Why haven't spiritual scientists undertaken research to find a fourth path? However, such questions are totally absurd as no science can be contrary to nature. Since eternity the eyes are used for the purpose of seeing. No science can make it possible to see through the ears. In the same way, there is a natural reason for the existence of only three paths since time immemorial. All the scriptures from the *Vedas* to the *Purāṇas* refer only to these three paths.

The first is *karma*, the path of action, the second is *jñāna*, the path of knowledge and the third is *bhakti*, the path of devotion; there is no fourth path. If there is any other path you may have heard of or read about, it is included within these three.

The reason for the existence of only three paths is that the Supreme Personality, *Brahman* has three personal powers. They are *Sat Brahman, Chit Brahman* and *Ānanda Brahman*. The nature of *Sat Brahman* is *karma*, that of *Chit Brahman* is *jñāna* and that of *Ānanda Brahman* is *bhakti*. As the individual soul is an eternal part of *Brahman* so it has only three natures, *karma, jñāna* and *bhakti*. When there is no fourth nature, how can there be a fourth path? Now let us consider each path in a little depth.

राधे राधे गोविंद गोविंद राधे। राधे राधे गोविंद गोविंद राधे॥

Karma

Let us begin with the path of *karma*.

The *Vedas* state,

andhantamaḥ praviśhanti ye'vidyāmupāsate
tato bhūya iva te tamo ya u vidyāyāṁ'ratāḥ

(*Iśha. Up.* 9)

"The person who follows the path of *karma*[1] attains ignorance." The reason for this is,

iṣhṭāpūrtaṁ manyamānā variṣhṭhaṁ
nānyachchhreyo vedayante pramūḍhāḥ
nākasya pṛiṣhṭhe te sukṛite'nubhūtvemaṁ
lokaṁ hīnataraṁ vā viśhanti

(*Muṇḍaka Up.* 1.2.10)

The consequence of *karma* is the attainment of celestial abodes; such an attainment is transitory and material, thus to

1. The performance of duties as prescribed in the Vedas according to one's cast and stage in life

practise *karma* is most unwise. This can never lead to the attainment of God or liberation from *Māyā*. The *Vedas* again state,

parīkṣhya lokān karmachitān brāhmaṇo
nirvedamāyān nāstyakṛitaḥ kṛitena

(*Muṇḍaka Up.* 1.2.12)

"The sages who have practically followed the path of *karma*, have concluded that it does not lead to liberation. It only results in the attainment of the celestial abodes." Some people, believing themselves to be scholars of the *Gītā*, say that in the *Gītā*, Śhrī Kṛiṣhṇa has recommended the path of *karma* to Arjuna. They say that He has clearly stated, "Arjuna! If you fight the war, you will attain one of the two. If you win, you will rule over this earth; and if you die bravely on the battlefield while performing your duty, then you will go to *svarga*. You stand to gain either way." However, Śhrī Kṛiṣhṇa further added that both *svarga* and the kingship of the earth are temporary and *māyika*, and result in bondage. When Arjuna heard this, he said, "That is the reason why I do not wish to perform *karma*." Śhrī Kṛiṣhṇa replied, "If you do not perform *karma* or the prescribed Vedic duties, it will be considered as irreligion and you will go to hell." In this way, Śhrī Kṛiṣhṇa explained to Arjuna that if he engaged in *karma*, he would attain the perishable joys of the celestial abodes or a temporary kingdom on earth, both of which are desired only by foolish people. If he did not engage in *karma*, then he would go to hell. So, Śhrī Kṛiṣhṇa instructed Arjuna, "Do not engage in *karma*; and do not avoid performing *karma* either. Do something which transcends both." Thus Arjuna did not perform *karma,* nor did he avoid performing *karma,* as either way he would have remained bound by the consequences of his actions. He would have been unable to attain freedom from material bondage. Rather, he accepted the path of surrender to God, which transcended both. The *Gītā* repeatedly proclaims that there is only one condition for liberation from *Māyā* and that is stated in this verse.

māmeva ye prapadyante māyāmetāṁ taranti te

(Gītā 7.14)

It means that only one who surrenders exclusively to God can cross over *Māyā*. Here, the word *'eva'* has been used, which emphasizes the fact that apart from surrender to God, there is no other way. With regard to *karma,* the *Gītā* clearly states,

yāmimāṁ puṣhpitāṁ vāchaṁ pravadantyavipaśhchitaḥ
vedavādaratāḥ pārtha nānyadastīti vādinaḥ

(Gītā 2.42)

"The result of *karma* is the attainment of celestial abodes, where there are greater pleasures than those found on earth. Such words of praise deceive foolish people, but the wise are not deceived." The same *Gītā* declares,

te taṁ bhuktvā svargalokaṁ viśhālam
kṣhīṇe puṇye martyalokaṁ viśhanti

(Gītā 9.21)

"The celestial abodes are attained only for a limited period of time, after which one has to return to this earth due to the bondage of past actions." Therefore, the path of *karma* is being condemned!

Now, let us reflect upon the significant words of Veda Vyāsa. In the *Bhāgavatam*, the great *jñānī* Uddhava questioned Lord Kṛishṇa, "O Lord! There are a number of paths being propagated by various spiritualists. Which of these are true and which are false? Why did so many paths come into existence? When a person hears and reads about thousands of different paths, he gets confused and cannot decide the right path to follow because he is ignorant. I beg you to resolve this confusion. A blind man cannot make a decision in matters relating to sight." Śhrī Kṛishṇa replied,

kālena nashṭā pralaye vāṇīyaṁ vedasaṁjñitā
mayā''dau brahmaṇe proktā dharmo yasyāṁ madātmakaḥ

tena proktā cha putrāya manave pūrvajāyasā
tato bhṛigvādayo'gṛihṇān saptabrahmamaharṣhayaḥ

tebhyaḥ pitṛibhyastatputrā devadānavaguhyakāḥ
manuṣhyāḥ siddhagandharvāḥ savidyādharachāraṇāḥ

kiṁdevāḥ kinnarā nāgā rakṣhaḥ kimpuruṣhādayaḥ
bahvayas teṣhāṁ prakṛitayo rajaḥ sattvatamobhuvaḥ

(Bhāg. 11.14.3 - 6)

"I have clearly stated in the *Vedas* the various means for My attainment but,

yābhir bhūtāni bhidyante bhūtānāṁ matayas tathā
yathāprakṛiti sarveṣhāṁ chitrā vāchaḥ sravanti hi

evaṁ prakṛitivaichitryād bhidyante matayo nṛiṇām
pāramparyeṇa keṣhāṃchit pākhaṇḍamatayo'pare

(Bhāg. 11.14.7 - 8)

"Those who read and contemplated the words of the *Vedas*, were of different types of nature. They had different *saṁskāras* accumulated over innumerable lifetimes. Their attitudes and interests were also different. As a result, those who were of a *sāttvika* temperament gave a *sāttvika* interpretation to the *Vedas;* those who had a predominantly *rājasika* temperament made a *rājasika* interpretation and those who were dominated by *tāmasa* made a *tāmasika* interpretation. Thus, various paths came into existence. Some paths also came about by tradition."

Suppose someone's ancestor began performing a ritual of his own invention. That tradition continues from generation to generation without anybody questioning it. In this way, baseless beliefs spring up. For example, in many Hindu families, important festivals like *Rāmanavamī* and *Janmāṣhṭamī* are not celebrated. If you ask them the reason for it, they tell you that the festival of *Janmāṣhṭamī* is not favourable for them. When you ask them how they reached that conclusion, they tell you that, someone in their family died while *Janmāṣhṭamī* was being celebrated several generations ago. So until today, they do not celebrate the festival, based on the superstitious fear that if they do, someone will die again! Consider the absurdity of their belief. The present creation is about two billion years old.

Obviously, we must have had thousands of ancestors, whereas there are only seven days in a week. All these thousands of ancestors must have died on each of the seven days. If by virtue of someone's passing away on a particular day, that day is considered inauspicious, then all seven days of the week should be so. But who is to explain this simple logic to them? Let us leave this point and come to the next question. In billions of years of ancestral history surely there must have been instances of a theft in the house when a bride arrived or someone died the day a large sum of money was inherited. The obvious answer will be that there are thousands of such examples that happen everyday. Then did anyone in the world ever declare that the bride or wealth was inauspicious? Now they will be silent. This means that God or religious occasions are the only dispensable things that can be branded inauspicious! Brides and wealth will never be considered 'inauspicious' because that would interfere with their material enjoyment! This is the foolishness of family traditions!

Some paths are created by hypocrites who disregard the devotional essence of the Vedic injunctions and retain the external form of the ritual. In this category we have mechanical repetition of scriptural verses, repetitive chanting using *japa* beads, visits to places of pilgrimage and so on. These hypocrites misguide the public, saying that if they simply chant so many names on the *japa* beads or perform certain traditional worship through a family priest or observe a certain fast, they will attain God after death. They initiate undeserving people as disciples with *mantras* and assure them, "You can now rest comfortably. I will take care of you. When you die, I will meet you at the gate of Vaikuṇṭha, the divine abode of Lord Vishṇu and take you inside." The poor disciple is beguiled and based on this guarantee, spends all his life engrossed in the world. After death, the guru and his disciple definitely go together, but not to Vaikuṇṭha. They end up in hell. Śhrī Kṛishṇa explained to Uddhava that because of all the above reasons, the words of the *Vedas* were misinterpreted and resulted in many false paths coming into existence. Śhrī Kṛishṇa elaborated on some of these paths,

dharmameke yaśhaśhchānye kāmaṁ satyaṁ damaṁ śhamam
anye vadanti svārthaṁ vā aiśhvaryaṁ tyāgabhojanam

(*Bhāg.* 11.14.10)

kechid yajñatapodānaṁ vratāni niyamān yamān
ādyantavantu evaiṣhāṁ lokāḥ karmavinirmitāḥ
duḥkhodarkās tamonishṭhāḥ kṣhudrānandāḥ śhuchārpitāḥ

(*Bhāg.* 11.14.11)

Some people insist that *dharma*, or the performance of scripturally prescribed duties should be followed in order to attain the great joys of the celestial abodes. Others refute this, stating that it is foolish to stifle our desires and suffer, in order to follow *dharma*, which ultimately results in the mere attainment of *svarga*. They say that one should endeavour for fame because that is the only thing that survives one after death. There are some who regard the attainment of fame as a waste of time, because fame is of no use to a person once he leaves the world. They claim that the best thing to do is to fulfil one's desires while living and enjoy life.

yāvajjīvet sukhaṁ jīvet

(Chārvāk)

"Enjoy life to the fullest, for who knows what happens after death." Some people strongly criticize this view, stating that it is foolish to waste this precious human life in sensual pleasures. The supreme way, is to follow the path of truth. We should speak only the truth and under no circumstances should we ever lie. By this, all problems will be solved and everyone from an individual to the world as a whole will attain peace and happiness.

Again, there are people who claim that there is nothing more to life than fulfilling one's selfish interests. In doing so, we should use both fair and foul means without any qualms, because this world has only been created to satisfy our self-interest. Such people say that it is foolish to sacrifice one's own self-interest to engage in the service of others or for rewards after death.

Other people claim that the secret of peace and happiness lies in renunciation. Acquisition of material objects results in suffering so we should learn to renounce our possessions. When we have no possessions, our miseries will also vanish. Possessions create illusory happiness and their loss creates sorrow. Others oppose this saying that the goal of life is to eat, drink and be merry. To renounce this world made by God for man's enjoyment is an insult to Him.

Then again, we have some who support the performance of *yajña* or sacrificial rites strictly according to the Vedic injunctions. They claim that everything on earth centres around food. The performance of *yajña* pleases the celestial gods who then send down rain. When there is proper rain, there will be good grains and all problems will be solved. However, there are those who criticize the burning of food-grains in sacrifices to acquire more food and claim that one should instead practise austerities to control the body and senses. Then the mind will automatically be at peace.

Yet others state that this is all ludicrous. Having come in this world, the most important work is charity. There are millions of people who are suffering in the world due to lack of basic necessities. We see in the world that someone is a billionaire and is misusing available resources, while in his very own neighbourhood, a poor man is dying for lack of proper medicine. If we can make charity our goal, then everyone will be happy.

Some people support the observance of fasts. Fasting will result in the attainment of celestial joys for considerable lengths of time. At the same time, food on the earth will be saved. We will benefit in both ways.

Again, there are people who say that all these views are wrong. They claim that we should be disciplined. Until we learn to adhere to discipline and put an end to frivolity, it is naive to hope for peace.

Lord Kṛiṣhṇa said, "O Uddhava! These practices and many others are very common in the world, but they are all wrong. The consequence of all these actions is either the attainment of pleasures of this world or of the celestial abodes and both of these have a beginning and an end. The ultimate result of this is that the soul will keep on revolving in the 8.4 million species of life. The celestial abodes are also full of sorrow as they are governed by *Māyā*. The Supreme Divine Bliss and Peace that you desire, cannot be experienced in any of the material abodes attained as a result of performing these actions."

dharmaḥ satyadayopeto vidyā vā tapasānvitā
madbhaktyāpetamātmānaṁ na samyak prapunāti hi

kathaṁ vinā romaharṣhaṁ dravatā chetasā vinā
vinā''nandāśhrukalayā śhudhyed bhaktyā vinā''śhayaḥ

(*Bhag.* 11.14.22 - 23)

"Religious principles, accompanied by truth and compassion have been accepted as perfect and supreme, but they do not completely purify the mind. Scriptural learning accompanied by the practice of austerity is supreme, but complete purification of the mind is impossible even through this." Therefore, mere performance of *karma*, cultivation of knowledge or practice of austerity and so on, cannot free us from the five material sheaths covering the soul, *pañchakoṣha*, the five afflictions, *pañchakleśha*, the consequences of the three types of actions, *trikarma*, and the three types of bodies, *trisharīra*, nor can they help us to attain Supreme Divine Bliss. Now let us look into the *Rāmāyaṇa*,

moha sakala vyādhina kara mūlā

(*Rāmāyaṇa*)

All men suffer from mental afflictions, the root cause of which is attachment. This gives rise to various other afflictions. Desire arises from ignorance. Fulfilment of desire leads to greed and non-fulfilment, to anger. In this way, desire, greed and anger are the root causes of all afflictions, just as *kapha, pitta* and *vāta* are considered the basic causes of all physical ailments.[1]

trividhaṁ narakasyedaṁ dvāraṁ nāśhanamātmanaḥ
kāmaḥ krodhastathā lobhastasmādetattrayaṁ tyajet

(*Gītā* 16.21)

"There are three gates leading to hell: desire, anger and greed." Among these three, desire is the main mental disease. In fact, one word 'desire' is enough, to refer to all three. However, when all three combine together at the same time, then like an attack of hysteria, any catastrophe is possible. Besides these, there are innumerable other mental ailments such as attachment, jealousy, hatred, pride and so on that constantly disturb the embodied soul.

---

[1] *kapha, pitta* and *vāta* refers to mucus, bile and wind in the body. According to Ayurveda an imbalance between the three is the primary cause of diseases of the body.

eka vyādhivaśha nara marahiṁ, ye asādhya bahu vyādhi

(Rāmāyaṇa)

Tulasīdāsa states that these ailments continuously torment the individual soul. On being asked for a cure, he stated that this was a very serious question because,

nema dharma āchāra tapa, yoga yajña japa dāna
bheṣhaja puni koṭina kariya, ruja na jāhiṁ hariyāna

(Rāmāyaṇa)

Following scriptural injunctions, performing religious duties, practising austerities, observing ritualistic sacrifices, being charitable, regular chanting of God's names on a set of beads and so on, cannot cure these afflictions. He therefore called these ailments 'incurable'.

ye asādhya bahu vyādhi

(Rāmāyaṇa)

This does not mean that there is no cure. What he meant was that '*karma*', cannot cure these mental ailments because its result is the attainment of '*svarga*', which is temporary and ultimately results in misery.

svargahu svalpa anta dukhadāī

(Rāmāyaṇa)

Therefore, it is indisputably established that our goal of attaining God, cannot be achieved by following this path. All this can be properly understood by the following examples which are related to Lord Rāma and His closest divine associates. Lord Rāma has been referred to as an embodiment of righteous conduct and morality. The purpose of His descension was to establish *dharma,* the proper performance of duties prescribed by the scriptures.

It is well known that Lord Rāma obeyed the instructions of His stepmother, Kaikeyī and went into exile to the forest for fourteen years. But we find His own brother, Bharata, renouncing his royal duties and retiring to the forest without the permission of his parents. Not only that, he scolded his mother with such foul language that even an enemy would not have used. He said,

hanyāmahamimāṁ pāpāṁ kaikeyīṁ duṣhṭachāriṇīm
yadi me dhārmiko rāmo nāsūyen mātṛighātakam

(Vālmīki Rāmāyaṇa)

"I would have murdered this wicked sinner Kaikeyī, if only someone could guarantee that my Beloved Rāma would not renounce me for this act." He went to the extent of saying to his mother,

na te'hamabhibhāṣhyo'smi durvṛitte patighātini

(Vālmīki Rāmāyaṇa)

"Kaikeyī! Murderess of your own husband! I do not even want to speak to you."

jo hasi so hasi muṁha masi lāī, āṁkha oṭa uṭhi baiṭhahu jāī

(Rāmāyaṇa)

"Go and smear charcoal on your face and get out of my sight." What is so astonishing is that, an ideal brother like Bharata is openly breaking the rules of righteous conduct towards his mother. In spite of this, Bharata was so dear to Lord Rāma that He clearly stated,

lakhana tumhāra sapaṭha pitu ānā
suchi subandhu nahiṁ bharata samānā

(Rāmāyaṇa)

"There is no brother equal to Bharata in the world." Now, let us observe the conduct of Lord Rāma's second brother, Lakṣhmaṇa. Before leaving for the forest, Rāma ordered Lakṣhmaṇa, "I am your elder brother, so you should obey my instructions and remain here. The situation also demands that you stay here, since Bharata and Śhatrughna have gone to their maternal grandparents. Our father is old and he is aggrieved about My departure." Lord Rāma is indirectly hinting about the gravity of the situation and the calamity that could befall the kingdom and the subjects in their absence.

jāsu rāja priya prajā dukhārī
so nṛipa avasi naraka adhikārī

(Rāmāyaṇa)

Further, Lord Rāma explained to Lakṣhmaṇa, "The king whose subjects suffer, goes to hell. According to *dharma*, or the rules of right conduct, your accompanying Me to the forest is not proper in any way." Now listen to Lakṣhmaṇa's reply,

naravara dhīra dharama dhuri dhārī, nigama nīti ke te adhikārī
dharama nīti upadesia tāhī, kīrati bhūti sugati priya jāhī

(Rāmāyaṇa)

"These rules of conduct of the scriptures are not for an ordinary person like me. Teach these rules of right conduct to those who desire worldly or celestial pleasures." If Lakṣhmaṇa, the brother of Śhrī Rāma, is not eligible to follow the rules of the scriptures, then who else is? Further, he said,

guru pitu mātu na jānauṁ kāū , kahahuṁ svabhāva nātha patiyāū

(Rāmāyaṇa)

"I do not know any father, mother or teacher apart from You. So I will not obey anyone else; I will come with You."

Now, let us look at the third brother, Śhatrughna. His name means 'the destroyer of enemies.' Against which powerful enemy did he display his valour?

lage ghasīṭana dhari dhari jhoṇṭī

(Rāmāyaṇa)

humaki lāta taki kūbari mārā

(Rāmāyaṇa)

He kicked the feeble hunchbacked woman, Mantharā, the maid servant who had poisoned Kaikeyī's mind against Lord Rāma, on her back. She fell on her face and her mouth began to bleed. Yet Śhatrughna did not leave her. Holding her by her hair, he angrily dragged her around. Is this the proper code of conduct for a prince?

Listen to one more astonishing instance. Even Sītā, the Mother of the Universe, did not accept the scriptural code of proper conduct. Lord Rāma advised Her, "Do not accompany Me to the forest. Stay back and look after My parents. Spend a few days at Your parents' home, and look after them as well. That is the highest duty for a married woman. Moreover, I am Your husband, and it is My desire that You stay here. A faithful wife should not hesitate to obey the instructions of her husband." In reply, Sītā gave Him a full lecture. She said, "Just as an object and its shadow can never be separated, I cannot stay away from You." Lord Rāma even went to the extent of warning Her,

jo haṭha karau prema vaśha vāmā,
to tuma dukha pāuba pariṇāmā

(Rāmāyaṇa)

"Listen, Sītā! If You stubbornly insist on accompanying Me, compelled by Your love for Me, You will face the dire consequences." This forewarning about the future could be considered a curse or a blessing! Nevertheless, Sītā did not pay heed and instead warned Rāma, "If You do not take Me along with You, then You will not find Me alive when You return." Is it not strange, that even though Yamarāja, the god of death, trembles before Goddess Sītā and She is saying, "You will not find Me alive!" Further, in the divine pastimes of Lord Rāma, we see that Sītā endured separation from Rāma most of the time after their stay at Pañchavaṭī.

All these acts that violated the codes of right conduct took place within the immediate family circle of Lord Rāma Himself. History is witness to the fact that the great devotee, Prahlāda disobeyed his father, even though the scriptures teach one to revere one's parents,

pitṛidevo bhava mātṛidevo bhava

"Respect your parents as the representatives of God." It is well known that the *Gopīs* disobeyed their husbands. Vibhīṣhaṇa disobeyed his elder brother, Rāvaṇa. King Bali renounced his preceptor, Śhukrāchārya. Tulasīdāsa refers to all these, without condemning them,

tajyo pitā prahlāda vibhīṣhaṇa bandhu bharata mahatārī
bali guru tajyo kanta brajavanitani bhe saba maṅgalakārī

(*Tulasīdāsa*)

All these divine personalities did not engage in *karma* or the prescribed duties of the scriptures. If *karma* alone could have led to the ultimate goal, then why would the Saints transgress it?

The scriptures prescribe duties for the four stages of life of human beings. A life of celibacy for a student, *brahmachārya*, the rearing of children for a family man, *gṛihastha*, a semi-retired life with one's wife in the forest, *vāṇaprastha* and finally a life of complete renunciation, *saṁnyāsa*. However, if liberation could be achieved without devotion to God simply by maintaining celibacy, the impotent would be the first to be liberated. If fulfilling the duty of having children could result in liberation, then cats, dogs and pigs would achieve it first. If mere renunciation of material objects and living in the forests, could take one to the ultimate goal, then the lion, cheetah and bear would be the first to reach it. The scriptures clearly condemn mere external practices as futile,

mīnāḥ snānaparāḥ phaṇī pavanabhuṅ meṣhaśhcha parṇāśhano,
nīrāśhaḥ khalu chātako hi nitarāṁ śhete bile mūṣhakaḥ
bhasmoddhūlanatatparaśhcha hi kharo dhyānānurakto bakas te
sarve nahi yānti mokṣhapadavīṁ bhaktiṁ binā śhrīhareḥ

(Sūkti)

"The fish live in the Ganges, the donkey smears its body with mud, the cows and buffaloes eat only grass, the rat lives in a hole in the ground, but even all these acts of external renunciation without devotion, does not qualify them for liberation."

Thus, the lives of Saints and the scriptures both substantiate the fact that mere performance of *karma* cannot result in the attainment of God.

A controversy now arises. If the performance of *karma* does not result in the attainment of God, then why should we bother to follow this path? Why then have the scriptures described the rules of *karma* in so much detail?

To understand the intricacies of *karma* it is necessary to know,

(i) *karma* (iii) *akarma or karma yoga*
(ii) *vikarma* (iv) *karma saṁnyāsa.*

Karma implies strict observance of all ritualistic actions specified by the *Vedas* and the scriptures, but without devotion to God. The main condition in *karma* is that there should not be the slightest deviation from the method prescribed in the *Vedas* and other scriptures, *smṛitis,*

duṣhṭaḥ śhabdaḥ svarato varṇato vā, mithyāprayukto na tamarthamāha sa vāgvajraṁ yajamānaṁ hinasti, yathendraśhatruḥ svarato'parādhāt

(Veda)

"If there is the slightest error in the pronunciation of even one syllable of a Vedic *mantra,* the performer of the sacrificial rites will be harmed, instead of being benefited." Once a demon forced some *ṛishis* to perform a sacrifice. The *mantra* to be recited during the ceremony was, ***'indraśhatrurvivardhasva'***. The meaning of this mantra is that *the enemy of Indra, the demons should prosper*. Retaining the original syllables of the *mantra,* the *ṛiṣhis* cleverly changed one accent of a single syllable. The demon was unaware of the importance of accents in the Vedic *mantras,* so he did not know that he was being deceived. The *yajña* was completed and the results given according to the *mantra*. When the demons attacked Indra and the other gods, the demons were all killed. This perplexed the demon who had conducted the *yajña* and he blamed God for being unjust. Then the secret behind the boon was revealed to the demon. When the *ṛiṣhis* had changed one accent in the recitation of the *mantra*, the whole meaning of the *mantra* had changed. It now meant, "Let the strength of Indra increase." As a result Indra was victorious. This is the outcome of ritualistic actions performed without compliance with the specified injunctions. If these injunctions are strictly adhered to, the ultimate result is the attainment of *svarga*, which has repeatedly been referred to as a temporary abode. This is the reason why we find mere ritualistic *karma* performed according to the scriptures being condemned.

Vikarma refers to non-observance of *karma* specified in the scriptures, as well as absence of devotion to God. This category includes those atheists who are totally materialistic and have a great contempt for God, the Saints and the scriptures. As a result of their bad deeds, they neither attain the heavenly abodes, nor God, but suffer in hell. Being extremely attached to sensual objects, they are undisciplined, and perform wilful actions. After death, they are born in demonic families.

āsurīṁ yonimāpannā mūḍhā janmani janmani
māmaprāpyaiva kaunteya tato yāntyadhamāṁ gatiṁ

(Gītā 16.20)

Thus, *vikarma* is far more condemnable than *karma*. Generally sinful actions are known as *vikarma* and virtuous actions are known as *karma*.

In fact, both virtuous actions as well as sinful actions result in bondage. The *Vedas* declare that the reward for virtuous actions, is *svarga*, celestial abodes and the result of sinful actions, is *naraka,* hell. A mixture of both, results in life on earth. The simplest way to understand the difference is, *svarga* is a prison of golden shackles, after which the individual is sent back to revolve in the 8.4 million species of life. Whereas hell is a prison of iron shackles. *Svarga* is merely an abode for enjoying the reward of our virtuous actions. No one has the right to perform fruit-yielding actions, *kriyamāṇa karma* either in the celestial abodes or in hell. So, both heaven and hell should be rejected.

Akarma refers to devotion to God with the mind, and physical performance of the ritualistic duties specified in the scriptures. This was the path recommended by Lord Kṛiṣhṇa to Arjuna in the *Gītā*. *Akarma* is also referred to as *karma yoga.* The Lord said to Arjuna, "If you engage in war, you will either be rewarded with celestial pleasures or an earthly kingdom, but if you do not take part in the war, it will be considered as *vikarma,* the result of which is hell. To transcend the bondage of these three, what you should do is, avoid 'fighting', and at the same time, avoid 'not fighting'. If you fight, it will be *karma,* and if you do not fight it will be *vikarma.* What you have to practise is, *akarma* or *karma yoga.*"

tasmāt sarveṣhu kāleṣhu māmanusmara yudhya cha

(Gītā 8.7)

"Keep your mind constantly attached to Me and engage in *karma,* action." The attachment of the mind to God with the body engaged in *karma,* is referred to as *karma yoga*. In the process of *karma yoga,* the result of devotion to God (constant attachment of the mind to God) is liberation from material bondage and attainment of Supreme Divine Bliss. There is no reward for the *karma,* as it is performed without attachment of the mind. Only that action which involves attachment of the mind, is rewarded or punished. When the mind is attached to God, then it obviously will not be attached to *karma.* In such a case there is no question of attaining the fruit of action or being bound by it. Thus *karma yoga* or *akarma* is highly recommended.

Karma saṁnyāsa means devotion to God with the mind, as is practised in *karma yoga,* but without physical involvement in duties. The reward for *karma saṁnyāsa* is the same as that of *karma yoga,* that is, liberation from material bondage and attainment of Supreme Bliss. As there is no performance of physical duties, the question of bondage does not arise. Thus, like *karma yoga, karma saṁnyāsa* is highly commendable.

Now the question arises, "When the reward for both *karma yoga* and *karma saṁnyāsa* is the same, that is, the attainment of God, then isn't the additional performance of *karma* by the *karma yogī* futile? When the *karma* he performs does not yield any reward, why make the extra effort and be burdened by it?" The answer has been given by Śhrī Kṛiṣhṇa to Arjuna in the *Gītā,*

saṁnyāsaḥ karmayogaśhcha niḥśhreyasakarāvubhau
tayostu karmasaṁnyāsāt karmayogo viśhiṣhyate

(Gītā 5.2)

"O Arjuna! both the *karma yogī* and *karma saṁnyāsī* are blessed, but the path of *karma yoga* is superior to *karma saṁnyāsa*." Listen to the reason for this,

yadyadācharati śhreṣhṭhas tattadevetaro janaḥ
sa yat pramāṇaṁ kurute lokas tadanuvartate

na me pārthāsti kartavyaṁ triṣhu lokeṣhu kiñchana
nānavāptamavāptavyaṁ varte eva cha karmaṇi

yadi hyahaṁ na varteyaṁ jātu karmaṇyatandritaḥ
mama vartmānuvartante manuṣhyāḥ partha sarvaśhaḥ

utsīdeyurime lokā na kuryāṁ karma chedaham
saṅkarasya cha kartā syāmupahanyāmimāḥ prajāḥ

(*Gītā* 3.21 - 24)

"Arjuna, it is a rule of the world that the actions of great personalities are imitated by others. Those great personalities set an example for others. You know that I have no selfish motive for any action. I am self contented, yet I engage in action, for if I did not perform actions, people would imitate Me and would fall into danger. Thus I engage in *karma* to set an example for humanity. That is why I consider the *karma yogī* to be superior to the *karma saṁnyāsī*. Therefore, I advise you Arjuna to become a *karma yogī* i.e. perform *karma* along with devotion."

Now there could still be a doubt concerning this subject. If the one who imitates the *karma yogī* benefits, why not the one who imitates the *karma saṁnyāsī*? What is the harm in imitating a *karma saṁnyāsī*? The simple answer is that the person who copies another usually imitates only his external behaviour and not the internal. When a person imitates a *karma yogī* he becomes a *karmī,* a performer of prescribed scriptural duties because he imitates that person's external actions, and not his devotion to God, which is internal. On the other hand, if a person were to imitate a *karma saṁnyāsī,* he would neither engage in *karma,* nor practise devotion to God. He would instead become a *vikarmī,* a sinner who rejects the duties prescribed in the scriptures.

Some people might still object saying that there is ultimately no difference between a *karmī* and a *vikarmī*. The person who imitates a *karma yogī* becomes a *karmī* and the person who imitates a *karma saṁnyāsī* becomes a *vikarmī*. But both the *karmī* and the *vikarmī*, attain neither liberation nor Divine Bliss. The *karmī* attains *svarga,* which is transitory and eventually results in suffering. This fact certainly appears to be true, yet the *karmī* is far better than the *vikarmī,* because he will not be negligent. Whenever he meets a true Saint who makes him understand the importance of practising devotion to God with the mind, along with the physical performance of *karma* offered to God, he will become a *karma yogī*. On the other hand, if a *vikarmī* happens to meet a a true saint, he will not accept any of his advice, because he has no faith or belief in the scriptures. Even if he accepts his words, it will be temporary, owing to his practice of being totally undisciplined for a long time. Thus, it is most unlikely that he will be devotionally inclined towards God. Besides this, the advantage of a *karmī* over a *vikarmī* is that social order and morality can be maintained through performance of scriptural duties, whereas a *vikarmī* will create a disturbance in society. This is the difference between imitating a *karma yogī* and imitating a *karma saṁnyāsī.*

From all this, it is obvious that only *karma* performed along with devotion to God is praiseworthy. Otherwise *karma* is condemnable. However, *karma* is still better than *vikarma*. There is one important point that needs to be reflected upon here. A *karmī* who violates the scriptural injunctions is duly punished, but the *karma yogī* is forgiven for any lapses he commits in the performance of *karma,* because he performs actions without attachment.

svalpamapyasya dharmasya trāyate mahato bhayāt

(*Gītā* 2.40)

To conclude, it should be kept in mind that, wherever the *Vedas* and other scriptures have criticized ritualistic actions, they refer to those actions which are totally devoid of devotion to God. When *karma* includes devotion, it is highly praiseworthy. It not only benefits the doer, but also the imitator.

Let us refer to the scriptures for clarification.

īśhā vāsyamidaṁ' sarvaṁ yat kiñcha jagatyāṁ jagat
tena tyaktena bhuñjīthā mā gṛidhaḥ kasya sviddhanam

(*Īśhā. Up.* 1)

"Actions should be offered to God."

yasya deve parā bhaktir yathā deve tathā gurau
tasyaite kathitā hyarthāḥ parkāśhante mahātmanaḥ

(*Śhvetā. Up.* 6.23)

"Only one who is equally devoted to God and Guru attains the supreme goal."

upāsate puruṣhaṁ ye hyakāmāste śhukrametadativartanti dhīrāḥ

(Muṇḍaka Up. 3.2.1)

"A person who does not attach his mind to any object except God through devotion attains freedom from *Māyā*." Thus, the *Vedas* have not condemned *karma yoga* but have condemned *karma* that is without devotion. In the *Gītā*, Lord Kṛiṣhṇa says to Arjuna,

vihāya kāmānyaḥ sarvān pumāṁśhcharati niḥspṛihaḥ
nirmamo nirahaṅkāraḥ sa śhāntimadhigachchhati

(Gītā 2.71)

"Only the person whose mind is not attached to any material object attains Supreme Peace." Again He states even more clearly,

yat karoṣhi yadaśhnāsi yajjuhoṣhi dadāsi yat
yattapasyasi kaunteya tat kuruṣhva madarpaṇam

(Gītā 9.27)

"Whatever you do, whatever you eat, whatever sacrificial rites you perform, whatever you give in charity, do it for Me alone. If your mind is attached to Me, then your actions will not bind you."

svakarmaṇā tamabhyarchya siddhiṁ vindati mānavaḥ

(Gītā 18.46)

"A man attains perfection when he performs his duties as an act of worship to God." Thus, it is obvious even from the *Gītā*, that mere performance of scriptural duties without devotion to God, cannot destroy the bondage of actions or lead to the attainment of Supreme Bliss. Let us come to the *Purāṇas*. Veda Vyāsa gives a precise definition of *karma*,

tatkarma haritoṣhaṁ yat

(Bhāg. 4.29.49)

"That alone is true *karma* which results in pleasing God." Again, at another place he declares that, if any *karma* does not give rise to love for the lotus feet of Lord Kṛiṣhṇa, then that *karma* is fruitless toil.

In other words, that action is condemnable,

dharmaḥ svanuṣhṭhitah puṁsāṁ viṣhvaksena kathāsu yaḥ
notpādayedyadi ratiṁ śhrama eva hi kevalam

(Bhāg. 1.2.8)

There are a number of verses emphasizing this very fact,

gṛiheṣhvavasthito rājan kriyāḥ kurvan gṛihochitāḥ
vāsudevārpaṇaṁ sākṣhādupāsīta mahāmunīn

(Bhāg. 7.14.2)

gṛiheṣhvāviśhatāṁ chāpi puṁsāṁ kuśhalakarmaṇām
madvārtāyāmānāṁ na bandhāya gṛihā matāḥ

(Bhāg. 4.30.19)

The Lord declares, "A family man who performs his daily duties with his mind completely engrossed in Me, remains disentangled from family life and is ever blissful, like King Janaka. Though living in a family, he is separate from it and attains Divine Bliss". The greatest ideal in this regard has been established by the *Gopīs*.

yā dohane'vahanane mathanopalepa
preṅkheṅkha nārbharuditokṣhaṇamārjanādau
gāyanti chainamanuraktadhiyo'śhrukaṇṭhyo
dhanyā brajastriya urukramachittayānāḥ

(*Bhāg.* 10.44.15)

The *Gopīs* performed all their household chores, singing the glories of their Beloved Kṛiṣhṇa and shedding tears of love for Him. Their supreme selfless devotion, made Śhrī Kṛiṣhṇa Himself their Eternal Servitor.

Finally, we also find this clarification in the *Rāmāyaṇa*,

so saba karma dharma jari jāū
jahaṁ na rāma pada paṅkaja bhāū

(*Rāmāyaṇa*)

"That *karma* or performance of duties is condemned, which is without devotion to God." It is only devotional actions, that result in liberation from material bondage.

tretā vividha yajña nara karahīṁ
prabhuhiṁ samarpi karma bhava tarahīṁ

(*Rāmāyaṇa*)

The *Rāmāyaṇa* again states,

japa tapa niyama yoga nija dharmā
śhruti saṁbhava nānā śhubha karmā
jñāna dayā dama tīratha majjana
jahaṁ lagi dharma kahe śhruti sajjana
āgama nigama purāna anekā
paṛhe sune kara phala prabhu ekā
tava pada paṅkaja prīti nirantara
saba sādhana kara yaha phala sundara

(*Rāmāyaṇa*)

"Repetition of the divine name, performance of all duties pertaining to the four orders and stages of life, all penance, austerity, knowledge, exercise of compassion, control of the senses and going on pilgrimage should result only in devotion to the lotus feet of the Lord." The *Rāmāyaṇa* goes to the extent of saying that even Brahmā, the creator should be ignored, if he is devoid of devotion,

bhaktihīna virañchi kina hoī

(*Rāmāyaṇa*)

All this evidence from the scriptures reveals the secret behind the apparent criticism of *karma* or performance of physical duties prescribed in the scriptures. Now let us go into the depth of both *karma* and devotion,

ṛiṇāni trīṇyapākṛitya mano mokṣhe niveśhayet

(*Manusmṛiti*)

Every individual soul is burdened with three debts. These relate to indebtedness to the celestial gods, the sages and the ancestors or forefathers. Without repaying these debts, no soul can attain liberation. Now if *karma* is renounced, as is done by the *karma saṁnyāsī,* how can liberation be attained without performance of the prescribed duties for repaying these debts? The answer to this question is given by Veda Vyāsa,

devarṣhibhūtāptanṛiṇāṁ pitṛiiṇāṁ
na kiṅkaro nāyamṛiṇī cha rājan
sarvātmanā yaḥ śharaṇaṁ śharaṇyaṁ
gato mukundaṁ parihṛitya kartam

(Bhāg. 11.5.41)

The person who is not devoted to God and who merely performs the required duties for repayment of the three debts specified by Manu will suffer a downfall. However, one who is devoted to God is not governed by the above law of repayment of debts. Thus his renunciation of *karma* is forgiven. Listen to the secret behind this.

Dharma, righteous action is of two kinds; one is superior *dharma* and the other, inferior *dharma.*

sa vai puṁsāṁ paro dharmo yato bhaktir adhokṣhaje
ahaitukyapratihatā yayā''tmā samprasīdati

(Bhāg. 1.2.6)

Devotion to God is superior *dharma* or *'para dharma',* the result of which is attainment of Supreme Bliss. Lower *dharma,* or *'apara dharma'* is mere performance of duties pertaining to one's social order, *varṇa* and stages in life, *āśhrama,* without devotion to God. The result of the performance of this inferior *dharma* is the attainment of the celestial abodes. *'Apara dharma'*, also referred to as *varṇāśhrama dharma*, is different for the four different castes, i.e. Brahmins, *Kṣhatriyas, Vaiśhyas* and *Śhūdras,* while *'para dharma'* is natural and is always the same for all the four castes. *'Apara dharma'* also varies according to one's stages in life. A *brahmachārī*, celibate student is instructed to stay away from women till he is twenty-five years old, but thereafter he is instructed to enter the *gṛihastha āśhrama*, i.e. to marry and have children in order to be free from the debt to his forefathers. Again, at the age of fifty he is instructed to leave his family and children, and retire to the forest with his wife, i.e. *vāṇaprastha āśhrama*. At the age of seventy-five, he is ordered to also leave his wife, and lead a life of total renunciation or *saṁnyāsa*, until death. Thus, he is alone again at the final stage of *saṁnyāsa*, as he was in the first stage of *brahmachārya*. Observe, there is a constant change in *'apara dharma'*, but *'para dharma'* or devotion to God is always the same for everyone, irrespective of the caste, or stage in life.

Another point worth considering is that, the scriptures have specially instructed people of every social order and every stage of life, to follow *'para dharma'* or devotion to God along with their respective *'apara dharma'* or physical duties. The *brahmachārī*, celibate student is advised to be devoted to God, so is the *gṛihasthī*, the family man, the *vāṇaprasthī*, the one who retires to the forest and the *saṁnyāsī*, the renunciate. The renunciate is expected to exclusively follow *'para dharma'* or devotion to God.

In the same way, every caste is instructed to practise devotion to God besides performing their respective duties. This is what is referred to as *karma yoga* in the scriptures. When physical duties are performed along with devotion to God, it is only the devotion that is rewarded. Liberation from material bondage and Divine Bliss can never be attained through the performance of external physical duties alone!

Someone may wonder that if it is absolutely necessary to practise devotion to God along with performing one's scriptural duties, then isn't it improper for the *karma saṁnyāsī* to totally renounce these duties especially when God Himself instructs everyone to follow the Vedic rules?

śhrutismṛitī mamaivājñe yasta ullaṅghya vartate
ājñochchhedī mama dveṣhī madbhakto'pi na me priyaḥ

(Vādhūla Smṛiti)

"One who does not follow the Vedic rules and regulations is My enemy. How can he be dear to Me?" But we have the answer to this question in the *Bhāgavatam*, where the Lord Himself refers to special exceptions,

ājñāyaivaṁ guṇān doṣhān mayā''diṣhṭānapi svakān
dharmān santyajya yaḥ sarvān mām bhajeta sa sattamaḥ

(Bhāg. 11.11.32)

"Although I Myself have laid down these Vedic injunctions and instructed people to follow them, stating that those who violate them shall be punished, yet the one who abandons these actions and devotes himself to Me alone, is extremely dear to Me." This obviously implies that the Vedic injunctions do not apply to the individual who is exclusively devoted to God. The *Vedas* declare,

sarve vedā yatpadamāmananti tapāṁsi sarvāṇi cha yad vadanti

(Kaṭha Up. 1.2.15)

"All the Vedic hymns inspire a person only towards God." The great Saint Śhāṇḍilya also declared,

na kriyā kṛityanapekṣhaṇājjñānavat

(Śhāṇḍilya Sūtras)

"Just as one who follows the path of *jñāna* is not obliged to perform *karma,* the devotee too does not necessarily have to perform *karma.*" This is the very reason why devotion has been declared as independent.

lakṣhaṇaṁ bhaktiyogasya nirguṇasya hyudāhṛitam
ahaitukyavyavahitā yā bhaktiḥ puruṣhottame

(Bhag. 3.29.12)

bhakti svatantra sakala sukha khānī

(Rāmāyaṇa)

anyābhilāṣhitāśhūnyaṁ jñānakarmādyanāvṛitam

(Bhakti Rasāmṛita Sindhu)

"*Bhakti* or devotion does not require the assistance of either *karma* or *jñāna.*"

There are several doubts that are likely to arise concerning *karma* and its renunciation by a person practising devotion. In the *Bhāgavatam,* it is stated that until a person is completely detached, he must follow *varṇāśhrama dharma* or duties pertaining to his social order and stage in life.

tāvat karmāṇi kurvīta, na nirvidyeta yāvatā
matkathāśhravaṇādau vā śhraddhā yāvanna jāyate

(*Bhāg.* 11.20.9)

This doubt is resolved by Veda Vyāsa himself. He says that everyone possesses the required detachment for the path of devotion.

na nirviṇṇo nātisakto bhaktiyogo' sya siddhidaḥ

(*Bhāg.* 11.20.8)

"To follow the path of devotion one must be neither too attached nor too detached." Almost everyone fulfils this condition, because no one can attain true happiness in the material world. Therefore, everyone is neither too attached nor totally detached.

The next question is, if everyone is neither too attached nor too detached and is therefore eligible to follow the path of devotion, then for whom are the elaborate rules of the *Vedas* been laid down?

matkathāśhravaṇādau vā śhraddhā yāvanna jāyate

(*Bhāg.* 11.20.9)

Veda Vyāsa replies that as long as a person does not have faith in the divine narratives of God, he can perform *karma* to build up this faith. Also, if a person desires to attain only *svarga*, he can engage in *karma*. Lastly, those who are extremely attached to the material world, should follow the path of *karma*.

According to the *Gītā*,

tasmāchchhāstraṁ pramāṇaṁ te kāryākāryavyavasthitau

(*Gītā* 16.24)

"Let the scriptures be the authority as to what is right and wrong. Each and everyone must follow the instructions of the scriptures."

It is also said in the *Gītā*,

yaḥ śhāstravidhimutsṛijya vartate kāmakārataḥ
na sa siddhimavāpnoti na sukhaṁ na parāṁ gatim

(*Gītā* 16.23)

"One who does not follow the instructions specified in the scriptures will not attain happiness, in his present life on this earth nor later. He cannot attain the Supreme Goal."

One who is '*kāmakārataḥ*', negligent of the scriptural injunctions because of his attachment to sensual objects, is to be condemned. But the devotee who neglects scriptural injunctions solely for the ultimate goal of attaining God is not condemnable." Veda Vyāsa declares,

tā manmanaskā matprāṇā madarthe tyaktadaihikāḥ
māmeva dayitaṁ preṣhṭhamātmānaṁ manasā gatāḥ
ye tyaktalokadharmāśhcha madarthe tān bibharmyaham

(*Bhāg.* 10.46.4)

The *Gopīs* had abandoned both worldly and Vedic duties. They even disobeyed their husbands, but were greatly loved by Lord Kṛiṣhṇa because they were selflessly and solely devoted to Him. The basic definition of virtue and sin given by the Lord Himself in the *Bhāgavatam* is as follows,

mannimittaṁ kṛitaṁ pāpaṁ maddharmāya cha kalpate
māmanādṛitya dharmo'pi pāpaṁ syān matprabhāvataḥ

(Veda Vyāsa)

"That sin which is performed for My sake, is not a sin, it is virtuous. But the virtuous action that is performed without remembrance of Me, is a sin." What can be more clear than this definition? Sage Nārada has declared that worldly and Vedic duties are hindrances in the path of devotion.

nirodhastu lokavedavyāpāranyāsaḥ
tasminnananyatā tadvirodhiṣhūdāsīnatā cha

(Nārada Bhakti Sūtra 8, 9)

"Devotional practice should be devoid of the impediments of worldly and Vedic duties. Secondly, there should be exclusive attachment to God. Thirdly, one should be indifferent to everything, except God." Indifference means neither love nor hate.

According to the *Vedas*,

dharmeṇa pāpamapanudanti

(Veda)

"Performance of scriptural duties destroys sins." When performance of scriptural duties is capable of destroying sins, why does it not bring about liberation from material bondage? Veda Vyāsa gives a wonderful explanation,

dharmaḥ satyadayopeto vidyā vā tapasānvitā
madbhaktyāpetamātmānaṁ na samyak prapunāti hi

(Bhāg. 11.14.22)

"Without devotion neither *dharma* combined with truth and compassion, nor knowledge combined with austerity, can completely purify the heart." The same truth is stated at another place,

taistānyaghāni pūyante tapodānajapādibhiḥ
nādharmajaṁ taddhṛidayaṁ tadapīśhāṅghrisevayā

(Bhāg. 6.2.17)

"Vedic actions, such as charity, sacrificial rites, penance, fasts and so on, do destroy sin but they cannot completely purify the heart." Some people argue that destruction of sins automatically implies purification of the heart, but it is not so. For example, suppose a person commits the sin of killing a cow. If he performs the various actions specified in the scriptures for atonement, it nullifies the effect of the sin, but it does not destroy that person's mentality or inclination to sin again. A person can sin again and continue to do so indefinitely, even while performing the prescribed actions for atonement. The heart can never be purified in this way.

Besides, it takes less time to sin and more time to atone. If we presume that all our present sins have been destroyed through actions of atonement, still all the accumulated innumerable sins of countless past lives can never be destroyed even if you engage in atonement for innumerable lives. How then can liberation be attained? Even a *jñānī* of the stature of Jagadguru Śhaṅkarāchārya wrote a very significant verse in this context,

śhuddhayati hi nāntarātmā kṛiṣhṇapadāmbhoja bhaktimṛite
(Śhaṅkarāchārya)

"The heart can never be purified without devotion to Lord Kṛiṣhṇa." And without this purification of the heart, there is no guarantee that external atonement for sins will prevent the person from sinning again.

The conclusion is that, mere performance of *karma* without devotion is not only incapable of liberating a person, but it does not even result in purifying the heart.

This is the reason why people who engage in *karma* without devotion, are deprived of a divine reward. A fish may live in the holy waters of the Ganges, but it cannot attain liberation without devotion. Yet naive people hope that by merely bathing once in these holy waters, they will reach the divine abode of Vaikuṇṭha. Such people only deceive themselves.

Some people argue that it does not matter whether you jump into fire willingly or you are pushed into it by force, the fire is bound to burn you in both cases. In the same way, a dip in the holy Ganges should yield the reward proclaimed in the scriptures. But those who have such doubts, should consider their own experience. Millions of people have bathed in the holy waters of the Ganges and the Yamuna, but have they become sinless? Have they become free from lust, greed, anger, jealously and so on? The answer is a definite, "No". It is such ignorant people who blemish the scriptures. A very simple example can put an end to your doubts.

Take a bottle and fill it with urine. Then close the bottle tightly and immerse it in the waters of the Ganges. After twenty-four hours, take the bottle out of the river and drink its contents. Will anyone drink it? No one will drink. Why not? Millions of people drink the water of this holy river. Your answer will be that because the bottle was sealed it still contains urine, and not the water of the Ganges. This is exactly what happens when you bathe in the Ganges. In which part of the body do your sins reside? They are all in the mind, aren't they? When you bathed in the Ganges, your mind was elsewhere. It was only your body that bathed. How then could those sins that were in your mind be washed away? The scriptures proclaim that if the mind unites with a pure entity, it becomes purified. Had your mind been attached to the holy Ganges, which is actually a divine power, then it would definitely have been cleansed. This obviously implies that, it is absolutely impossible to attain freedom from material bondage through *karma* that is devoid of devotion.

vāri mathe baru hoya ghṛita, sikatā te baru tela
binu hari bhajana na bhava tariya, yaha siddhānta apela

(Rāmāyaṇa)

"The impossible may become possible, but there can be no liberation without devotion to God." The *Rāmāyaṇa* again states,

jimi thala binu jala rahi na sakāī koṭi bhānti kou karai upāī
tathā mokṣha sukha sunu khagarāī rahi na sakai hari bhagati bihāī

(Rāmāyaṇa)

Māyā consists of three *guṇas* or modes - *sattva, rājasa* and *tāmasa.* In accordance with these three *guṇas,* there are three categories of actions. The fruit of *sāttvika* actions is *sāttvika,* of *rājasika* actions is *rājasika* and of *tāmasika* actions is *tāmasika.* The region to which the soul is sent after death depends on the fruits of his actions. For *sāttvika* actions, it is *svarga*; for *rājasika* actions, it is the earth; and for *tāmasika* actions, it is the lower regions of hell. But note, even the attainment of *svarga* through *sāttvika* actions is a material attainment, because *sattva guṇa* itself is a mode of *Māyā*.

Thus, it is obvious that any action within the category of the three *guṇas* cannot result in release from bondage. It is only God alone, who is beyond the realm of the three *guṇas.* If action, whether it be *sāttvika, rājasika* or *tāmasika,* is performed without devotion to God, then the result is nothing but suffering, because its origin is *Māyā*. The conclusion is that the scriptures recommend practice of *karma yoga,* which means constant attachment of the mind to God, along with physical performance of scriptural duties. If the mind is attached anywhere else apart from God, then it cannot be called *karma yoga*. *Karma yoga* is possible only when the mind is constantly attached to God without even a moment's separation from Him.

"yo māṁ smarati nityaśhaḥ"; "evaṁ satatayuktā ye"
"satataṁ kīrtayanto māṁ"; "teṣhāṁ nityābhiyuktānāṁ"

(Gītā)

All the above verses from the *Gītā* indisputably state that the mind should be constantly attached to God.

The problem before us now is, if the mind is attached to God constantly, how can we perform actions in the material world? The sense organs do not perform any action without the involvement of the mind. How *karma yoga* can be practised in daily life, will be explained in detail in a subsequent chapter dealing with *sādhanā*. For the present, it is sufficient to know that *karma yoga* implies ***"mana yāra meṁ tana kāra meṁ,"*** *Hands to work, mind to God*. Now, let us deal with the next path mentioned in the scriptures.

राधे राधे गोविंद गोविंद राधे। राधे राधे गोविंद गोविंद राधे॥

Jñāna and Jñānayoga

The subject of *jñāna* and *jñāna yoga* is very deep and vast nevertheless, we must discuss it briefly. In general, *jñāna*, knowledge is of two kinds - the first is verbal or theoretical knowledge and the second is practical or experienced knowledge. Mere book knowledge without practical experience is shallow and superficial.

Both theoretical and practical knowledge can be further classified into two: knowledge of material subjects and the other, knowledge of divine subjects. You are obviously familiar with theoretical knowledge of material subjects. For example, if a person has learned all about cooking from books and even delivers lectures on the subject, but has never practically cooked himself, he has only theoretical knowledge. Practical knowledge is doing the actual cooking.

Similarly, there is theoretical and practical knowledge of spirituality. A person with mere theoretical knowledge is one who memorizes the *Vedas* and other scriptures, and even delivers lectures on these subjects but has not practised any spiritual discipline. Such a person has no practical experience. A person with practical spiritual knowledge is one who actually follows a prescribed spiritual path and knows God through His Grace. We need to reflect on theoretical and practical spiritual knowledge in detail, because theoretical and practical material knowledge can never take us to our goal of attaining Divine Bliss. According to the *Vedas*,

tato bhūya iva te tamo ya u vidyāyāṁ' ratāḥ

(Veda)

"A person who possesses mere theoretical knowledge, suffers a great downfall."

The description of the man of knowledge, *jñānī* in the *Rāmāyaṇa* is so confusing, that even the greatest of scholars can be misled. Firstly, it is stated that the man of knowledge, a *jñānī* is specially dear to the Lord.

jñānī prabhuhiṁ viśheṣha piyārā

(Rāmāyaṇa)

Then it is said that, both the *jñānī* and *bhakta*, devotee are equal, that is, the *jñānī* is not specially dear to God,

gyānahiṁ bhagatihiṁ nahiṁ kachhu bhedā

(Rāmāyaṇa)

"There is no difference between the *jñānī* and the devotee." Again it is said,

bhagatihīna mohi priya nahiṁ soū

"The *jñānī* devoid of devotion is not dear to Me." At another place,

te jaṛa kāmadhenu gṛiha tyāgī
khojata āku phirahiṁ paya lāgī

(Rāmāyaṇa)

The *jñānī* has been compared to the fool who owns a *kāmadhenu,* the celestial cow, but does not drink its milk. He instead goes searching in the forests for the milk-like sap of a poisonous plant, swallow-wort. However even this criticism was not enough. Tulasīdāsa went a step further.

te śhaṭha mahāsindhu binu taranī
pairi pāra chāhahiṁ jaṛa karanī

(Rāmāyaṇa)

"The *jñānīs* are extremely foolish because they attempt to know God through the path of *jñāna,* which is like daring to cross the ocean without a boat." Tulasīdāsa uses even more shocking language here,

rāmachandra ke bhajana binu je chahaṁ pada nirvāṇa
gyānavanta api so nara paśhu binu pūñchha viṣhāṇa

(Rāmāyaṇa)

"The *jñānī* who desires to attain liberation through *jñāna,* is like a hideous beast that has no horns or tail." Now, what conclusion can we draw from this?

Yet, we also find the scriptures specially praising *jñāna*. The *Vedas* state,

ṛite jñānān na muktiḥ

(Veda)

"It is impossible to attain liberation without *jñāna*."

jñānādeva hi kaivalyam

(Veda)

"One can attain liberation only through *jñāna*."

The *Gītā* also states,

na hi jñānena sadṛiśhaṁ pavitramiha vidyate

(Gītā 4.38)

"There is nothing as pure as divine knowledge or *jñāna*."

jñānī prabhuhiṁ viśheṣha piyārā

(Rāmāyaṇa)

Further the *Gītā* agrees with the *Rāmāyaṇa* about the *jñānī* being specially dear to the Lord,

jñānī tvātmaiva me matam

(Gītā)

What conclusion can an ordinary man draw from these various viewpoints?

The truth is, wherever we find criticism of *jñāna*, it refers only to mere theoretical knowledge, which is extremely harmful. You may argue that it is impossible to attain practical experience without theoretical knowledge. That is true. Theoretical knowledge is necessary in the initial stage of spiritual practice in order to attain practical experience. But the problem is that, mere theoretical knowledge devoid of practical experience, results in fostering false pride which leads to a greater downfall than that suffered by a person who is ignorant. This pride is obvious if you observe a theoretical scholar at prayer reading a verse from the scriptures. Every word he utters is full of conceit. But when an ignorant man prays, ***"tvameva mātā cha pitā tvameva"*** *Oh Lord! You alone are my Father, You alone are my Mother,* the devotional feelings of his heart resound in his voice. The reason is that a simple minded person never thinks that he knows everything, but a scholar never forgets his scholarship of the scriptures.

It is false pride that is the greatest barrier between ourselves and God. When a theoretical scholar has no time to analyse the fact that he really has no factual comprehension, how is it possible for him to begin spiritual practice? His sole aim is to convince others of his scholarliness. He devotes his time trying to impress others, though he knows in his heart of hearts that he knows absolutely nothing. Therefore, mere scholarliness only enhances pride. Such a person cannot advance towards God but instead heads towards his own downfall. Therefore, the theoretical scholar is worse than the illiterate person, who with some faith, practises heartfelt devotion to God in some form. Therefore, mere theoretical knowledge is condemned. However, if this *jñāna* is used for devotional practice, it is extremely praiseworthy. Not only is theoretical *jñāna* praiseworthy when applied to practical *sādhanā,* but it is an absolute prerequisite to begin spiritual practice. There is no question of starting practical spiritual life without theoretical knowledge.

Some people claim that they do not agree with the fact that theoretical knowledge is indispensable. Rather, they believe only in the necessity of spiritual practice. To hold such a view is absolutely foolish. The mind is full of various doubts and confusions due to our mental impressions of innumerable past lives. These doubts need to be dispelled. Moreover there can be external and internal disturbances during spiritual practice. Theoretical knowledge is also necessary in order to free us from them. It is only upon attainment of perfection, that theoretical knowledge can be dispensed with. A person whose foot has been pierced by a thorn, should not curse all thorns, because he will require a bigger thorn to remove the smaller one that is stuck in his foot. Once he removes it, he can throw away both. In the same way, theory is initially necessary in spiritual practice to remove ignorance and attain realized knowledge. Once ignorance is dispelled, even theoretical knowledge can be dispensed with. However, if this theoretical knowledge of the scriptures is rejected in the beginning, the aspirant is bound to be unstable on the path. The *Vedas* declare,

nāvedavin manute taṁ bṛihantam

(Śhāṭhyāyanī Up.)

"Without theoretical knowledge of the scriptures, one cannot attain practical experience of God." Theoretical knowledge of God can become practical knowledge only when you practise devotion to God. Without devotion, the *jñānī*, theoretical man can never become a *jñāna yogī* that is, one who knows God. This is an irrefutable truth. Thus, just as devotion has been proved to be indispensable in the path of *karma*, it is equally indispensable in the path of *jñāna*. The truth is that, knowledge devoid of devotion is totally incapable of leading to genuine knowledge of God. Tulasīdāsa has criticized knowledge which is without devotion,

yoga kuyoga jñāna ajñānū jahaṁ nahiṁ rāma prema paradhānū

(*Rāmāyaṇa*)

"That knowledge which does not culminate in love for God is actually ignorance." Let us understand this through a worldly example. A servant of an officer kept a *pārasa*, a touchstone which changes iron into gold, on a table in his drawing room. When the officer returned home, he shouted angrily, "Who has put this useless stone on my table?" The servant replied, "Sir! While you were away, a *sādhu*, holy man came. He asked me to give this to you and mentioned that it is a touchstone." The officer said angrily, "You expect me to believe that this is really a touchstone?" He threw the stone out of the window. It fell on an iron object that was lying outside and that object turned into gold. The officer saw what had happened and was amazed. He was now convinced that it was actually a touchstone. He rushed out to pick up the stone and put it securely in his locker. He started dreaming of all the worldly pleasures he would now be able to acquire. His joy knew no bounds as he thought, "I can have as much wealth as I want. I can now become as great as God!" Just think, as long as the officer didn't know that the stone was an actual touchstone, he had no love for it. As soon as he discovered that it was genuine, he fell in love with it.

Similarly, firm faith in the words of the scriptures, knowledge related to God gives rise to love for God, and as this love increases, practical experience also increases. Therefore, anyone claiming to be a *jñānī* who is devoid of devotion to God, is really the most foolish man. His foolishness worsens as his false pride kills the natural desire to learn. Even Guru of the stature of Brahmā cannot make such a proud scholar understand the truth as he does not accept anything anyone says.

Veda Vyāsa has given a brief and beautiful definition of true knowledge,

sā vidyā tanmatir yayā

(Bhāg. 4.29.49)

"That alone is knowledge, which leads to devotion to God." He again states in the *Bhāgavatam,*

śhreyaḥ srutiṁ bhaktimudasya te vibho
kliśhyanti ye kevala bodhalabdhaye
teṣhāmasau kleśhala eva śhiṣhyate
nānyad yathā sthūlatuṣhāvaghātinām

(Bhāg. 10.14.4)

"One who desires to attain knowledge of the divine through the path of *jñāna* without pracitising devotion, is like the foolish woman who pounds and winnows empty husk in the hope of getting rice." Our goal cannot be attained even in our dreams through fruitless efforts of this kind. It is clearly stated in the *Gītā*,

māṁ cha yo'vyabhichāreṇa bhaktiyogena sevate
sa guṇān samatītyaitān brahmabhūyāya kalpate

(Gītā 14.26)

"The *jñānī* who attains the state of '*brahmabhūta*' and who has realized the 'self' or soul is called *ātmājñānī*. He attains it through non-dualistic devotion, that is, devotion to the Impersonal Aspect of God."

brahmabhūtaḥ prasannātmā na śhochati na kāṅkṣhati
samaḥ sarveṣhu bhūteṣhu madbhaktiṁ labhate parām

(Gītā 18.54)

"Although the *jñānī*, who reaches the state of '*brahmabhūta*' attains equanimity, that is, his desires come to an end and he does not suffer the pain of any loss, yet he does not attain complete knowledge of God. Therefore, he is subject to downfall even from this evolved state. However, once he attains Supreme Devotion (through practice of dualistic devotion, that is devotion to the Personal Form) complete knowledge is attained."

bhaktyā māmabhijānāti yāvān yaśhchāsmi tattvataḥ
tato māṁ tattvato jñātvā viśhate tadanantaram

(Gītā 18.55)

The partial knowledge that the *jñānī* attains as an *ātmajñānī*, as the knower of the 'self' or soul, reaches completion through devotion to the Personal Form of God and through this he comes to know God in totality. It is in this context, that the word, ***'abhijānāti'*** has been used, to indicate that the partial knowledge now reaches perfection. After attaining this perfect knowledge, the *jñānī* merges into *Brahman*. This is stated more clearly at another place in the *Gītā*,

jñānayajñena chāpyanye yajanto māmupāsate
ekatvena pṛithaktvena bahudhā viśhvato mukham

(Gītā 9.15)

"Different people worship Me in different ways but devotion is indispensable for everyone." From the words ***'mām upāsate'***, it is evident that even the *jñānī* has to practise devotion, be it dualistic, non-dualistic or any other form of devotion. It is again stated,

puruṣhaḥ sa paraḥ pārtha bhaktyā labhyas tvananyayā
yasyāntaḥ sthāni bhūtāni yena sarvamidaṁ tatam

(Gītā 8.22)

The Supreme Divine Personality, God is known only through single-minded devotion. The *jñānī* who is referred to as being dear to God is the *jñānī bhakta*.

chaturvidhā bhajante māṁ janāḥ sukṛitino'rjuna
ārto jijñāsurarthārthī jñānī cha bharatarṣhabha

(Gītā 7.16)

In this verse, Śhrī Kṛiṣhṇa has used the word ***'bhajante'*** which means 'devotion'. He states that four kinds of people worship Him. Three of them - the afflicted, the seeker of knowledge and the seeker of material possessions, are selfish devotees. The *jñānī* does not approach God with material desires, and so is very dear to Him. At another place, Arjuna asked Śhrī Kṛiṣhṇa the question,

evaṁ satatayuktā ye bhaktās tvāṁ paryupāsate
ye chāpyakṣharamavyaktaṁ teṣhāṁ ke yogavittamāḥ

(Gītā 12.1)

"Some people engage in non-dualistic devotion to realize the Formless Aspect of God. They desire to merge into *Brahman* through *jñāna yoga,* and lose their identity. Others engage in dualistic devotion to the Personal Form of God. They wish to retain their individual existence as eternal servitors of God. Which of these two do you consider superior?" The Lord replied that both would attain the divine goal, because ***"avyaktaṁ paryupāsate",*** both practised devotion, nevertheless, non-dualistic devotion to Impersonal *Brahman* is extremely difficult for embodied beings to practically pursue.

The following verse in the *Gītā* about liberation from *Māyā,* is the most significant one,

daivī hyeṣhā guṇamayī mama māyā duratyayā
māmeva ye prapadyante māyāmetāṁ taranti te

(Gītā 7.14)

The Lord declares, "My power *Māyā,* consisting of the three modes, can only be crossed by one who surrenders to Me." In other words, liberation cannot be attained through *jñāna* or *karma,* devoid of devotion to Śhrī Kṛiṣhṇa. At another place the *Gītā* states,

ananyachetāḥ satataṁ yo māṁ smarati nityaśhaḥ
tasyāhaṁ sulabhaḥ pārtha nityayuktasya yoginaḥ

(Gītā 8.14)

"One who absorbs his mind in exclusive and constant devotion to Me, attains Me very easily."

bahūnāṁ janmanāmante jñānavān māṁ prapadyate
vāsudevaḥ sarvamiti sa mahātmā sudurlabhaḥ

(Gītā 7.19)

"It is after constant efforts in millions of births that a *jñānī* surrenders to Me." It is only then that he can be said to be ***'sarvavit'***, one who realizes everything as God. The *Gītā* again states,

yo māmevamasammūḍho jānāti puruṣhottamam
sa sarvavid bhajati māṁ sarvabhāvena bhārata

(Gītā 15.19)

"After surrendering to Me, a *jñānī* attains complete divine knowledge and wholeheartedly worships Me." There is only one verse in the entire *Gītā* where Śhrī Kṛiṣhṇa says, "Even though I am unattainable, being divine, anyone who practises exclusive devotion to Me, can see Me, know Me and attain union with Me."

bhaktyā tvananyayā śhakya ahamevaṁ vidho'rjuna
jñātuṁ draṣhṭuṁ cha tattvena praveṣhṭuṁ cha parantapa

(*Gītā* 11.54)

Further Lord Kṛiṣhṇa promises at one place in the *Gītā,*

kaunteya pratijānīhi na me bhaktaḥ praṇaśhyati

(*Gītā* 9.31)

"O Arjuna! I promise that My devotee will never suffer a downfall." He does not take the same responsibility for *jñānīs* or *karmīs*. Again in the *Gītā* He says,

ye tu sarvāṇi karmāṇi mayi saṁnyasya matparāḥ
ananyenaiva yogena māṁ dhyāyanta upāsate

(*Gītā* 12.6)

teṣhāmahaṁ samuddhartā mṛityusaṁsārasāgarāt
bhavāmi na chirāt pārtha mayyāveśhitachetasām

(*Gītā* 12.7)

"I take responsibility for those who surrender all their actions to Me and worship Me with exclusive devotion. I liberate them from the endless cycle of birth and death." At another place in the *Gītā,* Lord Kṛiṣhṇa very clearly declares,

ananyāśh chintayanto māṁ ye janāḥ paryupāsate
teṣhām nityābhiyuktānāṁ yogakṣhemaṁ vahāmyaham

(*Gītā* 9.22)

"I take responsibility for those devotees who are exclusively devoted to Me. I give to them what they lack and I Myself protect what they have." In the entire *Gītā,* Lord Kṛiṣhṇa reveals His partiality at one place,

samo'haṁ sarvabhūteṣhu na me dveṣhyo'sti na priyaḥ
ye bhajanti tu māṁ bhaktyā mayi te teṣhu chāpyaham

(*Gītā* 9.29)

"O Arjuna! I am impartial towards all. No one is My enemy or friend, but I eternally reside in those who are devoted to Me and they reside in Me." The implication here is that the Lord constantly takes care of them.

Śhrī Kṛiṣhṇa again states,

ye yathā māṁ prapadyante tāṁstathaiva bhajāmyaham

(*Gītā* 4.11)

"Those who are naive, think Me to be desireless and self-contented, and therefore, a non-doer. This is true of My dealings with ordinary persons. But if someone surrenders to Me, I respond by serving him according to his degree and sentiment of surrender." The Lord takes care of surrendered souls as a mother takes care of a newborn child. The moment you acquire faith that the Supreme Lord serves insignificant living beings like us just by our surrender, you will surrender to Him immediately.

The Lord declares in the *Gītā*,

sarvadharmān parityajya māmekaṁ śharaṇaṁ vraja
ahaṁ tvā sarvapāpebhyo mokṣhayiṣhyāmi mā śhuchaḥ

(*Gītā* 18.66)

"After surrendering to Me, you don't have to think about the sins of your uncountable births in the past or the present.

From the very moment you completely surrender to Me, I become your governor and protector, and I redeem the sins of uncountable past lives and liberate you from *Māyā*. Do not worry. So abandon all other duties and surrender to Me." In other words, after a devotee surrenders to Śhrī Kṛiṣhṇa, He makes His devotee free from all worries eternally. He further says,

teṣhāṁ satata yuktānāṁ bhajatāṁ prītipūrvakam
dadāmi bhuddhiyogaṁ taṁ yena mām upayānti te

(Gītā 10.10)

"Those who are exclusively and constantly devoted to Me, receive that divine knowledge with My Grace, by which everything becomes known to them."

The Lord again declares in the *Gītā*,

api chetsudurāchāro bhajate māmananyabhāk
sādhureva sa mantavyaḥ samyagvyavasito hi saḥ

(Gītā 9.30)

"Even if a man's external actions appear evil, if he is exclusively devoted to Me, he is to be considered virtuous, because he has understood the truth about Me." It is on this basis that the so-called 'unrighteous' actions of Sugrīva and Vibhīṣhaṇa were ignored by Śhrī Rāma.

At one place in the *Gītā*, the Lord reveals the innermost secret of all secrets,

sarvaguhyatamaṁ bhūyaḥ śhṛiṇu me paramaṁ vachaḥ
iṣhṭo'si me dṛiḍhamiti tato vakṣhyāmi te hitam

(Gītā 18.64)

"Arjuna, because you are extremely dear to Me, I will reveal the most confidential of all secrets, which I do not reveal to others." What was this most intimate secret?

manmanā bhava madbhakto madyājī māṁ namaskuru
māmevaiṣhyasi satyaṁ te pratijāne priyo'si me

(Gītā 18.63)

"Arjuna, if you attach your mind to Me alone and remain devoted to Me, you will come to Me and remain eternally blissful."

From these verses of the *Gītā*, it should be absolutely clear that it is impossible to attain the goal of Supreme Bliss through *jñāna* alone which is, devoid of devotion. Non-dualistic worship of the Abstract, Formless, Attributeless Absolute is referred to as *'jñāna yoga'*. Dualistic worship of the Personal Form of God is referred to as *'bhakti yoga'*. Both the *jñāna yogī* and the *bhakti yogī* are blessed, because they practise devotion to God.

One most vital point to understand is that, a seeker cannot even enter the path of *jñāna* without *bhakti* or devotion. And even if he does, he is bound to fall on the way. If he somehow succeeds in attaining the state of a *jīvanmukta,* one who has realized the self he is still not free from the danger of material bondage. Let us understand the above points in depth.

The most vital thing to understand is that without devotion one cannot even enter the path of *jñāna.* The *Bhāgavatam* states,

nirviṇṇānāṁ jñānayogaḥ

(Bhāg. 11.20.7)

Only one who is totally detached and has attained tranquility of mind, patience and the capacity to discriminate between the eternal and the non-eternal, is eligible for the path of *jñāna*. Without dualistic devotion to the Personal Form of God, the purity of heart required to develop the qualities to enter on the path of *jñāna*, cannot be attained. Also, even if anyone has the eligibility to follow the path of *jñāna*, he will face immense difficulties on the path.

ye'nye'ravindākṣha vimuktamāninas
tvayyastabhāvādaviśhuddhabuddhayaḥ
āruhya kṛichchhreṇa paraṁ padaṁ tataḥ
patantyadho'nādṛitayuṣhmadaṅghrayaḥ

(*Bhāg.* 10.2.32)

tathā na te mādhava tāvakāḥ kvachid
bhraśhyanti mārgāt tvayi baddhasauhṛidāḥ
tvayābhiguptā vicharanti nirbhayā
vināyakānīkapamūrdhasu prabho

(*Bhāg.* 10.2.33)

One who follows the path of *jñāna* without practising devotion to God, falls spiritually, but one who follows the path of devotion does not suffer a spiritual downfall, because the Lord personally protects him. Thus, on one hand the devotee does not have to worry about anything and secondly, he does not fall from his path. Thirdly, even if a *jñānī* manages to attain the state of a *jīvanmukta,* and is engrossed in *nirvikalpa samādhi,* the unwavering blissful trance in which there is no consciousness of duality, there is still every possibility of his downfall. According to the *Vāsanā Bhāṣhya,*

jīvanmuktā api punarbandhanaṁ yānti karmabhiḥ

Even a *jīvanmukta* can be subject to material bondage again because he does not practise devotion to God, and is therefore deprived of protection from Him. We have the example of a *jīvanmukta* named Jaṛabharata, who had to become a deer in his next life because of his attachment to a fawn. The trance of the *jñānī* can be compared to a cave where *Māyā* does not enter. But as soon as this *jñānī* leaves his *samādhi* and ventures out into the external world, he is overpowered by *Māyā*. For example, a person who is being followed by bees, runs here and there to avoid being stung, but failing to do so, he jumps into a pond and keeps his head under the water. But how long can he stay in this position? As long as he does, he will be safe from the bees. But the moment he raises his head above the water, the bees will sting him. The state of *samādhi* of the *jñānī* is similar to this. The only state where there is no question of being bound by *Māyā* again is that of surrender, because in this state the devotee does nothing himself. The doer and governor of his actions is God Himself.

In the world of today, if any spiritual seeker goes to someone posing as a 'Saint', asking for a remedy for the disease of material existence; that so-called saint opens the entire dispensary of 'medicines' (various paths mentioned in the scriptures) and asks him to choose whatever he fancies. Now, ask that imposter a simple question. "If a patient knows how to diagnose his own problems, what is the need of going to a doctor?" All this is obviously a mere deception. The path to be followed by anyone is not a matter of personal choice, but is determined by the Guru according to his disciple's eligibility. The path of *jñāna* is only for a person who is totally detached from the world. The path of *bhakti* is for the one who is neither too detached, nor too attached to the world, and the path of *karma* is for the one who is extremely attached to the world.

Now you must have understood the three paths and the goal that one can attain by following each of them, and also the difficulties faced in each path. However, one thing is definitely evident and that is, devotion is indispensable in all the paths. No righteous action or knowledge can lead to the attainment of God without devotion.

The attainment of knowledge and detachment through devotion.

Knowledge and detachment, are considered essential prerequisites for attaining God. Now, the question arises that if someone follows the path of *bhakti,* how will he attain knowledge and detachment, and how will he progress without them? The answer to this question is given in the *Bhāgavatam,*

vāsudeve bhagavati bhaktiyogaḥ prayojitaḥ
janayatyāśhu vairāgyaṁ jñānaṁ cha yadahaitukam

(Bhāg. 1.2.7)

Knowledge and detachment are automatic by-products of devotional practice. One does not need to endeavour separately for them. Veda Vyāsa himself says,

> ***bhaktiḥ pareśhānubhavo virakti***
> ***ranyatra chaiṣha trika eka kālaḥ***
> ***prapadyamānasya yathāśhnataḥ syus***
> ***tuṣhṭiḥ puṣhṭiḥ kṣhudapāyo'nughāsam***
>
> *(Bhāg. 11.2.42)*

"When a person eats, the food automatically satiates his hunger and nourishes his body as well. Similarly, according to the degree of one's devotion to God, one attains natural detachment from the world as well as divine knowledge with God's Grace." In this way, devotion, knowledge and detachment go hand in hand. When a devotee attains perfection, that is he attains God, then he will have complete knowledge and complete detachment. Some people naively suggest that one should first attain detachment, then knowledge, and afterwards practise devotion. Some people recommend that one should first practise devotion then acquire knowledge, and finally attain detachment. Others state that knowledge is to be acquired first, then detachment and finally devotion. However, this is all childish talk. When you seriously reflect upon the above, you will be able to understand it correctly.

Another question arises with regard to the five material sheaths, *pañchakoṣha* that bind the individual soul. The scriptures state that liberation cannot be attained until they are destroyed.

How will the bondage of these five sheaths be burnt and destroyed by devotion? Veda Vyāsa replies,

animittā bhāgavatī bhaktiḥ siddhergarīyasī
jarayatyāśhu yā kośhaṁ nigīrṇamanalo yathā

(Bhāg. 3.25.33)

"In the fire of separation experienced through selfless devotion to Śhrī Kṛiṣhṇa, the five material sheaths burn away by themselves. Just as after eating, food is digested through the digestive fire. There is no need for any other extra effort." This implies that the path of devotion takes care of all the problems that one deals with. In other paths, it is not so. Veda Vyāsa states,

yat karmabhir yat tapasā jñānavairāgyataśhcha yat
yogena dānadharmeṇa śhreyobhiritarairapi

sarvaṁ madbhaktiyogena madbhakto labhate'ñjasā
svargāpavargaṁ maddhāma kathaṁchid yadi vāñchhati

(Bhāg. 11.20.32 - 33)

The fruits of *karma,* the celestial abodes the ultimate fruit of *jñāna,* liberation, that of *yoga,* the various *siddhis,* supernatural powers, God's divine abode or anything that any path can provide, can all be attained through devotion alone. God is quite reluctant to grant Divine Love, but is ready to give anything else asked for. Lord Rāma said to Kāgabhuśhuṇḍī,

kāgabhuśhuṇḍī māṅgu vara ati prasanna mohi jāna
aṇimādika sidhi apara nidhi mokṣha sakala sukha khāna

(Rāmāyaṇa)

"I am extremely pleased with you. Ask for any of the eight *siddhis,* yogic powers or nine types of *nidhis,* celestial treasures or anything else up to liberation." Kāgabhuśhuṇḍī cleverly replied, "Please do not be so pleased with me. All I want is Your Grace. If you truly want to grant me something, then grace me with Your most intimate power called 'Selfless Divine Love', which is glorified in all the scriptures, and which only a rare few souls attain with Your Grace.

avirala bhakti viśhuddha tava, śhruti purāṇa jehi gāva
jehi khojata yogīśha muni, prabhu prasāda kou pāva
..... dehu dayā kari rāma

(Rāmāyaṇa)

God is reluctant to bestow Divine Love, as He becomes eternally bound by the Love of His devotees.

According to Veda Vyāsa,

yaddurlabhaṁ yadaprāpyaṁ manaso yanna gocharam
tadapyaprārthito dhyāto dadāti madhusūdanaḥ

"Whatever is rare to attain, or impossible to attain, or even to conceive in the mind, can all be acquired without asking, by practising devotion. There is no need for any other separate endeavour to attain them."

राधे राधे गोविंद गोविंद राधे। राधे राधे गोविंद गोविंद राधे॥

Jñāna and Bhakti

There appear to be philosophical differences between the paths of *jñāna* and *bhakti* which actually do not exist. The *jñānī* considers the individual soul, *jīva* to be the Supreme Absolute, *Brahman.* He doesn't accept that there is a separate power named *jīva*. However, those following the path of *bhakti* consider the soul, *jīva* to be a separate power distinct from *Brahman*.

The second distinction is that the *jñānī* dismisses *Māyā* as an illusion and declares it to be indefinable. He does not accept *Māyā* as a power of God, but the devotee accepts *Māyā*, as a power of God. Therefore, where the *jñānīs* consider only *Brahman* to be the eternal entity, the *bhaktas* accepts three eternal entities - God, the individual soul and *Māyā*. Thus it appears that the paths of *jñāna* and *bhakti* differ from each other.

Śhaṅkarāchārya

The primary preceptor and propagator of the path of *jñāna* was the first *Jagadguru*, Śhaṅkarāchārya. In his commentaries, he has tried to establish that the individual soul, *jīva* is not a distinct entity from *Brahman* and that there is no factual existence of the power called *Māyā*. The *jīva*, individual soul itself is *Brahman*. *Brahman* is the Indivisible Absolute Truth, devoid of differences with any entity within and outside Itself. It is indifferent and a witness and towards all. It is pure consciousness, devoid of form, qualities or attributes. The world is an illusion and *Māyā* is indefinable. The individual soul is only a shadow - reflection of *Brahman* and is the same as *Brahman*. The soul is compared to the space contained in a pot, while *Brahman* is compared to universal space. When the pot is destroyed that the veil of ignorance is lifted from the soul, the soul realizes its true identity as *Brahman*.

His principal declaration was, "***tattvamasi***," *You are that Brahman*. By hearing and repeatedly contemplating this truth, one attains realization of the knowledge, "***ahaṁ brahmāsmi***," *I am that Brahman*, which is the ultimate stage of the path of *jñāna*. *Māyā*, *avidyā* and *ajñāna* are one and the same. *Māyā* performs various kinds of deluding activities with the power derived from *Brahman*.

Rāmānujāchārya

Jagadguru Rāmānujāchārya's philosophy is exactly opposite to that of Śhaṅkarāchārya. He held that there is one entity, God, who has simultaneous internal distinctions, *svagatabheda*, which are the *jīvas*, souls and *jagata*, the material world. *Brahman*, according to him is not without qualities. He is the Ocean of Knowledge, Bliss and Grace. Knowledge and Bliss are His pre-eminent attributes. The world comprised of the sentient and insentient beings is His special form. The word *'nirguṇa'* which was interpreted by Śhaṅkarāchārya, to mean 'attributeless', was interpreted by Rāmānujāchārya as, "one who is devoid of the material *guṇas - sattva, rājasa* and *tāmasa*." The world has emanated from God. Therefore, it is not an illusion. *Māyā* is a power of God and is inherent in Him.

The soul, *jīva* is an infinitesimal part of God, as a spark is of fire. It is minute in size, while *Brahman* is all-pervading. The *jīva* is ignorant, while *Brahman* is all-knowing and all-powerful. The *jīva* is a part of *Brahman*, hence it has an eternal identity. It is only in the context of experiencing the Bliss of *Brahman* equally, that the *jīva* can be accepted to be equal to *Brahman*. Devotion is the only means to attain liberation. The *jīva* is a servant of God. It is the greatest offence for the *jīva* to claim himself to be *Brahman*, or the Master. *Māyā* is a power of God, and is dependent upon Him. Ignorance deludes the *jīva*, but not *Brahman*. This philosophy of Rāmānujāchārya is referred to as *'viśhiṣhṭādvaita'* or 'Qualified Non-Dualism'.

Rāmānujāchārya has laid great emphasis on *'prapatti'*, complete surrender to God. Everything should be entrusted to Him. Constantly thinking favourably about God, rejecting everything unfavourable and surrendering to His will, is *prapatti*. The *jīva* must offer his very being to God, and direct all his affections to Him. It is only by the Grace of God that the *jīva* can attain Eternal Peace. Therefore, we must detach ourselves from all the objects of the senses, and surrender to God alone. Rāmānujāchārya has expressed this in the following verse,

sarvadharmāṁśh cha santyajya sarvakāmāṁśhcha sākṣharān
lokavikrāntacharaṇau śharaṇaṁ te'vrajaṁ vibho

(Rāmānujāchārya)

"O Lord, of infinite universes! I have renounced my father, mother, sister, brother, friends, elders, wealth, homeland, house and all my desires, to take complete shelter at Your lotus feet."

According to Rāmānujāchārya, God resides as a witness in everyone's heart. He is the Supreme Being, the Creator and Lord of the universe. The individual soul is His eternal servitor, so the supreme goal of the soul, *jīva* is to destroy self-pride and surrender to God. Our comprehension of the world is false, just as that of a person who mistakes a rope to be a snake in the dark. God is our eternal Father and Mother. Our duty as His children is to attain His Grace. One's tongue should be engaged in chanting God's name, and one's body, mind and wealth should be engaged in His service. Rāmānujāchārya said that we should constantly beg forgiveness for all our sins with utmost humility. Then, the causelessly merciful Lord will forgive all our sins and we will attain Eternal Divine Bliss.

Nimbārkāchārya

Jagadguru Nimbārkāchārya also propounded a philosophy that is devotion-oriented. He held that the *jīva* are both different and non-different from *Brahman*. God is both the efficient and material cause of the world. The metal, gold and gold earrings are both the same. Yet the person who knows what gold is, still has a curiosity to know about the earrings. Thus, there is a dualistic difference. *Chit* is the enjoyer, the soul and *achit* the enjoyable, material world. Both are dependent on *Brahman*, so they are non-different from Him. But they have opposite characteristics from Him, therefore they are also different from Him. It is only through devotion to God, that the individual soul can attain Supreme Bliss and liberation. In other words, it is only when the individual considers himself as the servitor and God as the Master and he engages in devotion to Him, that liberation can be attained. Nimbārkāchārya's theory is called '*dvaitādvaita*', or Dualistic Non-Dualism. According to him, God is all-powerful, and His Personal Form is the supreme form. Even though He manifests Himself in the form of the world, He remains in His original identity. He is beyond both the world and the three *guṇas*. He is ultimately responsible for the creation, sustenance and dissolution of the world. He is the material and efficient cause of this creation. He is the cause and the world is the effect. The souls, *jīvas* are an eternal part of *Brahman*, and are an effect of Him. The purpose of creation is that the individual souls can attain the Divine Grace and Vision of God. Eternal freedom from all sufferings and the attainment of Supreme Divine Bliss, is only possible through the attainment of God. Devotion is the sole means to attain Him. Although God is both Personal and Impersonal, yet the means to attain Supreme Bliss, is *bhakti* or devotion. When the individual soul, *jīva*, leading a moral life and chanting the divine names, attributes and pastimes of the Lord, acquires a true longing for Him, he surrenders to a bonafide Guru. The path taught by the Guru alone brings about the manifestation of Perfect Devotion in the purified heart. This Perfect Devotion enables the individual soul to attain God and become eternally fulfilled. In this way even Nimbārkāchārya's philosophy is that of dualistic devotion.

Mādhvāchārya

Jagadguru Mādhvāchārya was also of the opinion that all three entities declared by the *Vedas* - God, the individual soul and *Māyā* are to be accepted. All the verses of the *Vedas* that relate to non-dualism declaring the soul to be identical with *Brahman* are secondary and not primary. According to his philosophy, devotion alone can lead to the attainment of God and liberation. It is a total delusion to state or believe that the individual soul is God, because it is evident that God possesses every kind of perfection whereas the individual soul is imperfect. God is all-pervading, and the individual soul, *jīva* is not. He is all-powerful, and the soul possesses only insignificant powers. God is the creator and is omniscient, whereas the souls have originated from Him and possess limited knowledge. Mādhvāchārya's philosophy is called *'dvaita vedānta'*, Dualism.

He suggests that one should constantly engross oneself in remembrance of God, so that this remembrance remains even at the time of death. It is said that the pain of death is worse than the sting of thousands of scorpions put together. Bile, mucus and wind choke the throat. Being bound by various kinds of ties of attachment, the individual becomes extremely agitated. In such a state, there is total forgetfulness of God. Mādhvāchārya stated that every individual receives happiness and sorrow according to his own actions. Therefore, he should not forget God in times of happiness and should realize His Grace even in times of misery.

One should remain steadfast in the authentic path prescribed by the *Vedas* and scriptures. Every auspicious action should be performed with humility and constant remembrance of God, as He alone is our All-in-All. Our precious time should not be wasted in futile worldly affairs, but instead be used in the constant remembrance of God. There is nothing higher than thinking about, hearing, meditating on and glorifying God. The mere attempt to engross oneself in the remembrance of the lotus feet of the Lord, destroys all sins. When a mere attempt has such a great effect, then everything can be attained with factual remembrance.

Madhvāchārya says, "I make a solemn promise that only God is the Supreme Entity. Had God not been the Supreme Entity the world would not have been subordinate to Him. Had the world not been subordinate to Him, the living beings would have constantly experienced Bliss since the world would have been the Supreme Entity.

Vallabhāchārya

Vallabhāchārya's commentary also expresses the view that both God and the soul are separate entities, and attaining God is the ultimate goal of every soul. He established the path called *'puṣhṭi mārga'*, which is another word for pure *bhakti*. He had great faith in the narration of the divine pastimes, *līlās* of Lord Kṛishṇa described in the *Bhāgavatam*. He declared that the *Gītā*, *Bhāgavatam* and the *Brahma Sūtras* support the path of *puṣhṭi*. He particularly stressed upon devotion imbued with loving affection and referred to *puṣhṭi* as the symbol of God's Grace. He laid emphasis on devotion with sentiments of *vātsalya bhāva*, loving God as one's child. Chanting of the divine name has a special place in the path of *puṣhṭi*. Vallabhāchārya opposed Śhaṅkarāchārya's doctrine of *māyāvāda*[1]. He proved that the soul is as real as *Brahman*, yet it is a part of *Brahman* and is His servitor. So it has the natural sentiments of servitude, friendship, parenthood and amorous love towards Him. The soul can never attain peace without devotion to God. Vallabhāchārya believed in the infinitesimal nature of the soul. He declared that the world

---

[1] *māyāvāda* – The theory of *māyāvāda* holds everything other than Brahman to be an illusion.

has emanated from *Brahman,* so it is as real as Him. The Supreme Soul is *'sākāra',* that is, He posesses form. Although Vallabhāchārya, like Śhaṅkarāchārya, supported the doctrine of *advaita,* he established the theory of *'śhuddhādvaita',* 'pure non-duality of *Brahman* and the soul', and inspired souls towards the attainment of Divine Love. He held that renunciation of the fruits of Vedic and worldly actions are compulsory. The ultimate aim of the soul is to serve the Supreme *Brahman,* Śhrī Kṛiṣhṇa. Renouncing all egoism and attachments to the world, one should attain the Grace of Lord Kṛiṣhṇa by offering oneself completely and exclusively to Him through devotion. Vallabhāchārya has written an extremely beautiful verse which contains the essence of his philosophy,

sahasraparivatsaramita-kālajātakṛiṣhṇaviyogajanitatāpa
kleśhānandatirobhāvo'haṁ bhagavate kṛiṣhṇāya
dehendriyaprāṇantaḥkaraṇāni taddharmāṁśhcha
dārāgāraputrāptavittehāparāṇi ātmanā
saha samarpayāmi dāso'haṁ śhrīkṛiṣhṇa! tavāsmi

(Vallabhāchārya)

"True liberation is nothing but uniting with Śhrī Kṛiṣhṇa of Goloka. *'Pushṭi'* or spiritual nourishment, is that which manifests Divine Love in our hearts. The basis for *'pushṭi'* is Divine Grace." Vallabhāchārya was in favour of total renunciation of family life. In case this was not possible, then one should offer all of one's actions to Śhrī Kṛiṣhṇa.

Śhrī Chaitanyadeva Gaurāṅga Mahāprabhu

Gaurāṅga Mahāprabhu, the descension of Śhrī Rādhā also propagated the path of selfless devotion to God. The essence of devotional practice is contained in his *'Aṣhṭapadī'*, the eight verses, which is like an ocean of knowledge concentrated in a little pot. Some refer to Śhrī Chaitanya as the descension of Lord Kṛiṣhṇa. He exemplified the message of devotion to Lord Kṛiṣhṇa, by practising devotion himself. His love-lorn condition reached a climax in the last six years of his life, which were spent in the intense *bhāva*, ecstatic feelings of Śhrī Rādhā. During that period, all the expressions of the highest state of Divine Love, *'Mahābhāva'*, manifested in him. His divine association transformed great Monists, such as Vāsudeva Sārvabhauma and Prakāśhānanda, into loving devotees of Lord Kṛiṣhṇa. Śhrī Chaitanya laid great emphasis on *saṅkīrtana* or chanting of the divine name as the highest means, and spread his message of devotion to Lord Kṛiṣhṇa through *saṅkīrtana*. The eight verses he wrote contain the purest and most beautiful philosophy which is extremely dear to me. You too will find them inspiring.

chetodarpaṇamārjanaṁ bhavamahādāvāgninirvāpaṇam
śhreyaḥ kairavachandrikāvitaraṇaṁ vidyāvadhūjīvanam
ānandāmbudhivardhanaṁ pratipadaṁ pūrṇāmṛitāsvādanam
sarvātmasnapanaṁ paraṁ vijayate śhrīkṛiṣhṇasaṅkīrtanam

(Śhikṣhāṣhṭaka)

"The glorification of the divine names and qualities of Lord Kṛiṣhṇa through chanting, is the supreme means. There is no other spiritual discipline that can be compared to it. It cleanses the mirror of the mind and extinguishes the blazing fire of suffering in the form of the repeated cycle of birth and death. The chanting of Lord Kṛiṣhṇa's name is like the radiance of moon-beams which causes the lily of eternal good to blossom and which swells the tide of the Ocean of Bliss. It is the very life of all transcendental knowledge. Every utterance of the divine name gives full taste of its nectarine sweetness that swells in the hearts of the chanters, like a surging ocean of everlasting Bliss and Peace."

This verse also describes the seven stages of devotion that a spiritual aspirant goes through.

1. *chetodarpaṇamārjanam.* In the first stage of *bhakti*, the heart is purified to some extent, personal ego is lessened, which is replaced with devotional humbleness, and the devotee begins to feel his relationship with Śhrī Kṛiṣhṇa as His natural servant.

2. *bhavamahādāvāgni nirvāpaṇam.* This is the second stage of *bhakti*. In this stage, the fire of material and sensual desires, that gives rise to physical and mental agony, is extinguished.

3. *śhreyaḥ kairavachandrikāvitaraṇam.* This is the third stage of *bhakti*. Worldly happiness is called *'preya'*; divine happiness is called *'śhreya'*. The true pleasure of devotion blossoms forth in the heart of the devotee through the radiance of Śhrī Kṛiṣhṇa name. Just as the water lily blossoms in the cool moonlight, not in the scorching heat of the sun; accordingly, the real bliss of the soul is evolved by the cool effulgence of the divine name, not by the heat of sensual enjoyments.

4. *vidyāvadhūjīvanam.* This is the fourth stage of *bhakti.* Knowledge of *māyika* objects is gained through *apara vidyā,* and knowledge of God is gained through *para vidyā.* The true knowledge that "Śhrī Kṛiṣhṇa is the supreme God" comes in this stage.

5. *ānandāmbudhivardhanam.* Śhrī Kṛiṣhṇa is the Supreme Divine Bliss and so is His name. Through the all-virtuous divine name, the soul, which is a fraction of Śhrī Kṛiṣhṇa, becomes blissful. This is the fifth stage of *bhakti.*

6. *pratipadaṁ pūrṇāmṛitāsvādanam.* This is the sixth stage of *bhakti.* Both Śhrī Kṛiṣhṇa and His *bhakti* are the absolute Bliss of Divine Love. Therefore, this *bhakti* gives the fullest experience of devotional Bliss at every step. The blissful experiences of both the *jñānī,* whose goal is the Impersonal *Brahman* which is the effulgence of the divine body of Śhrī Kṛiṣhṇa, and the *bhakta,* devotee of Lord Viṣhṇu Who is omnipresent in the world, are both incomplete.

7. *sarvātmasnapanaṁ.* This is the seventh stage. In this stage, the soul becomes free of *māyika* impurities and, totally drowned in Śhrī Kṛiṣhṇa's love, he obtains his true divine form as an eternal servant of Śhrī Kṛiṣhṇa.

In addition to these descended Divine Masters, numerous other Saints like Tulasīdāsa, Sūradāsa, Mīrābāī, Nānaka, Tukārāma, Hita Harivaṁśha, Vyāsa, Lalita-Kiśhorī, Nāgarīdāsa, Paramānandadāsa and so on, have propagated only the philosophy of devotion.

Therefore, apart from Śhaṅkarāchārya, virtually every other Saint has taught dualistic devotion though they may have worded their philosophies differently. Therefore, this should be universally accepted. In reality, even Śhaṅkarāchārya practised devotion to Śhrī Kṛiṣhṇa towards the end of his life. For the purification of the mind and intellect he has said,

śhuddhayati hi nāntarātmā kṛiṣhṇapadāmbhojabhaktimṛite

(Śhaṅkarāchārya)

"It is impossible to purify the mind without devotion to Śhrī Kṛiṣhṇa."

Śhaṅkarāchārya composed beautiful verses of prayer to the Lord,

satyapi bhedāpagame nātha! tavāhaṁ na māmakīnas tvam
sāmudro hi taraṅgaḥ kvachana samudro na tāraṅgaḥ

(Śhaṅkarāchārya)

"O, Lord..." Observe, he uses the word 'Lord' *Nātha* for the Impersonal *Brahman*, which obviously means that he considered himself as the Lord's servant. He admitted, "Although it is true that there is no difference between the soul and *Brahman*, yet there is some difference - the soul originates from *Brahman*, but *Brahman* does not originate from the soul, just as the waves arise from the ocean, but the ocean does not arise from the waves."

matsyādibhiravatārairavatāravatā sadā vasudhām
parameśhvara paripālyo bhavatā bhavatāpabhīto' ham

(Śhaṅkarāchārya)

"O Saviour of the universe! You have descended in innumerable forms such as *Matsya, Kachchhapa, Varāhā* and so on from time to time for the deliverance of fallen souls. Will You not deliver me from the fearful clutches of *Māyā*?" Śhaṅkarāchārya, here accepts that he is in the grip of material afflictions and begs the Lord to protect him. These are the true inner feelings of his heart. One of Śhaṅkarāchārya's disciples questioned him,

mamukṣhuṇā kiṁ tvaritaṁ vidheyam

"What should be done immediately by a person who desires liberation?"

satsangatir nirmamateśhabhaktiḥ

Śhaṅkarāchārya replied that he should seek the association of a Saint, break the bonds of his material attachment, and attach his mind to God. The disciple again asked, **"kiṁ karma kṛitvā na hi śhochanīyam,"** *What is that action which a wise man performs, for which he never has to regret?* Śhaṅkarāchārya replied,

kāmāri - kaṁsāri - samarchanākhyam

(Śhaṅkarāchārya)

"Only the one who practises devotion to Śhrī Kṛiṣhṇa is carefree." In fact Śhaṅkarāchārya, the unrivalled propounder of *Advaita Vedānta,* advised his own mother to practise devotion to Lord Kṛiṣhṇa, and blessed her with a vision of the Lord. Now, listen to his next proclamation,

kāmyopāsanayārthayantyanudinaṁ kiñchit phalaṁ
svepsitam kechit svargamathāpavargamapare yogādiyajñādibhiḥ
asmākaṁ yadunandanāṅghriyugaladhyānāvadhānārthinām
kiṁ lokena damena kiṁ nṛipatinā svargāpavargaiśhcha kim

(Śhaṅkarāchārya)

"Those naive people who perform actions with the selfish desire for the attainment of celestial abodes, may do so. Those who desire liberation through the path of *jñāna* or *yoga* may pursue that goal, but I have nothing to do with these two paths. I wish to become a bumble bee to enjoy the sweet nectar of the lotus feet of Śhrī Kṛiṣhṇa who is an ocean of infinite Bliss. I do not desire worldly or celestial pleasures, nor do I desire liberation. I am a *Rasika* who enjoys the Bliss of Divine Love!" If you read the verses below, it should become clear how great a *Rasika* Saint Śhaṅkarāchārya was,

yamunānikaṭataṭasthita vṛiṇḍāvanakānane mahāramye
kalpadrumatalabhūmau charaṇaṁ charaṇopariṣṭhāpya
tiṣhṭhantaṁ ghananīlaṁ svatejasā bhāsayantamiha viśhvam
pītāmbaraparidhānaṁ chandanakarpūraliptasarvāṅgam
ākarṇapūrṇanetraṁ kuṇḍala yugamaṇḍitaśhravaṇam
mandasmitamukhakamalaṁ sakaustubhodāramaṇihāram
valayāṅgulīyakādyānujjvalayantaṁ svalaṅkārān
galavilulitavanamālaṁ svatejasāpāstakalikālam
guñjāravālikalitam guñjāpuñjānvite śhirasi
bhuñjānaṁ saha gopaiḥ kuñjāntarvartinaṁ namata
mandārapuṣhpavāsita mandānilasevitaparānandam
mandākinīyutapadaṁ namata mahānandadaṁ mahāpuruṣham
surabhīkṛitadigvalayaṁ surabhiśhatairāvṛitaḥ paritaḥ
surabhītikṣhapaṇamahāsurabhīmaṁ yādavaṁ namata

(Śhaṅkarāchārya)

"Lord Kṛiṣhṇa is sitting with one leg crossed over the other, under a divine wish-fulfilling tree, in a most beautiful flowery bower in Vṛindāvana, on the banks of the river *Yamunā*. His complexion, as blue as a new rain-bearing cloud, illuminates the world with its lustre. He is dressed in yellow robes and His entire body is anointed with sandalwood and camphor. His large, captivating eyes appear to reach almost to His ears, which are adorned with glittering earrings. There is a gentle, enchanting smile on His face. He is wearing necklaces of precious stones, pearls and the *kaustubha* gem, as well as garlands of forest flowers. The radiance and lustre of His body enhances the splendour of His bracelets, rings and other ornaments. Around His neck a *vunamālā*, a garland of various fragrant flowers, *pārijāta, kunda, mandāra,* lotus interspersed with *tulasī* leaves is gently swinging to and fro. His very brilliance and beauty drive away the sinful effect of the dark age of *Kali Yuga*. His curly black locks embrace His head like twining creepers, and the humming bees, attracted by these nectarean vines of Love, enhance the scene. He is sitting in the flowery bower and eating with His playmates, the cowherd boys. Meditate upon that Supreme Personality, Śhrī Kṛiṣhṇa, the bestower of the highest Bliss. He is caressed by the gentle breeze made fragrant by *mandāra* flowers, and the divine river *Gangā* resides at His lotus feet. His divine fragrance pervades the entire atmosphere. Even the cows are attracted to His captivating beauty and the sweet strains of the soul-stirring ethereal music pouring out from His flute. Bow to Śhrī Kṛiṣhṇa, the descendant of *Yadus*, who drives away the fears of the gods and terrifies the demons."

Śhaṅkarāchārya composed most of his poems in praise of Lord Kṛiṣhṇa. They show the extent to which his devotional heart yearned for a sight of his beloved Lord. Saints often preach unusual philosophies, depending upon the time, place and circumstances. We find that Lord Buddha went to the extent of denying the authority of the *Vedas* and even God. In fact, he described the soul as a changeable entity and not eternal. In the same way, the *Advaita* philosophy propounded by Śhaṅkarāchārya was mainly necessitated by the age in which he lived. He had to restrain the influence of Buddhism and ritualism which were gradually promoting atheism. He refuted both these beliefs with his great intellectual skill, but he himself continued to practise devotion. From this you can see how different his practice was from his teaching.

To say that *Māyā* is a delusion cannot be the solution. The fact that, it is a power of God, is not hidden from the scholars of the *Vedas* and other scriptures.

māyāṁ tu prakṛitiṁ vidyān māyinaṁ tu maheśhvaram

(Śhvetā. Up. 4.10)

Māyā is a power of God. The *Advaita* doctrine which accepts only one entity, *Brahman*, can be disproved by mere logic. For instance, let us consider from when the individual soul has been overpowered by ignorance and for how long he will be in this state. If it is claimed that ignorance has been there since eternity and will continue forever, this means that it will never end. If this is accepted as true, it automatically proves that there are two eternal entities *Brahman* and *avidyā*, ignorance, and not one, as is the contention of the *Advaitīs*.

If it is claimed that this ignorance had a beginning and will end one day, then another problem will arise. It will mean that the individual soul was once perfect, i.e. *Brahman*, before being overpowered by ignorance. When the individual soul that was once *Brahman*, could be overpowered by ignorance, then there is no benefit in re-attaining its original state as *Brahman* through spiritual practice, because ignorance could overpower Him again!

manuṣhyānāṁ sahasreṣhu kaśhchid yatati siddhaye
yatatāmapi siddhānāṁ kaśhchin māṁ vetti tattvataḥ

(Gītā 7.3)

"It is only after constant efforts in thousands of lives that we can attain perfection." Thus, if this state were to be temporary and ignorance were to overpower the soul again, resulting in re-entry into the cycle of birth and death, then all that efforts would be futile. Therefore, this philosophy too is unacceptable.

If it is stated that it had a beginning one day, but will stay forever, then the problem is even worse, because this would imply that a soul can never be liberated and the question of performing one's prescribed duties would not arise. The person who practises spiritual discipline would always remain ignorant, and so would the person who engages in wicked and evil actions. This view is totally unacceptable.

Finally, if it is stated that it never had a beginning but would be destroyed one day, i.e. creation will end, then there would be a problem again. This would be a direct refutation of the *Vedas* which declare creation to be eternal. Therefore, this philosophy is also unacceptable.

Now which of these theories is acceptable to the *Advaitīs*? They may not have any answer to this question. If a person happens to see a rope lying in the dark, it may scare him if he mistakes it for a snake. But it is impossible for a person to think that he himself is a snake. Besides, the knowledge that 'I am *Brahman*', is constant and complete. How can ignorance overpower this knowledge?

Therefore, the only philosophy that can be universally accepted is that the individual soul has been overpowered by ignorance due to *Māyā* since beginningless time, but this ignorance will not stay forever. It can be terminated some day through the practice of devotion. However, it should be remembered that the power, *Māyā* is eternal and can never be destroyed, but we can individually be liberated from its bondage.

nāsato vidyate bhāvo nābhāvo vidyate sataḥ

(Gītā 2.16)

"That which is existent can never cease to be." *Māyā* is an eternal power of God. Therefore, it is madness to think in terms of its destruction. Had this been possible, then the innumerable descensions of God and the Saints since time immemorial would have destroyed *Māyā* once and for all, and freed everyone from its clutches. Thus, *Māyā* can never be destroyed. It is absolutely impossible to do so. Nevertheless, even though it cannot be destroyed, one can be eternally liberated from it.

There is one more point that requires reflection. In the *Brahma Sūtra* there is an important aphorism.

jagadvyāpāravarjam

(Brahma Sūtra 4.4.17)

Even if the soul realizes *Brahman,* he cannot perform the task of creation. It is further said,

bhogamātrasāmyaliṅgāchcha

(Brahma Sūtra 4.4.22)

It is only with respect to the experience of Divine Bliss that the soul is considered equal to *Brahman.*

Apart from this all the self-realized souls who, merged in the Impersonal Form of God, *Brahman* retained their own individual identity.

evamevaiṣha saṁprasādo'smāchchharīrātsamutthāya paraṁ jyotīrupa sampadya svena rūpeṇābhiniṣhpadyate

(Chhān. Up. 8.12.3 ; 8.3.4)

The *Vedas* again state,

brahmavid āpnoti param

(Taitti. Up. 2.1)

The person who knows *Brahman,* realizes *Brahman.* If we accept this contention of the *Advaitīs* that the soul is *Brahman* then what is the necessity of attaining anything higher?

Besides this, not one of the *jñānīs* referred to in history, ever became omnipresent. They meditated upon *Brahman* and merged into *Brahman.* Some people state,

yathā nadyaḥ syandamānāḥ
samudre' staṁ gachchhanti nāmarūpe vihāya
tathā vidvān nāmarūpād vimuktaḥ
parāt paraṁ puruṣhamupaiti divyam

(Muṇḍaka Up. 3.2.8)

Just as when a river, flows into the sea it loses its form, similarly, the soul loses its form when it merges in *Brahman.* Applying worldly logic, they say that the river loses its form forever by acquiring the same salty nature as the ocean. Using this example, they have propounded a philosophy, which factually contradicts the actual meaning of the Vedic verses. The *Advaitīs* need to consider that if the water in the ocean is only salty, then where does the sweet rainwater come from which pours down from the clouds? After all, the clouds draw water from the same ocean. Therefore it is not right to say that an entity which once existed, the soul, can ever cease to be. And if we accept the argument of the *Advaitīs* that the river was never a river but always the ocean, then what was the need for it to merge into the ocean? Can the river itself not become the ocean? How is it that the *Advaitī* does not become all-powerful and omnipresent on realizing his identity with

Brahman? Why does he have to attain union with *Brahman* when he himself is *Brahman*? Why does the above verse of the *Muṇḍaka Upaniṣhad* say that the *jñānī* merges in *Brahman*?

It is thus evident that the only purpose behind establishing the philosophy of *Advaitavāda* was the circumstances prevailing at that time. This is proved beyond doubt, since Śhaṅkarāchārya personally engaged in devotion to Śhrī Kṛiṣhṇa. If there are any doubts remaining, then the following examples will dispel them completely. I am now going to present some examples of *paramahaṁsa jñānīs,* who were liberated from *Māyā* and had realized Impersonal *Brahman,* but afterwards were irresistibly attracted to the Bliss of Divine Love of the Personal Form of God. Nobody instructed them to do so, nor did they make any special effort to attain this Bliss. They were naturally and spontaneously attracted to the Personal Form of God. Why they were overwhelmed will be explained now.

Brahmānanda and Premānanda

(The Bliss of the Impersonal Brahman and the Bliss of Divine Love)

It would be completely inappropriate to say that the Bliss of *Brahman* experienced by the *jñānīs* in their state of divine trance is lesser, limited or *māyika* and bliss of Divine Love related to the Personal Form of God experienced by *bhaktas* is greater or divine. *Brahman* or the Absolute Truth is One and is always transcendental and immeasurable. He is the abode of

Divine Bliss. The seeker who attains Him, no matter in which aspect – Personal or Impersonal, will attain unlimited Divine Bliss for eternity. Nevertheless, the Bliss of Divine Love of the Personal Form, has a special distinctive quality that overwhelms and attracts even the mind of *paramahaṁsas*. This distinctive nature of Divine Love can be understood through certain worldly examples.

If someone sees a person smelling the stem of a rose bush instead of the rose, he naturally considers him foolish. Although the flowers, stems and so on, are all parts of the rose plant, it is evident that in comparison to the stem, the rose flower has a special distinctive quality. The branches of a sandalwood tree have a lovely fragrance. Now use your imagination to think how exquisite the fragrance of the flower of the sandalwood tree would be, if the tree happened to have flowers. In this way, the special distinction in the fragrance that would exist between the branch and flower of a sandalwood tree, would give us some idea of the difference between the Bliss of the Impersonal and Personal aspects of God.

Let us consider a second example to understand this point. If a person were to eat the branch of a mango tree instead of the fruit, he will be considered foolish. Although the fruits, branches and so on, are parts of the mango tree itself, there is a special sweetness and flavour in the fruit, which is absent in the branch. Using this example, let us come to the sugarcane plant. The stem of this plant itself is very sweet. Now imagine how remarkably sweet the fruit of the plant would be. From these examples, to a certain extent we can imagine the difference between the Bliss of the Impersonal Absolute and the Personal Form of God. This is the reason why Veda Vyāsa declares,

muktānāmapi siddhānāṁ nārāyaṇaparāyaṇaḥ
sudurlabhaḥ praśhāntātmā koṭiṣhvapi mahāmune

(Bhāg. 6.14.5)

"There is rarely one fortunate *paramahaṁsa* among millions, who attains this Bliss of Divine Love." It is again stated both in the *Bhāgavatam* and *Rāmāyaṇa*,

ātmārāmāśhcha munayo nirgranthā apyurukrame
kurvantyahaitukīṁ bhakimitthambhūtaguṇo hariḥ

(Bhāg. 1.7.10)

jīvanamukta brahmapara charita sunahiṁ taji dhyāna
je hari kathā na karahiṁ rati tinake hiya pāṣhāna

(Rāmāyaṇa)

"Those who have attained the state of *paramahaṁsas*, become irresistibly attracted to Lord Kṛiṣhṇa." There is definitely some remarkable speciality in the Personal Form.

chayastviṣhāmityavadhāritaṁ purā
tataḥ śharīrīti vibhāvitākṛitim
vibhur vibhaktāvayavaṁ pumāniti
kramādamunnārada ityabodhi saḥ

(Sūkti)

Once the Sage Nārada was descending to Dvārikā from the celestial abode. The people of Dvārikā looked up and saw a bright effulgence descending from the sky to the earth. When Nārada Jī drew closer, they could perceive a shimmering form in the midst of an aura of light. On his descending to the earth, they recognized him as Nārada Jī. In the same way, there are three inseparable aspects of *Brahman,*

vadanti tattattvavidas tattvaṁ yajjñānamadvayam
brahmeti paramātmeti bhagavāniti śhabdyate

(Bhāg. 1.2.11)

"That one Supreme Truth manifests in three ways - as *Brahman, Paramātmā* and *Bhagavān."* The first, the all-pervading Impersonal *Brahman,* performs no actions and is the object of worship of the *jñānīs. Brahman* can be compared to the effulgence seen in the distance by the residents of Dvārikā. The aim of the *jñānīs* is to attain liberation by merging into this Divine Effulgence. The second manifestation is *Paramātmā* or Supreme Soul, who dwells in the heart of every living being and keeps a record of our uncountable actions of innumerable lifetimes. It is He Who dispenses the fruits of actions and also notes each and every action of our present life. He is the object of worship of the *yogīs*. The *yogīs* have a closer experience than the *jñānīs* of the same Supreme Being. This is like the shimmering form seen by the residents of Dvārikā. The third manifestation bestows Grace by descending in His Personal Form on this earth. The Personal Form can be experienced with all the senses. This manifestation of God is the one that is most intimately experienced. The worshippers of this manifestation, *Bhagavān,* are called *bhaktas* or devotees.

The *Gītā* states,

tapasvibhyo' dhiko yogī jñānibhyo'pi mato'dhikaḥ
karmibhyaśhchādhiko yogī tasmād yogī bhavārjuna

(*Gītā* 6.46)

yogināmapi sarveṣhāṁ madgatenāntarātmanā
śhraddhāvān bhajate yo māṁ sa me yuktatamo mataḥ

(*Gītā* 6.47)

The *yogī* is superior to the ritualist (one who practises austerities) and the *jñānī*, but even superior to the *yogī*, is the *bhakta*." All three, the *yogī*, the *jñānī* and the *bhakta*, attain the same Supreme Being. All three are liberated and all three attain complete fulfilment, by experiencing unlimited Divine Bliss for eternity. Nevertheless, they are known differently based on the proximity of their experience to that same Supreme Being. It is on this basis that they are referred to as *jñānīs*, *yogīs* or *bhaktas*.

If the Bliss experienced by the *jñānīs* is compared to that of seeing a mango, then that of the *yogī* could be compared to smelling it, and that of the devotee can be compared to the combined bliss of seeing, smelling and tasting the fruit.

The Bliss of Impersonal *Brahman* and the Bliss of Divine Love are not two different things. Let us take an example to understand this. A pregnant mother experiences joy merely feeling the presence of her yet unborn child and already considers herself a mother. Having remained childless for a long time and desperately desirous of having a child, she feels great joy just knowing about her pregnancy. Subsequently, this joy increases with each passing month with the anticipation of the coming child, even though she cannot see, touch, or witness its activities as yet. On the actual birth of her child, she considers the joy she had experienced during pregnancy to be negligible in comparison, because she now actually sees the physical form, of her child who has name, qualities and actions. There is definitely a distinctive pleasure experienced now, and no mother in the universe would prefer to revert to the previous experience of having the child back in her womb. The first experience of pleasure was mental, but now she can enjoy the child with all her senses. These two experiences can be used to compare the Bliss of Impersonal *Brahman* with the Bliss of experiencing Divine Love of a Personal Form of God who has qualities, names, form, pastimes and who can be experienced with all the senses.

If these examples are not enough to understand the distinction between these two kinds of Divine Bliss, let us look at the examples of some *paramahaṁsas,* who were initially absorbed in the Bliss of the Impersonal Absolute but were irresistibly drawn to the Bliss of Divine Love of the Personal Form.

First let us go to the creator Brahmā and listen to his analysis of *jñāna* and Divine Love, because he has been declared to be storehouse of knowledge. It is he who manifests the *Vedas* prior to creation. He is also the first instructor of divine knowledge. This creation is his work, and even a blade of grass from it cannot be analysed or duplicated by the greatest minds of the universe without the Grace of God. How can one even measure the extent of Brahmā's intelligence? Today's scientists only add and subtract from the existing substances in the universe for their inventions, whereas Brahmā created this vast elaborate universe out of nothing! There are no actual creators today even among the greatest of scientists. The only true creator is Brahmā!

You might object saying that scientists today have created a myriad of things. This is just your confusion, because scientists do not create anything new. At best, they may discover something that was hidden before. There may be fire in water and they may develop a technique to manifest it, but they cannot do it unless it was already present there. Research simply means searching for and finding that which already exists. Columbus did not create America, he discovered it. Anyway, even the rules governing Brahmā's creation cannot be fully understood, so the question of competing with him just doesn't arise. The reason is that this astonishing creation, which is the work of Brahmā, is manifested by the power he received from God. That very Brahmā declares,

ṣhaṣhṭhivarṣhasahasrāṇi mayā taptaṁ tapaḥ purā
nandagopabrajastrīṇāṁ pādareṇūpalabdhaye
tathāpi na mayā prāptāstāsāṁ vai pādareṇavaḥ

(Vṛihadvāmana Purāṇa)

"Even though I performed austerities for sixty thousand celestial years to receive the foot-dust of the cowherd boys and

Gopīs of Braja who are ever-immersed in the Bliss of Divine Love, yet I failed." Isn't it astonishing? The personality who revealed the *Vedas* and created our world, performed severe penance in order to attain the foot-dust of the illiterate cowherd boys and *Gopīs* of Braja. Yet he did not succeed! You might be familiar with this event from the *Bhāgavatam*.

Five thousand years ago, the Supreme Personality, Lord Kṛiṣhṇa descended on this earth. When Brahmā heard of His descension, he immediately went to find out if this was actually God. Just as a person who knows little cannot test an expert, so the greatest expert cannot evaluate one who is all-knowing. The *Vedas* define God,

yaḥ sarvajñaḥ sarvavidyasya jñānamayaṁ tapaḥ

(Muṇḍaka Up. 1.1.9)

"God is All-Knowing and All-Powerful." Just as it is ludicrous for the main switch of a house to challenge the source of its power - the powerhouse, so it is ridiculous of a Brahmā, the governor of a single universe, to test the Creator of uncountable universes.

saṁkhyā chet rajasāmasti na viśhvānāṁ kadāchana

(Devī Bhāgavatam)

"It may be possible to count the grains of sand on the earth, but it is impossible to count the innumerable *brahmāṇḍas* (universes)."

bhinna-bhinna prati loka vidhātā
bhinna viṣhṇu śhiva manu disi trātā

(Rāmāyaṇa)

According to the *Rāmāyaṇa*, each *brahmāṇḍa* has three governors, Brahmā, Vișhṇu and Śhaṅkara. As there are innumerable *brahmāṇḍas*, there are also innumerable Brahmās, Vișhṇus and Śhaṅkaras. All of them are governed by the Supreme Governor, Lord Kṛișhṇa. Therefore, the attempt of the Brahmā of this universe, to test the Lord of uncountable universes, Śhrī Kṛișhṇa, was an unauthorized and foolish attempt. When Brahmā saw Him playing and eating with His illiterate playmates, he could not understand how the Supreme *Brahman*, Lord Kṛișhṇa, could behave in such a child-like manner. Thus, doubting Lord Kṛișhṇa's true identity, he used his power to hide the cows, calves and playmates of Lord Kṛișhṇa in a mountain cave in order to test Him. He returned to his abode only to find that he had been replaced by another Brahmā. This was the secret doing of Śhrī Kṛișhṇa to teach him a lesson. Humiliated, he returned to Braja and found Lord Kṛișhṇa engaged in His pastimes with exactly the same cows, calves and cowherd boys, down to every last detail exactly as before. He rushed to the cave where he had hidden the boys and calves and was shocked to see the same boys and calves, still lying in the trance in which he had left them. Brahmā was bewildered and could not grasp the reality of the situation. The more he thought about it, the more his mind reeled in confusion and he fell unconscious. Brahmā had wanted to fool the Omnipresent Lord, but he himself was made a fool of. Admitting his own ignorance and insignificance, he asked for forgiveness and surrendered to Lord Kṛișhṇa.

Lord Kṛishṇa graced him with divine vision, with which he saw all the boys and calves as expansions of Kṛishṇa Himself and thus he was able to grasp the secret of Lord Kṛishṇa's divine pastimes. Realizing the truth, he repented and prayed to Lord Kṛishṇa for forgiveness,

tadastu me nātha sa bhūribhāgo
bhave'tra vānyatra tu vā tiraśhchām
yenāhameko'pi bhavajjanānāṁ
bhūtvā niṣheve tava pādapallavam

(*Bhāg.* 10.14.30)

aho bhāgyamaho bhāgyaṁ nandagopabrajaukasām
yanmitraṁ paramānandaṁ pūrṇaṁ brahma sanātanam

(*Bhāg.* 10.14.32)

tadbhūribhāgyamiha janma kimapyaṭavyām
yad gokule' pi katamāṅghrirajo' bhiṣhekam
yajjīvitaṁ tu nikhilaṁ bhagavān mukundas
tvadyāpi yatpadarajaḥ śhrutimṛigyameva

(*Bhāg.* 10.14.34)

"O Lord! I have committed a grave offence. I did not realize that these cowherd boys are immersed in the ecstasy of Divine Love. I shall consider myself truly fortunate if I am allowed to be born even as a blade of grass or a bird in Braja, so that I may be graced with the foot-dust of the residents of this divine land. I have no words to praise the tremendous good fortune of Your playmates, who have You, the Almighty, All-Powerful Supreme Personality Himself as their Eternal Friend."

Who could be a greater *jñānī* than Lord Śhaṅkara! He has the reputation of being pleased easily. Everyone knows that he is the bestower of liberation and he is the supreme in knowledge of *Brahman*. He is capable of destroying the universe simply by opening his third eye. Lord Śhaṅkara always remains absorbed in a divine trance in his abode, Mount Kailāśha. On hearing that God had descended to earth as Śhrī Rāma, a prince of Ayodhyā, he put on the garb of an ascetic and roamed the streets of Ayodhyā hoping to be blessed with a vision of His Beloved Lord. And when the same Supreme Lord Rāma descended as Lord Kṛiṣhṇa, Śhaṅkara rushed to Gokula, disguised as an ascetic and stubbornly sat at Mother Yaśhodā's door, begging for a glimpse of her divine child. She refused, thinking that her child would be scared by his fearsome appearance. Mother Yaśhodā, in her innocence and out of love for her divine son was worried that this ascetic with a garland of skulls and snakes around his neck, would scare her child. This is the very child, about whom the *Vedas* say,

bhayādasyāgnistapati bhayāt tapati sūryaḥ
bhayādindraśhcha vāyuśhcha mṛityurdhāvati pañchamaḥ

(*Kaṭha Up.* 2.3.3)

"In fear of Him, fire burns, in fear of Him the sun shines, the clouds rain and the wind blows. In fear of Him death stalks about to kill."

Disheartened, Lord Śhaṅkara went to the banks of the Yamunā crying out to the Lord, "You are causelessly merciful and lovingly indulgent towards Your devotees. Won't you give me a glimpse of Your divine form? You can do anything."

Śhrī Kṛiṣhṇa is governed by His law as declared in the *Gītā*,

ye yathā māṁ prapadyante tāṁs tathaiva bhajāmyaham

(Gītā 4.11)

"I serve the devotee exactly according to the sentiment with which he worships Me and to the degree of his surrender." It is also His declaration,

jo tū dhāve eka paga to maiṁ dhāūṁ sāṭha
jo tū karro kāṭha to maiṁ lohe kī lāṭha

"If you take one step towards Me, I take sixty running strides towards you." According to this rule, on hearing Lord Śhaṅkara's crying, the Performer of infinite playful pastimes, Śhrī Kṛiṣhṇa, also reciprocated by crying. His mother had never seen Him crying like this before. Mother Yaśhodā, along with the other women was convinced that this was connected somehow to the ascetic, who must have cast a spell on her child. She immediately went out searching for him. Finding the ascetic on the banks of the Yamunā, she begged him to come and see her child, Kṛiṣhṇa Who was calling him. Lord Śhaṅkara understood that this was Śhrī Kṛiṣhṇa's response to his crying. And sure enough, the moment their eyes met, the so-called spell was removed. It is also well-known that Lord Śhaṅkara assumed a Divine *Gopī*-Form to gain entrance into the *Mahārāsa*. So here again we have the example of a divine personality absorbed in the blissful trance of the Impersonal Absolute, abandoning that trance and craving for an experience of Divine Love. Who could be a greater *jñānī*, than Lord Śhaṅkara?

However, both Brahmā and Śhaṅkara are manifestations of God known as *Guṇāvatāra*. Do we have any examples of *paramahaṁsas* in the category of the *jīva* or individual souls? There is an example in *Satya Yuga*, of the leaders among *paramahaṁsas* – the four eternally liberated brothers, Sanaka, Sanandana, Sanātana and Sanaṭa Kumāra. They could travel anywhere in the universe at will. Once they went to the abode of Mahavișhṇu, Vaikuṇṭha. The divine fragrance of the *tulasī* leaves offered at the Lord's feet, entered their nostrils and ended their absorption in the Impersonal Absolute. They were overwhelmed with Divine Love. Veda Vyāsa describes this in the *Bhāgavatam*,

tasyāravindanayanasya padāravinda
kiñjalkamiśhratulasīmakarandavāyuḥ
antargataḥ svavivareṇa chakāra teṣhām
saṅkṣhobhamakṣharajuṣhāmapi chittatanvoḥ

(Bhāg. 3.15.43)

These *paramahaṁsas* then begged the Lord for a boon,

kāmaṁ bhavaḥ svavṛijinairnirayeṣhu naḥ syāch
cheto'livad yadi nu te padayo rameta
vāchaśhcha nastulasivad yadi te'ṅghriśhobhāḥ
pūryeta te guṇagaṇairyadi karṇarandhraḥ

(Bhāg. 3.15.49)

"O Lord, we are ready to reside even in hell, as long as our minds can remain absorbed in Your lotus feet." What does this plea for absorption of the mind in Divine Love, even at the cost of going to hell, imply? There is surely a unique sweetness in the nectar of Divine Love.

In *Tretā Yuga*, the leader of the *jñānīs* was King Janaka who was given the title of *'Videha'*, which means one who is completely oblivious to his body. It is well-known that, even if one hand of his were to be put on the breast of a beautiful woman and the other in a blazing fire, his meditation on the Impersonal Absolute would remain totally unaffected. When he saw Śhrī Rāma for the first time, he was irresistibly drawn to His divine beauty!

mūrati madhura manohara dekhī, bhayeu videha videha visekhī

(Rāmāyaṇa)

The Bliss of his realization of Impersonal *Brahman* paled into insignificance before the superior Bliss of the Personal Form of Lord Rāma. He admitted,

inahiṁ vilokata ati anurāgā, barabasa brahmasukhahiṁ mana tyāgā

(Rāmāyaṇa)

"I feel so much intense attraction towards this beautiful divine form, that it is causing my mind to reject the Bliss of the Impersonal Absolute." How is it that he gave up a Divine Bliss which is supposed to be an eternal attainment? Did his mind get attracted to some form of material pleasure? No, what he was experiencing was an even sweeter form of Divine Bliss, which he became spontaneously attracted to. Janaka then said,

brahma jo nigama neti kahi gāvā, ubhaya rūpa dhari kī soi āvā

(Rāmāyaṇa)

"My mind which is absorbed in the Bliss of the Impersonal Absolute doesn't get the least attracted to anything else because all other pleasures are illusory, limited, *māyika* and temporary. But if my mind is now getting attracted to Śhrī Rāma, He must be my Impersonal *Brahman* in a Personal Form. The Supreme Being that I had so far considered imperceptible to the senses and impossible to interact with, has now come in a Form that I can see, experience and have a loving relationship with."

In *Dvāpara Yuga*, the leader of the *jñānīs* was Uddhava. He was fully satisfied in the Bliss of the Impersonal. Lord Kṛiṣhṇa sent him to the *Gopīs* to make him realize the unique distinction of the Bliss of Divine Love as compared to the Bliss of Impersonal *Brahman*. Uddhava went to give knowledge to the *Gopīs* but ultimately rejected that very knowledge and returned humbled and overwhelmed by the experience of the Bliss of Divine Love imparted to him by the *Gopīs*. Praising the *Gopīs* to Śhrī Kṛiṣhṇa, he asked for a boon,

āsāmaho charaṇareṇujuṣhāmahaṁ syāṁ
vṛindāvane kimapi gulmalatauṣhadhīnām
yā dustyajaṁ svajanamāryapathaṁ cha hitvā
bhejur mukundapadavīṁ śhrutibhir vimṛigyām

(Bhāg. 10.47.61)

"O Śhrī Kṛiṣhṇa! I would consider it my greatest fortune to be born as a creeper, a bush or a tree in Vṛindāvana in order to attain the foot-dust of these *Gopīs.* My human birth seems to have been wasted when I compare myself to these *Gopīs* who have reached such an exalted state. This is a state that the personified Vedic hymns even after performing countless austerities, have not been able to reach."

Now let us look at the composer of the *Vedānta* and the *Purāṇas,* Veda Vyāsa. Even after revealing the *Purāṇas* and the *Vedānta,* he still felt dissatisfied. He was advised by Sage Nārada, that Ultimate Peace could only be attained by remembrance of Śhrī Kṛiṣhṇa's divine names and pastimes. Showing off one's scholarship is one thing and being immersed in Divine Love, quite another. Then Veda Vyāsa composed the *Bhāgavatam* in which he related Śhrī Kṛiṣhṇa's pastimes, and attained the Bliss he was longing for. He then stated,

bile batorukramavikramānye,
na śhṛiṇvataḥ karṇapuṭe narasya
jihvāsatī dārdurikeva sūta,
na chopagāyatyurugāyagāthāḥ

bhāraḥ paraṁ paṭṭakirīṭajuṣhṭam,
apyuttamāṅgaṁ na namen mukundam
śhāvau karau no kurutaḥ saparyāṁ,
harer lasatkāñchanakaṅkaṇau vā

varhāyite te nayane narāṇāṁ,
liṅgāni viṣhṇor na nirīkṣhato ye
pādau nṛiṇāṁ tau drumajanmabhājau,
kṣhetrāṇi nānubrajato harer yau

tadaśhmasāraṁ hṛidayaṁ vatedaṁ,
yad gṛihyamāṇair harināmadheyaiḥ
na vikriyetātha yadā vikāro,
netre jalaṁ gātraruheṣhu harṣhaḥ

(Bhāg. 2.3.20 - 24)

"The ears that do not listen to Śhrī Rādhā-Kṛiṣhṇa's glories are no better than snake-pits. The voice that does not sing the glories of Śhrī Rādhā-Kṛiṣhṇa is like the croaking of a frog (which invites the snake called Time, to devour it). That crowned head of a king, who does not bow before Lord Kṛiṣhṇa is a mere burden. The senses that are not engaged in service of the Lord are not praiseworthy rather they are extremely contemptible. That heart is as hard as a thunderbolt, which does not melt on hearing the glories of the Lord and there are no tears of joy or appearance of ecstatic symptoms. What more can I say? The person who has not become immersed in love for Śhrī Kṛiṣhṇa, is as good as dead."

Now let us look at Śhukadeva Paramahaṁsa, who was as spiritually evolved as his father Veda Vyāsa. He was an extraordinary personality in the history of India. It is said that He chose to stay in his mother, Piṅgalā's womb for twelve years, because he did not want to come under the influence of *Māyā.* When he finally emerged, it was as a *paramahaṁsa*. He set off immediately for some unknown destination. His father Veda Vyāsa followed him calling out, "Son! Son!" He could not hear his father calling out to him, because a *paramahaṁsa's* trance cannot be penetrated by any external material sound. This was his exalted state at birth!

yaṁ pravrajantamanupetamapetakṛityaṁ
dvaipāyano virahakātara ājuhāva
putreti tanmayatayā taravo' bhinedus
taṁ sarvabhūtahṛidayaṁ munimānato' smi

(Bhāg. 1.2.2)

Śhukadeva Paramahaṁsa went further and further into the forest, with his father following him. On the way, Veda Vyāsa came across a scene,

dṛiṣhṭvānuyāntamṛiṣhimātmajamapyanagnaṁ
devyo hriyā paridadhur na sutasya chitram
tadvīkṣhya pṛichchhati munau jagadustavāsti
strīpumbhidā na tu sutasya viviktadṛiṣhṭeḥ

(Bhāg. 1.4.5)

Some celestial maidens were bathing unclothed in a lake and on seeing Śhukadeva Paramahaṁsa they did not make any efforts to cover themselves. But on seeing Veda Vyāsa, they immediately put on their clothes. This astonished Veda Vyāsa, who scolded them saying, "You covered yourselves for me, an old man, but not for my son, who is a youth. Why is that?" The women replied, "Please forgive us for saying so, but we had to cover ourselves before you, because you are a Saint of the *'haṁsa'* category and your son is a *'paramahaṁsa'*." Veda Vyāsa asked them, "Can you tell me the difference between a *haṁsa* and a *paramahaṁsa*? How could you tell that he is a *paramahaṁsa* and I am a *'haṁsa'*? This implies that you have more insight than both of us." The women replied, "O sage! It's not true. We are far less qualified than you, but we have heard the description of a *paramahaṁsa* from the *Vedas*.

yatra hi dvaitamiva bhavati taditara itaraṁ jighrati taditara itaraṁ paśhyati taditara itaraṁ śhṛiṇoti taditara itaramabhivadati taditara itaraṁ manute taditara itaraṁ vijānāti yatra vā asya sarvam ātmaivābhūttatkena kaṁ jighrettatkena kaṁ paśhyettatkena kaṁ śhṛiṇuyāttatkenakamabhivadettatkena kaṁ manvīta tatkena kaṁ vijānīyāt yenedaṁ sarvaṁ vijānāti taṁ kena vijānīyādvijñātāramare kena vijānīyāditi

(Bṛihad. Up. 2.4.14)

The *haṁsa* experiences duality, he is conscious of his own self as well as the outside world, which he can see, hear, smell, think and know. However, the *paramahaṁsa* who is beyond duality, only experiences his own self everywhere. He does not see, hear, smell, think of, or know anyone else."

The women judged the state of these two Saints, by the expression in their eyes. When Śhukadeva was looking in their direction, there was no change of expression. There was no love, no anger or astonishment. However, they saw a change in Veda Vyāsa's expression, which proved his state of duality. Furthermore, he also questioned them. The *paramahaṁsa* experiences nothing and therefore who would he question? The *haṁsa* does not experience material duality as we do, rather he experiences duality from a divine perspective. He sees what is true and what is false, rather for him, the false can never predominate the truth. According to the *Rāmāyaṇa,*

jaṛa chetana guṇa doṣhamaya viśhva kīnha karatāra
santa haṁsa guṇa gahahiṁ paya parihari vāri vikāra

"The *haṁsa* sees both the real and the unreal, but chooses only the real and rejects the false, the same way a swan (*haṁsa*) extracts only milk from a mixture of milk and water."

Śhukadeva Paramahaṁsa went into the jungle and Veda Vyāsa returned home. Subsequently, Veda Vyāsa wrote the *Bhāgavatam*. A disciple who had memorized a verse from this scripture, found Śhukadeva Paramahaṁsa absorbed in a state of trance in the jungle and recited that verse into his ear. Śhukadeva's unwavering trance came to an end. It is important to note here that no material sound can be heard by a person absorbed in the Bliss of the Impersonal Absolute. But the sound of this verse was heard! This is a divine secret which only God's intimate *Rasika* Saints can understand. Śhrī Kṛiṣhṇa's divine pastimes have a magical effect only on persons of the spiritual level of Śhukadeva Paramahaṁsa. An ordinary worldly soul is unable to experience the Bliss of these pastimes. Anyway, Śhukadeva followed that disciple and heard the entire *Bhāgavatam* from his father, Veda Vyāsa, Note here, that from the highest level of *jñāna*, the *paramahaṁsa* stage, Śhukadeva again began at the first stage of devotional practice which is 'listening'!

According to the philosophies of *Mīmāṁsā, Vedānta, Nyāya, Vaiśheṣhika, Sāṁkhya* and the *Yoga Sūtras* of *Patañjali* after listening to spiritual knowledge, *śhravaṇa,* contemplation, *manana* and then absorption in it, *nididhyāsana,* one attains the state of a *paramahaṁsa,* which was the state Śhukadeva had already attained. Then why did he go back to the initial stage of spiritual practice, that of listening? The answer is,

harerguṇākṣhiptamatirbhagavān bādarāyaṇiḥ
adhyagānmahadākhyānaṁ nityaṁ viṣhṇujanapriyaḥ

(Bhāg. 1.7.11)

One who has attained perfection on the spiritual path through listening, reflection and absorption, still gets attracted to hearing and chanting the names, qualities, etc. of God, which are actually fully enjoyed at the stage of perfection on the dualistic path of Divine Love. A spiritual aspirant listens at a different level. His listening assists him in keeping his mind in God. But Saints of the spiritual level of Śhukadeva Paramahaṁsa listen to them to enjoy the Bliss of Divine Love. This is a confidential secret and is the distinctive feature of Divine Love for a Personal Form of God. Divine Non-Duality, is transcendent to material duality, and in this state, the *paramahaṁsa* enjoys the Bliss of the Impersonal Absolute, but beyond this experience is the sweetness of Divine Duality or the ecstasy of Divine Love which is experienced by devotees who have attained Perfection. Śhukadeva Paramahaṁsa says,

sarvavedāntasāraṁ hi śhrībhāgavatamiṣhyate
tadrasāmṛitatṛiptasya nānyatra syādratiḥ kvachit

(Bhāg. 12.13.15)

The essence of all Vedānta philosophies, *Ādvaita*, *Viśhiṣhṭādvaita*, *Dvaitādvaita*, *Dvaita*, etc. is that, your mind should be attached to Śhrī Kṛiṣhṇa's name, form, qualities, pastimes, associates, abode and so on in order to attain Divine Love through God's Grace. After attaining Divine Love you again enjoy the Bliss of those very names, qualities and pastimes in such a way that the sweetness of the nectar of Divine Love continues to increase every moment for the rest of eternity. Now, if someone like Śhukadeva, who was a *paramahaṁsa* since birth became so overwhelmed after hearing just one verse from the *Bhāgavatam,* then what can be said about other *jñānīs*?

You might be curious to know the verse that captivated Śhukadeva Paramahaṁsa. It is the following verse,

aho bakīyaṁ stanakālakūṭaṁ
jighāṁsayā pāyayadapyasādhvī
lebhe gatiṁ dhātryuchitāṁ tato'nyaṁ
kaṁ vā dayāluṁ śharaṇaṁ vrajema

(Bhāg. 3.2.23)

"O, causelessly merciful Śhrī Kṛiṣhṇa, if I leave You, who else could I love? I become overwhelmed when I hear that You granted Your abode and the status of a mother to Pūtanā, who had intentionally applied poison on her breasts and with a desire to kill You, forced You as a Child to suckle them. You are all-knowing and grant the result of people's inner sentiments. Yet, ignoring her evil intention, You only considered the fact that she had offered her breasts to You as a mother would, and rewarded her accordingly!"

Philosophically, the deliverance of Pūtanā was justified because she was overwhelmed on seeing the divine beauty of, Śhrī Kṛiṣhṇa; and on receiving His touch her joy knew no bounds. Her deliverance was not against divine law because her mind had become totally absorbed in Him. Some people object saying that her mind was united with Him in hostility. However, no matter what the reason was for her deliverance, behind it was the Causeless Grace of the Lord.

Now let us look at the foremost of *jñānīs* of our age, *Kali Yuga* - Śhaṅkarāchārya. I have already established earlier that he was a devotee of Śhrī Kṛiṣhṇa, but wrote non-dualistic commentaries with the intention of refuting the atheistic Buddhist doctrines and ritualistic *Mīmāṁsā* or *Karma* doctrines. Most philosophers describe him as a *Rasika* Saint in the guise of an *Advaita* scholar. His intellectual writings are far removed from his internal feelings. Great divine personalities perform various actions for the welfare of the world in different circumstances, for different sets of people. Śhrī Kṛiṣhṇa performed diverse actions like instigating the war of *Mahābhārata* and performing *Mahārāsa*, in different circumstances, for different sets of people. Both actions were solely for universal benefit. The actions of Saints, like the actions of God, are of various levels and one should only look at the intention and not judge their external actions.

One *paramahaṁsa*, observing the contradictory qualities in God exclaimed,

> ***gopālāṅgaṇakardame viharase viprādhvare lajjase***
> ***brūṣhe gosutahuṁkṛitaiḥ stutipadair maunaṁ vidhatse satām***
> ***dāsyaṁ gokulakāminīṣhu kuruṣhe svāmyaṁ na dattātmasu***
> ***jāne kṛiṣhṇa tvadīyapādayugalaṁ premaikalabhyaṁ param***
>
> *(Sūkti)*

"O Śhrī Kṛiṣhṇa, the *Vedas* describe you as All-Knowing, All-Seeing, All-Powerful, the Governor of All, the Well-Wisher of All, and the Lord of All, then how did You become so helpless before your devotees. Though ignorance cannot even come near You, how did you do the following things? Can the All-Knowing Lord be deluded? Oh, Śhrī Kṛiṣhṇa! In spite of being the Lord of countless universes, You still choose to play in the mud of the courtyard of one house, of one village named Nandagaon, of one district, Mathura, of one state of one country, India, in one planet in one of those uncountable universes! And, at the same time You are reluctant to appear at Vedic sacrificial ceremonies conducted by learned Brahmins strictly according to scriptural injunctions. You respond to the grunts of the calves of Gokula by speaking to them, and remain silent when Vedic hymns, praising your glories are recited by great learned scholars. You are present in the deities in temples, but remain silent when wise men recite your glories with Vedic verses. These scholars would be thrilled to hear even a word of abuse from You, but You don't even do that!"

Once there was a Muslim *fakīra* who worshipped God with great fervour. His knees were sore from offering prayers to Him day and night. Another Muslim *fakīra* happened to observe his worship and sarcastically asked him whether he had met God, or if his prayers were still unheard. The first *fakīra* respectfully replied, "I have not met God as yet. But tell me, have you met Him?" The second *fakīra* said, "I meet Him every day." The first *fakīra* believed him and eagerly said, "Please do me a favour then. Ask God whether He has liked any of my prayers." The *fakīra* assured him, "I will definitely find out and tell you tomorrow." The next day he came to the first *fakīra* and said, "Well, I asked God and He said that He did not like even one of your prayers." The moment the first *fakīra* heard this, he began dancing with joy. The second *fakīra* was really astonished to see this reaction. He kept repeating that God had not liked any of his prayers, but instead of being disheartened, these words made the *fakīra* fall unconscious in ecstasy. When he regained consciousness, the second *fakīra* was curious to know the reason for his joy. The *fakīra* replied, "When God said that He did not like any of my prayers, it means that He must have heard each and every one of them. I am indeed fortunate that He has been witness to the prayers of a worthless sinner like me."

In the same way, the learned men who recite invocations to the deity in the temple, would be thrilled to hear even a word of reprimand from God, but there is no response whatsoever. Again, He, the Supreme Lord, who hesitates to enter the *samādhi* of great self-realized souls even as their Master, is seen serving the illiterate village girls of Gokula as their devoted servant and dancing to their tune! Why did all these extraordinary things happen? It is all due to the glory of Devotion. The Lord declares in the *Bhāgavatam*,

na tathā me priyatama ātmayonir na śhaṅkaraḥ
na cha saṅkarṣhaṇo na śhrīr naivātmā cha yathā bhavān

(Bhāg. 11.14.15)

"My devotees are more dear to Me than My son Brahmā, My grandson Śhaṅkara, My brother Balarāma or even My Own Divine Consort, Mahālakṣhmī. In fact, even My soul is not so dear to Me." He states again,

ahaṁ bhaktaparādhīno hyasvatantra iva dvija
sādhubhirgrastahṛidayo bhaktairbhaktajanapriyaḥ

(Bhāg. 9.4.63)

"I am the servant of My devotees. They have taken complete possession of My heart. I am not independent, but subject to their control."

nirapekṣhaṁ muniṁ śhāntaṁ nirvairaṁ samadarśhanam
anubrajāmyahaṁ nityaṁ pūyeyetyaṅghrireṇubhiḥ

(Bhāg. 11.14.16)

"I follow My devotees, so that I may be purified by their foot-dust."

One *paramahaṁsa* declares,

nigamatarau pratiśhākhaṁ mṛigitaṁ militaṁ paraṁ brahma
militaṁ militamidānīṁ gopavadhūṭīpaṭāñchale naddham

(Sūkti)

"That *Brahman*, who with great difficulty was found as a divine effulgence scattered in the various branches of the four *Vedas*, is seen in one place completely bound to the hem of the dresses of the *Gopīs*."

dhanyā gokula kanyā vayamiha manyāmahe jagati
yāsāṁ nayanasarojeṣhvañjanabhūto nirañjano vasati

(Sūkti)

"The great fortune of these *Gopīs* is beyond description, because the Formless *Brahman* resides as *kājala,* collyrium in their eyes."

Referring to the very special fortune of Mother Yaśhodā, the great Sage Nārada said,

kiṁ brūmustvāṁ yaśhode kati kati sukṛitakṣhetravṛindāni pūrvam
gatvā kīdṛigvidhānaiḥ kati kati sukṛitānyarjitāni tvayaiva
no śhakro na svayambhūr na cha madanaripur yasya lebhe prasādam
tatpūrṇaṁ brahma bhūmau viluṭhati vilapat kroḍamāroḍhukāmam

(Sūkti)

"O Yaśhodā! I have no words to praise your great fortune. To tell you the truth, I am confused because there is no spiritual discipline described in the *Vedas* or other scriptures, by which one can attain the special position you have been blessed with. The Supreme Personality, Whose Grace is sought after by Brahmā, Śhaṅkara, Indra and others, is rolling on the ground in tantrums, wanting to be carried in your arms, and you are scolding Him, 'I cannot spare time from my household chores now. Are You a special child that You always have to be carried around? Go, run outside and play with Your friends.'"

The conclusion is that although the Bliss of Impersonal *Brahman* and the Bliss of the Supreme Personality endowed with form is eternally one and the same, yet there is an indescribable special sweetness in the Bliss of Divine Love, which makes even the *paramahaṁsas* merged in the Bliss of the Impersonal Absolute, totally spellbound.

Only one in billions is eligible to follow the path of *jñāna*. For those who are, there is always the danger of a spiritual downfall because there is no protection from God, and out of those who luckily attain the Bliss of the Impersonal, it is one rare fortunate soul in billions who is able to experience the sweetness of Love in Divine Duality!

राधे राधे गोविंद गोविंद राधे। राधे राधे गोविंद गोविंद राधे॥

Impersonal, Personal God and The Secret of Descension

Some people question the concept of a personified descension of God because they believe that God is only an impersonal entity. But the scriptures clearly proclaim God possesses contradictory qualities. The *Vedas* state,

ajāyamāno bahudhā vījāyate

(Veda)

"He, the Supreme Being, is without a body, yet He has a form: He is unborn, yet He takes innumerable births."

dve vāva brahmaṇo rūpe mūrtaṁ chaivāmūrtaṁ cha

(Bṛihad. Up. 2.3.1)

God has two aspects, Impersonal and Personal. Now the question is, if God possesses a form, how can He possibly pervade subtle things? Besides this, if He did have a form, He would have been seen in the world at one time or another. Actually, the soul is formless.

bālāgraśhatabhāgasya śhatadhā kalpitasya cha
bhāgo jīvaḥ sa vijñeyaḥ sa chānantyāya kalpate

(Śhvetā. Up. 5.9)

chinmātraṁ śhrī harer aṁśhaṁ sūkṣhmamakṣharamavyayam

(Veda)

Just as a formless soul assumes a body, God also assumes a form. The difference is that the individual soul being under the control of *Māyā,* assumes a material body and the body he acquires is in accordance with his past actions. On the other hand, God takes on a divinely blissful form according to His own free will through His Power *Yogamāyā,* in order to shower Divine Bliss on individual souls. To raise the objection that if God had a form, He would surely have been visible to us sometime, is naive, because God's form is divine, whereas our vision is material. A divine form can never be perceived with material vision. It is only when an individual attains eligibility through the practice of devotion that he attains divine vision through God's Grace, whereupon he sees the divine form of God everywhere. The experience of Saints provides evidence of this truth.

Isn't it silly to presume that the Almighty, All-powerful Supreme Being who creates innumerable universes and countless subtle elements, merely with a smile, cannot take a form Himself? God has innumerable, incomprehensible divine powers. When He has such unlimited powers, what is so surprising about His assuming a form? We have examples of formless substances taking form in the material world itself. The *Vedas* describe the manifestation of the material elements in the following sequence.

tasmād vā etasmādātmana ākāśhaḥ sambhūtaḥ
ākāśhādvāyuḥ vāyoragniḥ agnerāpaḥ adbhyaḥ pṛithivī
pṛithivyā oṣhadhayaḥ oṣhadhībhyo'nnam

(Taitti. Up. 2.1)

"God created the element space. Now space does not have the property of touch, but from space came air, which possesses the quality of touch. From air came fire, from fire came water, from water came the element, earth. From the earth came the trees and herbs, and from the trees and herbs came food..." Observe, from the formless element space which is devoid of even the quality of touch, we have the earth, which contains the properties of touch, taste, smell, sound and so on. Now isn't it absurd to argue that the Almighty, All-Powerful God Himself cannot assume a form?

Some people raise a childish objection that, in the world when a cloud releases rainwater, it ceases to exist and when a cloud is formed, its cause, the vapour, ceases to exist. In the same way, the omnipresent, formless, absolute will not remain all-pervasive if He assumes a Personal Form. Their fear is that the formless *Brahman* will cease to exist, but this fear is groundless. Material causes have different powers of action, whereas God has unlimited powers which are capable of doing anything. That is why He is referred to as the Cause of all causes and the Almighty. If material causes had powers that could enable them to do anything and everything, they would no longer be referred to as material. Therefore, using material reasoning for the All-Powerful and All-Capable God is naive.

Some people give another argument. They state that if God is All-Powerful, He can also destroy Himself. The possible implication of these people may be that, if God were to get into an agitated state some day, He could destroy Himself and we would be free from all control. We could then freely engage in sinful activities without fear of punishment. Such people are obviously ignorant of the fact that every power acts according to its nature, never against it. Observe, fire is said to be capable of burning everything.

kā nahiṁ pāvaka jari sake

But the fact that fire burns everything, does not mean that it can burn itself. This is absolutely impossible because it is contrary to its nature. An acrobat can never climb on his own shoulders and walk.

Then again, some people question that if God can create countless universes, can He not make countless Gods in the same way? They probably think that if many Gods were to come into being, there would be competition between them, and in this process they would get special advantages. But this is impossible. To think that the existence of many Gods will result in benefits as we get in worldly competition, is absurd because this is against spiritual law. Besides, God does in fact assume innumerable forms. There have been countless descensions in each *Brahmāṇḍa*. Even in one descension, He assumed many forms to perform various *Līlās*. For example in *Mahārāsa* Śhrī Kṛiṣhṇa assumed innumerable forms which were His own expansions. All these assumed forms were obviously God Himself. After assuming these innumerable forms in one descension, He again becomes One. If the intent of the questioner is that God could create another God like Himself who could work independently, then this is just a thinking of a material mind. It is absolutely impossible because such an action would be against God's nature. God does not perform any material action based on attachment and animosity, nor does He perform any unnecessary action.

Thus, divine powers cannot function contrary to their nature, just as fire cannot burn itself. If they did, then it would mean that God is under the control of His Own powers. But as God is the Master and Governor of all His powers, these arguments have absolutely no place here. The Personal Form and the Impersonal Aspect of God have been clearly referred to in all the scriptures from the *Vedas* to the *Rāmāyaṇa*. This truth is also well-known in the world. To doubt this is absurd. Besides, it has already been pointed out that worship of the formless *Brahman* is extremely difficult for embodied beings. First, one has to meet the strict criteria of eligibility for entering the path of *jñāna*. Secondly, actual practice on the path is extremely difficult and there is a vast difference in the Divine Bliss experienced in the state of ultimate attainment as compared to the Bliss of Divine Love. Nevertheless, if someone is determined to worship the Impersonal *Brahman*, then he can do so only after meeting the required qualifications which have been specified by the scriptures. However, we are discussing the path of devotion to a Personal Form of God here.

The Secret of Descension

Although people accept the possibility of the Impersonal Absolute assuming a Personal Form, some question the necessity of God's descension in a Personal Form. They argue that God is Almighty, so He can perform all the necessary actions even without descending. Therefore, the secret behind His descension needs to be understood. There are innumerable reasons for the descensions of God. No one can limit them.

hari avatāra hetu jehi hoī, idamitthaṁ kahi jāta na soī

(Rāmāyaṇa)

To state that the purpose of God's descension is limited to a specific reason is absurd. The actual secret can be understood only by God Himself. Nevertheless, various reasons have been given by different people according to their own interest. In my opinion, the most important reason for the descension of God is only, 'Causeless Mercy'.

Since God is free from attachment and aversion, and is completely self-contented, He has nothing to gain from anyone, therefore everything He does is solely for the benefit of others.

His causelessly merciful nature is well-known to all. It is because of this nature that He manifests Himself in different forms.

It is very simple to explain how He showered His Causeless Grace upon the souls by His descension. There are rigid qualifications to enter the path of *jñāna* or non-dualistic devotion to the Impersonal Aspect of God. Such a person who fulfils these qualifications is so rare that there may be only one in millions. Śhaṅkarāchārya declared the following condition to become eligible.

śhuddhayati hi nāntarātmā kṛiṣhṇapadāmbhojabhaktimṛite

(Śhaṅkarāchārya)

It is impossible to attain the purification of the heart required to enter the path of *jñāna* without devotion to Lord Kṛiṣhṇa. Without this purification how can a person become eligible to qualify for the path of *jñāna*? Further, of those who do manage to become eligible, very few manage to attain liberation. Therefore, the causelessly merciful nature of God is the only reason behind all His descensions. It is through these descensions that the innumerable names, attributes, qualities and pastimes of the Personal Form are revealed to us. By taking their help, innumerable sinful material souls have crossed the ocean of material bondage and attained eternal Divine Bliss. We have the striking example of a great sinner like Vālmīki, whose uncountable sins prevented him from uttering the word 'Rāma'! He too became a great Saint even though he recited God's name in reverse manner. It is in this context that Veda Vyāsa wrote,

bhave'smin kliśhyamānānām avidyākāmakarmabhiḥ
śhravaṇasmaraṇārhāṇi kariṣhyanniti kechana

(Bhāg. 1.8.35)

Constant contact with this world of form and qualities has caused living beings to have a natural inclination towards forms and qualities. So, God descends on earth to provide a divine form and divine qualities for living beings to absorb their minds in Him. As a result, innumerable souls have been blessed eternally.

Another important reason that is even more appealing to me is,

tathā paramahaṁsānāṁ munīnām amalātmanām
bhaktiyogavidhānārthaṁ kathaṁ paśhye mahi striyaḥ

(Bhāg. 1.8.20)

God descends on earth in His Personal Form for the *paramahaṁsas,* who worship formless *Brahman* so that they may be attracted to the superior Bliss of Divine Love. We have ample evidence of great *paramahaṁsas* such as the Sanatakumāras, Janaka, Śhukadeva and others, who had attained Bliss of the Impersonal *Brahman,* yet were irresistibly drawn to the Bliss of Divine Love. In spite of this evidence, people deny the necessity of God's descension in Personal Form. Had there been no evidence of so many descensions, then the followers of the Formless Absolute would have loudly proclaimed that there is no Personal God. Although, there is no difference between the Impersonal Aspect and the Personal Forms, yet God descends with form in order to grace the devotees enjoying the Bliss of *Brahman* with the nectar of Divine Love. By this, He also proves that both His Impersonal Aspect and Personal Forms are one. If they were not the same, then why would these completely contented *paramahaṁsas* be irresistibly attracted to the Personal Form?

barabasa brahma sukhahiṁ mana tyāgā

(Rāmāyaṇa)

Although, both Personal and Impersonal Forms are one, nevertheless the *paramahaṁsas* who were devoid of any material desires were irresistibly attracted to the Personal Form of God, who is a manifestation of a superior level of Divine Bliss.

Besides these, there are other prominent reasons for the descension of God, such as establishing righteousness, the destruction of demons and the protection of holy men. In addition to these, there could be innumerable other reasons. Even in the world, when you go to some place you try to do many things at one time. Then how is it possible to count the reasons for God's descension. The main point to remember is that, during His descensions, God graces many individual souls. Hearing about this, other souls are inspired to surrender to Him. Thus, they progress speedily with undivided faith.

The next important point about descension is that, all the descensions of God are divine.

janma karma cha me divyam

(Gītā)

According to this statement in the *Gītā*, both the birth and actions of God are divine. It is a different matter, that both His form and actions appear to be material to unqualified souls who are bound by *Māyā*. But the truth is that all the descensions of God are divine and eternal. None of these descensions are greater or lesser. You cannot make fractions of God. He is complete and unchanging, always, everywhere and in all circumstances. Veda Vyāsa clearly states,

sarve pūrṇāḥ śhāśhvatāśhcha dehāstasya parātmanaḥ

(Padma Purāṇa)

Generally those who worship God make the mistake of claiming that the form of God they worship is superior and the other forms of God are inferior. This is one of the greatest transgressions against God and is called *nāmāparādha* or spiritual transgression in the scriptures. We should not commit this mistake, even accidentally. If God could be divided into parts, then He would surely not be God.

Now let us reflect upon the path of devotion to attain God.

राधे राधे गोविंद गोविंद राधे। राधे राधे गोविंद गोविंद राधे॥

Bhakti Yoga

ālodya sarvaśhāstrāṇi vicharya cha punaḥ punaḥ
idamekaṁ suniṣhpannaṁ dhyeyo nārāyaṇo hariḥ

(Skandha Purāṇa, Mahābhārata)

saba kara mata khaganāyaka ehā,
kariya rāma pada paṅkaja nehā
jahaṁ lagi sādhana veda bakhānī
saba kara phala hari bhagati bhavānī

(Rāmāyaṇa)

The unanimous verdict of all the scriptures is that *Bhakti*[1] is the ultimate attainment. Now we need to know the means to attain it. You will be surprised to know that Divine Love, which overwhelms even the *paramahaṁsas* in special ecstasy, is not something that can be practised, nor does it

---

[1] The Saints and scriptures speak of two types of *Bhakti* (devotion)– The first is *sādhanā bhakti* or preparatory devotion. It is practised to purify the heart completely to receive the second type of *Bhakti*.

The second *Bhakti*, is Siddha Bhakti know as Perfect Devotion, Divine Love, *(Prema)* or Supreme *Bhakti*. It is the most intimate of God's Personal Powers. This is attained only upon complete purification of the heart, by the Grace of the Guru.

come by itself. Divine Love is actually the name of one of the most intimate powers of God. It is He alone who possesses this Divine Power. There is no price that can be paid for this priceless attainment. The *Rāmāyaṇa* clearly states,

avirala bhakti viśhuddha tava, śhruti purāṇa jehi gāva
jehi khojata yogīśha muni, prabhu prasāda kou pāva

(Rāmāyaṇa)

"The greatest sages and *yogīs* seek Divine Love, but it is attained only by some rare fortunate souls, and that too, only through Divine Grace." The pre-requisite for attaining Divine Grace is *Sādhanā Bhakti*, preparatory devotion. But first, it is important to understand what this Supreme *Bhakti*, Divine Love is.

The Essentials of Bhakti

In the *Chaitanya Charitāmṛita* which contains the life history of Lord Gaurāṅga, it is stated,

kṛiṣhṇera anantaśhakti tāte tina pradhān
chichchhakti māyāśhakti jīvaśhakti nāma
antaraṅgā bahiraṅgā taṭasthā kahi jāre
antaraṅgā svarūpa-śhakti sabāra ūpare

(Chaitanya Charitāmṛita)

"The Supreme *Brahman*, Śhrī Kṛiṣhṇa possesses innumerable powers, of which three are prominent. One is *Chit Śhakti*, the second is *Māyā Śhakti*, and the third is *Jīva Śhakti*. *Chit Śhakti* is an internal power, *Māyā Śhakti* is an external power, and *Jīva Śhakti* is an intermediate power. *Chit Śhakti* being the internal, intimate power, is the supreme amongst these." This fact has also been mentioned in the *Viṣhṇu Purāṇa,*

viṣhṇuśhaktiḥ parā proktā kṣhetrajñākhyā tathā' parā
avidyākarmasaṁjñānyā tṛitīyā śhaktiriṣhyate

(Viṣhṇu Purāṇa 6.7.61)

hlādinī-sandhinī-saṁvit tvayyekā sarvasaṁsthitau
hlādatāpakarī miśhrā tvayi no guṇavarjite

(Viṣhṇu Purāṇa 1.12.68)

Chit Śhakti, also known as *Svarūpa Śhakti,* is classified into three categories,

sat-chit-ānandamaya kṛiṣhṇera svarūpa
ataeva svarūpa śhakti hoya tin rūpa
ānandāṁśhe hlādinī sadaṁśhe sandhinī
chidaṁśhe saṁvit jāre jñana kari māni

(Chaitanya Charitāmṛita)

The three categories are *Sat, Chit* and *Ānanda*. This is why *Brahman* is referred to as *Sachchidānanda*. From the *Sat* aspect originates the Power *Sandhinī,* from the *Chit* aspect originates the power *Saṁvit,* and from the *Ānanda* aspect originates the power *Hlādinī*. The *Hlādinī Śhakti* surpasses the other two powers in sweetness. It is because of this power that God remains ever-blissful even while creating innumerable material universes and maintaining a record of each individual's actions. In a worldly family consisting of perhaps five to ten people, even a husband

and wife cannot get along without being upset with each other. They always remain disturbed by frictions that arise between them, several times a day. Yet, God keeps a record of each one of the innumerable actions, of the innumerable lifetimes, of innumerable souls, in the innumerable universes and dispenses the fruits accordingly, but He is never disturbed! He is ever-blissful due to His Personal Power, *Hlādinī Śhakti*. Now listen to what the *Chaitanya Charitāmṛita* says about Divine Love,

hlādinī sāra aṁśha tāra prema nāma

(Chaitanya Charitāmṛita)

The absolute essence of this *Hlādinī Śhakti* is Divine Love or *Bhakti*. To summarize, of all the innumerable powers of God, three are foremost: *Svarūpa Śhakti, Jīva Śhakti,* and *Māyā Śhakti*. From among these three, *Svarūpa Śhakti* is supreme, and it consists of three aspects: *Sat*, *Chit* and *Ānanda* of which *Ānanda* is foremost. The essence of this Supreme power, *Ānanda,* is *Hlādinī Śhakti,* and the essence of *Hlādinī Śhakti* is *Prema,* Divine Love, also referred to as *Bhakti* or Perfect Devotion. It is the sweetest and the most intimate of all God's powers. Why wouldn't God come under its control? This is why the *Rasika* Saints when they come face-to-face with God, have asked for this intimate power, Divine Love. Even though the Lord stands personally before them, they do not ask for God Himself. They only desire *Avirala Bhakti, Nirbharā Bhakti, Parā Bhakti,* or *Premā Bhakti.* These are all different names for Divine Love, which God very reluctantly gives to a devotee. Nevertheless if a devotee absolutely insists, He is bound to give it.

Now the question is, how can this rarest, most precious of all attainments be acquired? It is not attained through practice, nor does it come by itself. Some people are constantly engaged in efforts to attain that *Bhakti* or Divine Love on the strength of their own spiritual practice, while some sit back and do nothing, on the pretext that Perfect Devotion is not something that can be practised; it will come whenever it is supposed to come. Both of them are wrong. Devotion can never be attained through spiritual practice alone nor through being indolent. The *Vedas* state that one has to practise devotion in order to attain God's Grace. It is only then that one will receive His most intimate power, Divine Love.

tapaḥ prabhāvād devaprasādāchcha

(Śhvetā. Up. 6.21)

yamevaiṣha vṛiṇute tena labhyas tasyaiṣha ātmā vivṛiṇute tanūṁ' svām

(Kaṭha Up. 1.2.23)

We have to practise devotion in order to attain Supreme *Bhakti* which comes only through God's Grace. The *Rāmāyaṇa* mentions the following condition for the devotion that has to be practised by us,

mana krama vachana chhāṁṛi chaturāī
bhajatahiṁ kṛipā karata raghurāī

(Rāmāyaṇa)

"To attain God's Grace practise devotion with sincerity, abandoning all deceit and worldly desires." This is a prerequisite to attaining Divine Love, the essence of *'Hlādinī Śhakti'*.

Sādhanā Bhakti

(Preparatory Devotion)

Now we need to make a deeper study of the devotion that we have to practise, because Supreme *Bhakti* will automatically be attained through God's Grace afterwards. Besides, we cannot comprehend the *Bhakti* that is attained through God's Grace because it is divine, and therefore, inconceivable.

First, we will analyse the word *'Bhakti'*. One derivation is from *'bhajanaṁ bhakti'*, which refers to Perfect Devotion; and the other derivation is from, *'bhajayate bhaktiḥ'*, which is preparatory devotion. Let us now understand the characteristics of preparatory devotion.

anyābhilāṣhitāśhūnyaṁ jñānakarmādyanāvṛitam
ānukūlyena kṛiṣhṇānuśhīlanaṁ bhaktiruttamā

(Bhakti Rasāmṛita Sindhu)

guṇarahitaṁ kāmanārahitaṁ pratikṣhaṇavarddhamānam

(Nārada Bhakti Sūtra 54)

sarvopādhivinirmuktaṁ tatparatvena nirmalam
hṛiṣhīkeṇa hṛiṣhīkeṣha sevanaṁ bhaktiruchyate

(Nārada Pāñcharātra)

ahaitukyavyavahitā yā bhaktiḥ puruṣhottame

(Bhāg. 3.29.12)

There are three main points to be understood from these verses. Firstly, one should be devoid of all desires. Secondly,

Bhakti should not be assisted by *karma, jñāna, tapaśhcharyā* or other means. Thirdly, one should actively serve Lord Kṛiṣhṇa by favourable feelings of devotion through the relationships of *śhānta bhāva,* reverence, *dāsya bhāva,* servitude, *sakhya bhāva,* friendship, *vātsalya bhāva,* parent-hood and *mādhurya bhāva,* amorous love.

The first point requires serious study and reflection, because in my opinion, it is the reason for our failure to practise devotion, and is the greatest impediment that blocks our progress. Once this is understood, the path of *Bhakti* will be smooth and we will speedily progress towards our goal.

Devotion is possible only when all kinds of desires are abandoned. In reality, it is the mind that has to practise devotion because the mind alone is the cause of bondage and liberation. If the mind is preoccupied with desires for worldly or celestial attainments, how can you possibly engage it in devotion? You have only one mind. You can either have desires for material attainments, or a desire for the divine. It is totally impossible to have both kinds of desires simultaneously in one mind. Most people who believe in God never seriously reflect on this point, but it definitely needs serious consideration.

1. Bhakti should be devoid of desires

What are the various kinds of desires that need to be abandoned in preparatory devotion? The simplest and most satisfactory answer to this question is, any desire apart from the desire for Lord Kṛiṣhṇa. The desires that have to be abandoned are of four kinds: *dharma,* performance of scriptural duties, *artha,* wealth, *kāma,* sensual pleasures and *mokṣha,* liberation. The first three - *dharma, artha* and *kāma* together are also referred to as *bhukti* because they relate to the material realm, and *mokṣha* or liberation which is a divine attainment is referred to as *mukti.* In short, we have to abandon two kinds of desires, *'bhukti'* and *'mukti'.*

Some people may find the renunciation of the second kind of desire, *mukti,* to be quite puzzling. To renounce all material pleasures attainable up to the abode of Brahmā is understandable, but to renounce *mukti* or liberation seems quite strange. Listen to what the *Rasika* Saints declare,

bhuktimuktispṛihā yāvat piśhāchī hṛidi vartate
tāvat bhaktisukhasyātra kathamabhyudayo bhavet

(Rūpa Gosvāmī)

"So long as the two witches in the form of *bhukti* and *mukti* reside in the heart of an individual soul, the Supreme Goddess of Devotion cannot manifest herself." Between the two, *bhukti* and *mukti,* the witch called *bhukti* is not as dangerous as the witch called *mukti,* because it is possible to be free from her clutches. If a fortunate soul happens to meet a *Rasika* Saint, surrenders to him, and practises devotion, he can experience the nectar of Divine Love. On the other hand, if anyone falls into the clutches of the witch named *mukti,* he attains liberation and merges into *Brahman.* Then there is absolutely no chance of his experiencing the nectar of Divine Love, because once liberation is attained, it is attained forever. There is no question of experiencing duality again.

You might point out that, there are examples of millions of *paramahaṁsas* such as Sanaka, Sanandana, Janaka and the others, who became *Rasika* Saints and enjoyed the Bliss of Divine Love. The reason is that, as long as the *paramahaṁsa* is in the physical body, he does not merge in God. It is only when the body is given up, that he merges into *Brahman*. Thereafter, he cannot assume a body, and without a body, it is impossible to experience the Bliss of Divine Love. Thus, the witch *mukti* is obviously worse than *bhukti*. So, desires up to and including the desire for liberation have to be abandoned.

It is often seen that even before starting spiritual practice people have countless desires in their hearts which they place before God and call themselves selfish devotees, *sakāma bhakta* and expects God to fulfil their desires. Such people are merely selfish and not devotees. This is not the definition of a *sakāma bhakta*! A *sakāma bhakta* is a 'devotee' who has practised devotion to God. People who have only worldly desires and claim to be *sakāma bhakta* are only selfish and not true devotees. These people with selfish material desires can in no way be compared to the examples of *sakāma bhaktas*, like Draupadi, Gajarāja and the others.

Devotion, which is practised while harbouring material desires has many dangers.

First, it is apparent that, the aspirant is not yet sure where true happiness lies - in the world, or in God? If it is in the world, then what is the need for God? And if it is in God alone, why desire worldly things? Actually, God and the material world of *Māyā* are opposing entities. To accept that God is the only source of Bliss and still have material desires, is like approaching fire to keep yourself cool. If our goal is to attain happiness, then going to God, Who is the source of happiness and asking Him for the world which is a source of misery, evidently implies that we still have hopes of getting unlimited happiness from this world. When our goal itself is not right, then how can we practise devotion, let alone attain Perfection? Worldly things simply add fuel to the fire of material desires. In addition, false pride increases on attaining them. This is the main cause for our turning away from God.

Second, remember that, when material possessions are acquired by people according to their own destiny, they misunderstand it to be due to the Grace of God. And when they do not receive these possessions due to their destiny, they think it is a sign of God's anger. Thus a person will be a believer as long as he acquires worldly possessions, and when he is deprived of them, he will become an atheist. Therefore, it is in the best interest of a spiritual aspirant to totally renounce all desires for material objects in devotional practice.

Third, God does not break His law by granting possessions contrary to what is destined for each individual. If someone claims that God always listens to his selfish prayers and fulfils them, then he is a fortunate exception for whom God has violated His own law. Now, why doesn't he ask God for God Himself, once and for all, so that the desire to ask again and again comes to an end? To repeatedly ask for the world where there is no happiness, where fulfilment of desires results in the emergence of more formidable desires, only brings about harm. It is only when we ask for a vision of God or Divine Love that the root cause - desire itself will end forever and the individual soul will become completely fulfilled. But all this is only imagination. People just lie that God fulfils their every desire, because they ignorantly think that any benefit received as a result of one's destiny is due to God's Grace. There is some benefit in this belief because the individual realizes God's Grace on this basis. But the harmful consequence of this belief is that, when the material desires are not fulfilled, this faith in God immediately disappears.

Fourth, when we understand from the scriptures that God is omniscient and whatever He does, is for our benefit, then why do we interfere and ask Him for anything? Being ignorant, we do not really know what is best for us. Therefore, if we remember that God is all-knowing and leave everything on Him, then the disease of asking will never arise.

Fifth, the scriptures declare that each individual is bound by the consequences of his actions. Whatever worldly happiness (which is actually sorrow) is destined for each person will be given to him according to his fate, consequences of past actions awarded to him in the present life. We read in the scriptures about the untimely death of Daśharatha, the father of the All-Powerful, Almighty Personality, Lord Rāma. But Lord Rāma did not save him. Abhimanyu, the nephew of Lord Kṛiṣhṇa and son of Arjuna, could not be saved from an untimely death by both these great personalities together. Surely we don't think ourselves to be greater than Daśharatha and Abhimanyu! Then why do we expect that the irrevocable divine law governing destiny will be broken for us?

Sixth, understand that, a lack of material possessions is actually God's Grace, because in this state a person is not intoxicated with pride arising out of possession of material things. Therefore, we should desire this blessed state. What is the use of asking God for worldly things that distract us and cause us to promptly forget Him?

Besides these, there are countless other hindrances that arise with material desires which prevent you from practising devotion, or surrendering to a Saint. If this happens, how can you progress spiritually? So, all desires including the desire for *mokṣha,* also known as *mukti* or liberation must be renounced. We should only desire what is truly in our self-interest and that is selfless Divine Love for God. Tulasīdāsa states,

svāratha sāṁcha jīva kara ehā
mana krama vachana rāma pada nehā

(Rāmayaṇa)

Our true self-interest lies in pleasing God keeping our desires in line with God's will, which is the purest form of practical devotion.

Desire and Love: Desire is opposed to Love. To constantly want, is desire and to constantly give, is Love. The process of give and take is a business. Wherever there is any desire to receive from one's beloved, this is not Love. Where one is not satisfied even after having given everything but has an ever-increasing desire to give, that is Love. So, no one in the world can love in the true sense of the word, because each and everyone is naturally selfish. Everyone desires their own happiness therefore, there is always a constant desire to receive, and not give. When both sides are intent on taking, how long can a relationship be amicable? This is the reason why a wife and husband, a father and son clash several times a day. Wherever parties are set upon receiving, conflict is inevitable, and wherever there is a clash, the farce which goes by the name of worldly 'love' is exposed for what it truly is, and their love comes to an end. Love based on selfish desires constantly decreases, whereas Divine Love constantly increases. Desire is a form of darkness, and Love is the form of light. The *Chaitanya Charitāmṛita* gives a beautiful definition of desire and Love.

kāmera tātparya nija sambhoga kevala
kṛiṣhṇa-sukha tātparya prema to prabala
loka dharma, veda-dharma, dehadharma, karma
lajjā, dhairya, deha sukha, ātma sukha marma
sarvatyāga karaye kare kṛiṣhṇera bhajana
kṛiṣhṇa sukha hetu kare premera sevana
ataeva kāme preme bahuta antara
kāma andhatama prema nirmala bhāskara

(Chaitanya Charitāmṛita)

"To want one's own happiness is desire and can be compared to darkness, and the desire to only please one's Beloved, is Love, and can be compared to sunshine."

Observe the bird called the *chātaka*. This bird is a beautiful example of selfless love. It loves its beloved all the year round, while we worldly people run to places of worship and to Saints only when we have some worldly desires. The moment our worldly wants are fulfilled, we never think of going again. We are too preoccupied with material pleasures to even think of God. If someone asks you, "Why have you stopped going to places of worship, or to Saints?", you arrogantly reply, "I have no need for all that external show. I attain everything from within."

The reality is that, we are actually worshippers of worldly desires. We have not yet understood anything about the subject of God. We should learn a lesson from the bird, *chātaka*. This bird is always devoted to its beloved, the rain cloud. It lives only on the rain drops falling in the autumn asterism, *Svātī*, and does not drink any other water. We too must love the Lord exclusively and constantly in the same way, and our every desire should be focused on pleasing Him alone.

jāche bāraha māsa piye papīhā svāti jala

(Tulasīdāsa)

Wherever there is love in the world, there is always an inherent selfishness. The moment that self-interest is harmed, the love comes to an end and even results in enmity. But the love of the *chātaka* is different. It is unselfish,

pavi pāhana dāmini garaji, jhari jhakori khari khījhi
roṣha na priyatama doṣha lakhi, tulasī rāgahi rījhi

(Tulasīdāsa)

Tulasīdāsa wrote that the beloved of the *chātaka* bird is very cruel-hearted. The *chātaka* begs for a few rain drops, but instead its beloved thunders and sends down lightning and hailstones upon it, thereby insulting and teasing it. But the *chātaka* neither resents this cruel behaviour, nor is it angered by it. In fact it never thinks about the imperfections of its beloved, but instead derives ever-increasing pleasure from its every action. We should learn a lesson from this by not getting upset or angry when any worldly calamity befalls us, and instead we should consider it as the Grace of God.

To continue with the story of the *chātaka*. Once, the *chātaka*, weary and exhausted with hunger and thirst, flew to a tree to rest in its shade. Then it thought, "This tree is nourished by underground water and not water from my beloved. To rest in its shade, amounts to infidelity." So it flew out into the scorching heat of the sun again. Dizzy and half-unconscious, it sat on the branch of another tree on the banks of the river Ganges, where it was seen by a hunter and was shot. As it fell into the river it thought, "I was true to my love all my life. In my dying moments I can drink the water of the Ganges and attain liberation." But as soon as this thought crossed its mind, it sternly reproached itself, "It would be a blemish on the purity of my love, to accept water from any other source." So turning its beak upwards, lest it swallowed any drop of the Ganges water, it remained true to its love till the very end.

badhyo badhika paryo punya jala ulaṭi uṭhāī choñcha
tulasī chātaka prema-paṭa maratahuṁ lagī na khoñcha

(Tulasīdāsa)

We have to learn from the *chātaka* not to fall into the trap of liberation and deprive ourselves of Divine Love.

bhakti karata soi mukti gusāīṁ
anaichchhita āvata bari āīṁ

(Rāmāyaṇa)

Mukti is automatically attained by one who practises devotion. When devotion itself leads to liberation from *Māyā,* why be deprived of the nectar of Divine Love? On the other hand, if we fall into the trap of liberation, it is impossible to attain the Bliss of Divine Love, as liberation means losing oneself completely in the Formless, Attributeless *Brahman,* whereas one automatically attains liberation upon attaining Divine Love.

Like the *chātaka,* our ultimate aim should be exclusive ever-steady devotion to our Beloved, Śhrī Kṛiṣhṇa. Our intense love and service to Him should be entirely for the sake of pleasing Him.

In true love, one should not base one's love upon the virtues of one's Beloved, because even this is a desire. This is why, when we love someone in the world because of a particular quality, the moment that quality ends, so does our love. If we love someone because of beauty or wealth, the moment that person loses these qualities, our love comes to an end.

It is mentioned in the *Rāma Charita Mānasa* that, when Pārvatī was performing austerities to get Lord Śhaṅkara as her husband, some great *yogīs* came to discourage her and said, "Why do you love Lord Śhaṅkara? He wears a snake and a garland of skulls around his neck, lives in a cremation ground and has ghosts for company. In addition, he is an ascetic and also heartless. Why don't you love Lord Viṣhṇu instead? He is always surrounded by auspicious things. Pārvatī replied, "All this may be true, but I do not love Lord Śhaṅkara, because of his qualities."

janma koṭi lagi ragari hamārī
baraum̐ śhambhu na tu rahaūm̐ kuvārī

"It is my firm decision to make Lord Śhaṅkara my husband even, if it takes me uncountable lifetimes, or I will remain unmarried."

śhambhu sakala avaguṇa bhavana, viṣhṇu sakala guṇa khāna
jākara mana rama jāhi sana, tāhi tāhi sana kāma

"It may be that Lord Śhaṅkara has bad qualities and Lord Viṣhṇu has all good qualities but I am determined to marry Lord Śhaṅkara because my mind is absorbed in him alone."

Even though there is no question of God's qualities or powers coming to an end, nevertheless the nature of love is that it doesn't look at external qualities. Whether He behaves lovingly or rudely, it is pleasing to a devotee. Gaurāṅga Mahāprabhu says,

āśhliṣhya vā pādaratāṁ pinaṣhṭu mām
adarśhanān marmahatāṁ karotu vā
yathā tathā vā vidadhātu lampaṭo
matprāṇanāthas tu sa eva nāparaḥ

(Śhikṣhāṣhṭaka)

"O Śhyāmasundara! Hear my challenge. You can act in one of the three ways, You may accept me as Your lover and embrace me, or kill me as an enemy, or act indifferent to me and torment me endlessly. I will love You with the same intensity in all three kinds of behaviour. I have no objection to any behaviour of Yours as I have unconditionally accepted You as the Lord of my life." In other words, he did not love Śhrī Kṛiṣhṇa hearing about His quality of being causelessly merciful or anything else. Love is that which exists without seeing the qualities of the beloved. It is practised simply because He alone is Your Beloved. It is the nature of the living being to love. One should not think beyond this, no matter what the consequences may be.

Once, a Saint in Vṛindāvana was engrossed in the Bliss of Divine Love. All of a sudden he saw his Beloved Śhrī Kṛiṣhṇa standing in front of him. He ran forward to embrace Him, but Śhrī Kṛiṣhṇa ran away. The devotee followed Him, but he had hardly run a few yards, when his long matted hair got entangled in a thick bush, and at that moment Śhrī Kṛiṣhṇa disappeared from his sight. The Saint frantically tried to disentangle his hair, but then a thought came into his mind, "Maybe my Beloved Śhyāmasundara likes to see me in this pose. I have not deliberately entangled my hair, if I disentangle it for my own happiness, then that may not fulfil the wish of my Beloved. It may hurt Him. So I am not going to disentangle it". He remained standing for seven days in this pose.

Śhyāmasundara's heart is extremely tender. The one who knows this secret, never leaves Him. On the seventh day, Śhyāmasundara came in disguise and said, "O *Bābājī!* You are very lazy. Can't you disentangle your own hair?" The Saint said, "A third person shouldn't interfere in the matters of a husband and wife. Please go your own way. What does it matter to you?" Śhyāmasundara said, "It does matter. That is why I came here." The Saint said, "I don't understand what you mean." Śhrī Kṛiṣhṇa said, "I am your Beloved." The Saint answered, "My Beloved Śhyāmasundara is Madanamohana, Rādhāramaṇa, the Beloved of Śhrī Rādhā Rānī, the One Whose beautiful form is curved at three places." Lord Kṛiṣhṇa accepted defeat and appeared in His true form. Seeing Him, the Saint was overwhelmed. When Śhyāmasundara lifted His hand to disentangle the Saint's hair, the Saint stopped Him, "Hey! Touching another's wife is a sin." Śhrī Kṛiṣhṇa said, "Even now, you consider yourself another's wife?" The Saint said, "Yes. I will not believe You until Śhrī Rādhā Rānī Herself comes and testifies, *Yes, He is My Beloved.*" The Saint took full advantage of this opportunity, he had now to make Śhrī Kṛiṣhṇa do whatever he desired. Thus, Śhrī Rādhā Rānī also came, the problem was resolved, and his hair was disentangled. This is a glimpse of selfless Love.

2. Devotion should not be assisted by karma and jñāna.

The second condition of preparatory devotion is that it must not be obstructed by *karma, jñāna, yoga,* austerity or similar practices. In other words, devotion is independent. It does not require the support of *karma* or *jñāna*. However, they remain as an adjunct to devotion.

3. Devotion should be practised with favourable sentiments.

We should not devote ourselves only to God. This might sound shocking to you. Does this mean we should worship the celestial gods, human beings and demons along with God? This is not what is meant here. If we worship Śhrī Kṛiṣhṇa as a Supreme Almighty Personality, we will feel fear, hesitation and distance. This will become a hindrance in establishing a close relationship with Him. *Rasika* saints have emphasized devotion to Lord Kṛiṣhṇa through intimate relationships such as we have in the material world. These relationships of the devotee and God are known as '*bhāvas*'. There are five '*bhāvas*': *śhānta, dāsya, sakhya, vātsalya* and *mādhurya*. All the aspects of Love, i.e. God as our king, master, friend, child and beloved have been established in order to make us feel closer to God.

Each succeeding *bhāva* is superior to the previous one. *Dāsya bhāva* is superior to *śhānta bhāva. Sakhya bhāva* is superior to *dāsya bhāva, vātsalya bhāva* is superior to *sakhya bhāva,* and *mādhurya bhāva* is superior to *vātsalya bhāva. Śhānta bhāva* is the lowest, as it is the relationship between a subject and a king. Awe and reverence dominate this relationship, so it has generally been rejected by *Rasika* Saints. In *dāsya bhāva,* the relationship is closer, as the devotee considers himself as a servant and the Lord as his master. *Sakhya bhāva* or friendship is more close than servitude, because in this *bhāva* the devotee considers God as his friend. In *vātsalya bhāva,* the devotee has greater privileges than in *sakhya bhāva,* because here the devotee loves the Lord as his little child. *Mādhurya bhāva* is the closest of all relationships, as it is that intense sweet love that exists between a lover and her beloved.

We can understand this from worldly examples. Even in the world, the closest relationship is that of a lover with her beloved, less close is that of parents with their child, even less close is the relationship between friends, the servant's relationship with the master is even lesser, and finally the relationship of a subject with his king is the least close. One important point to note here is that, *mādhurya bhāva* incorporates within it the remaining four sentiments. Just as earth, water, fire, air and space are considered to be incorporated in the element, earth, so in *mādhurya bhāva,* we can think of God as our beloved, son, friend, master, or king whenever we wish. The highest *Rasika* Saints do not give much importance to the *śhānta bhāva* therefore, we generally find devotees of the other four sentiments; *dāsya, sakhya, vātsalya* and *mādhurya.*

Vātsalya bhāva includes four sentiments. Just as water contains the elements water, fire, air and space, similarly in *vātsalya bhāva* we can consider Śhrī Kṛiṣhṇa as our son, friend, master and king, but not our beloved.

Sakhya bhāva includes three sentiments. Just as fire contains fire, air and space, similarly *sakhya bhāva* includes friendship, servitude and the feeling of a subject for a king. However, we cannot consider Śhrī Kṛiṣhṇa as our beloved or son.

In *dāsya bhāva*, we can consider Śhrī Kṛiṣhṇa as our master or king. Here the relationship of a friend, son, or beloved is excluded. In *śhānta bhāva*, we can consider Śhrī Kṛiṣhṇa only as king, just as space has only one element, space. In *śhānta bhāva* we cannot consider Him as your master, friend, son or beloved.

Only these five relationships are acceptable in devotion. If you look upon God as God, then you will feel "I am an ordinary living being and He is All-Powerful, how can I love Him?" This will create fear in your relationship.

These feelings are also experienced in the world and one can get an idea of this even though a beloved's relationship in the world is selfish. The wife regards her husband as her beloved, but along with this, she has a motherly heart and expresses *vātsalya bhāva* at the time of serving food. A husband may have experienced that if he eats less occasionally his wife acts as a mother, "You are not eating or drinking anything these days. You are getting weaker. Have some more," and so on.

The wife is also a friend. She is always ready to give an opinion on matters even where she has no right and in matters where she has a right, she boldly gives her advice. A husband takes only the advice of his wife in confidential matters, and he does not discuss these with anyone else. Lastly, the feeling of servitude is self evident in this relationship.

Thus a glimpse of these five relational feelings can be seen even in selfish worldly love. But the reality can only be seen in totality in the divine amorous sentiment. One point I would like to emphasize here is that, although a wife has all five feelings towards her husband, she does not refer to these relationships by name. A wife shouldn't start calling her husband 'son', otherwise a conflict could be stirred up at home. However, there is no such limitation in the divine realm; we can address God in any way.

hā nātha! ramaṇa! preṣhṭha! kvāsi kvāsi mahābhuja
dāsyāste kṛipaṇāyā me sakhe! darśhaya sannidhim

(Bhāg. 10.30.40)

"Oh Lord! Oh my dear One! Oh, One with powerful arms! Oh most Beloved One! Where have You gone? Reveal Yourself to Me, Your loving servant as I am, distressed and heart-broken."

Everything can be said in the divine realm because there is no worldly formality. You don't have to think or worry. "If I call my, husband 'son' it is a sin." This is not a sin in the divine world.

In *śhānta bhāva* there is a predominance of reverence, and no significant manifestation of loving feelings. The real sweetness of Divine Love begins in *dāsya bhāva*. A devotee in *dāsya bhāva* says,

pañchatvaṁ tanuretu bhūtanivahāḥ svāṁśhe viśhantu sphuṭam
dhātāraṁ praṇipatya hanta śhirasā tatrāpi yāche varam

tadvāpīṣhu payas tadīyamukure jyotis tadīyāṅgana-
vyomni vyoma tadīyavartmani dharā tattālavṛinte' nilaḥ

(Sūkti)

"Oh Lord! When I die, it is my desire that all the five elements of this material body should be used in serving You. Let the element of water mix with the water You bathe in. Let the element of light, fire mix in the mirror You use. Let the element of space merge in the space of the courtyard where You play. Let the element of air mix with the air near You, so that it may serve as a breeze to cool You in summer. Let the element of earth mix with the earth in the path upon which You tread." Thus, this devotee desires that his body should be useful in service even after his death. This is *dāsya bhāva*. There are more formalities than privileges in this relationship. The liberties that the devotee can have with God are limited. Bharata states in the *Rāmāyaṇa*,

sira bala chālauṁ uchita asa morā
saba te sevaka dharma kaṭhorā

(Rāmāyaṇa)

A servant's duty is to bow his head, wherever his Lord places His feet. When Lakṣhmaṇa accompanied Lord Rāma to the forest, to avoid stepping on the footprints of Lord Rāma, he had to walk on thorns and rugged paths. But for an ordinary person this is extremely difficult.

nūpure tvabhijānāmi nityaṁ pādābhivandanāt

(Vālmīki Rāmāyaṇa)

When Lakṣhmaṇa was asked to recognize Sītā's jewellery, he expressed his inability to do so, because he could only recognize Her anklets, which he had seen when paying obeisance to Her. Lakṣhmaṇa did not recognize any of Sītā's other ornaments because his eyes had always remained ever devoted to Her holy feet. Imagine, how impossible this seems! How could a servant possibly stay with his mistress day and night and not look beyond her feet. That is why it is said that the formalities of servitude are difficult even for *yogīs* to follow.

sevādharmaḥ paramagahano yogināmapyagamyaḥ

It is almost impossible for an ordinary man to follow these formalities. However, all etiquette is discarded in the intensity of love.

prabhu tarutara kapi ḍāra para

(Rāmayaṇa)

The monkeys during the descension of Śhrī Rāma were devotees of *dāsya bhāva*. But they sat on top of the trees, while Śhrī Rāma sat below them. This breach of etiquette happened because they were absorbed in Divine Love. Due to this, they were not conscious of what formality they should follow with their Lord. This breach of propriety is often quoted in the world in defence of people's improper behaviour. However, it should be kept in mind that such a breach is pardonable only when a devotee is completely absorbed in love. Otherwise, it will be transgression. Even Lord Rāma was so absorbed in their love that He was unaware that, He, being their Master, was sitting below His servants. He was not even conscious that He should be chastising them for their behaviour. Such is the absorption in the love of *dāsya bhāva*! Lord Rāma said to Hanumāna,

pratyupakāra karauṁ kā torā
sanamukha hoi na sakata mana morā
sunu suta tohiṁ urina maiṁ nāhīṁ
dekheuṁ kari vichāra mana māhīṁ

(*Rāmāyaṇa*)

"O Hanumāna! I can never free Myself of My indebtedness to you." In the *Vālmīki Rāmāyaṇa* He declares,

ekaikasyopakārasya prāṇān dāsyāmi te kape
śheṣhasyehopakārāṇāṁ bhavāma ṛiṇino vayam

(*Vālmīki Rāmāyaṇa*)

"I can repay one of your debts by giving My life, but I will still remain bound by countless other debts." Thus, in the spiritual realm even *dāsya bhāva* is glorified.

In *sakhya bhāva*, there is greater intimacy and speciality in the Bliss of Divine Love as compared to *dāsya bhāva*. Although the friends of Lord Kṛiṣhṇa in Braja were illiterate villagers, Śhrī Kṛiṣhṇa would be overjoyed when they would call Him 'Kanuā'. Seeing them displeased or annoyed would make Him unhappy. He would snatch morsels of food from them and eat with great relish. Even the creator Brahmā was confused when he saw this *līlā*, pastime. These cowherd friends never thought, not even in their dreams, that their friend Kṛiṣhṇa was God. If they had the slightest inkling that He was God, the sweetness of their love would have diminished. They would often defeat Him in games and demand that He become their horse, so that they could enjoy riding on His back. When they would playfully kick Him, urging Him forward, Śhrī Kṛiṣhṇa would be so overcome with ecstasy, that tears of joy would flow from His eyes.

At the time Śhrī Kṛiṣhṇa lifted the Govardhana Hill in order to save Braja from the devastating rainfall sent by Indra, the cowherd boys, who had also applied their staffs with full strength to the underside of the hill, said to each other, "Look Śhrīdāmā, Madhumaṅgala, we are applying our full strength with our sticks to this mountain, but take a look at that Kanhaiyā! All He is doing is just touching the mountain with a single fingertip of one hand!" Śhrī Kṛiṣhṇa became overwhelmed with love, hearing his friends make fun of Him in this way. But all such behaviour is forgiven only in the ecstasy of Divine Love, otherwise there are limits which are inappropriate to cross even in the relationship of friends.

A devotee of *vātsalya bhāva* definitely enjoys greater intimacy and authority than one of *sakhya bhāva*. The authority a mother has over her child is well-known to all. Mother Yaśhodā tied Lord Kṛiṣhṇa to a grinding mortar and threatened to beat Him with a stick. The Supreme Lord cried, trembled and pleaded to be spared this beating. "Oh *Maiyā*, mother forgive me this time. I promise never to eat mud again."

Once Mother Yaśhodā bathed and dressed Śhrī Kṛiṣhṇa, and sent Him out to play. Śhrī Kṛiṣhṇa ran straight to the muddiest part of the courtyard and playfully smeared Himself with mud.

When His mother saw Him in this dishevelled state only minutes after she had bathed Him, she was angry and scolded Him,

paṅkābhiṣhiktasakalāvayavaṁ vilokya
dāmodaraṁ vadati kopavaśhādyaśhodā
tvaṁ śhūkaro' si gatajanmani pūtanāre
rityuktisasmitamukho' vatu no murāriḥ

(Sūkti)

"It seems to me that You must have been a pig in Your last life!" Little Kṛiṣhṇa smiled to Himself remembering His descension as a Boar, the Śhūkarāvatāra. His mother had hit upon the truth without knowing the reality. Thus a devotee of *vātsalya bhāva*, reaching the heights of parental love, is totally oblivious of the majesty of Lord Kṛiṣhṇa. However, there are limits which a devotee of *vātsalya bhāva* cannot consciously transgress.

The last and most intimate of all relationships is *mādhurya bhāva*, in which the devotee enjoys all privileges and has complete authority over Lord Kṛiṣhṇa. The selfless amorous Divine Love of the *Gopīs*, is known to all. It was this selfless Love that made the Supreme *Brahman,* Kṛiṣhṇa forget His Godliness and become their eternal servitor. Lord Kṛiṣhṇa longed to hear these illiterate maidens of Braja, call Him a thief, a flirt and so on. He even went to their houses to be insulted in this manner. These *Gopīs* are supreme amongst all Saints. Brahmā, Śhaṅkara and great *paramahaṁsas,* entreat the Lord to make them creepers, trees, etc. in Vṛindāvana, in order to be blessed with the holy foot-dust of these *Gopīs*. The *Bhāgavatam* declares that even the Vedic hymns in personified form could not attain the exalted state of these *Gopīs*.

nāyaṁ shriyoṁ' ga u nitāntarateḥ prasādaḥ
svaryoṣhitāṁ nalinagandharuchāṁ kuto' nyāḥ

(Bhāg. 10.47.60)

Even Mahālakṣhmī, the eternal consort of Mahāviṣhṇu could not attain the nectar of Divine Love that the *Gopīs* attained.

yadvāñchhayā śhrīrlalanācharattapo
vihāya kāmān suchiraṁ dhṛitavratā

(Bhāg. 10.16.36)

Mahālakṣhmī could not gain entrance to the divine-dance, *Mahārāsa*, even though she performed severe penance for a long time. There is a beautiful verse in the *Bhāgavatam*, which gives a glimpse of the selfless Love of the *Gopīs*. The *Gopīs* in separation from Śhrī Kṛiṣhṇa say,

yatte sujātacharaṇāmburuhaṁ staneṣhu
bhītāḥ śhanaiḥ priya dadhīmahi karkaśheṣhu
tenāṭavīmaṭasi tad vyathate na kiṁsvit
kūrpādibhir bhramati dhīr bhāvadāyuṣhāṁ naḥ

(Bhāg. 10.31.19)

"O beloved Śhyāmasundara! We place Your extremely tender feet gently on our hearts, out of fear that our hard breasts may in some way hurt them. And we cannot bear to see you walking bare foot on the stony paths in the woods, because You are our very life!" What tender, selfless emotions are expressed by the *Gopīs*. It would melt the heart of the most hard-hearted person. This is the supremacy of the Love of the *Gopīs*.

By now you must have understood that the selfless amorous feelings of the *Gopīs* is the sweetest of all devotional sentiments. Practising devotion along these lines guarantees one the attainment of the highest Divine Bliss. The factual meaning of *mādhurya bhāva* is, "He is my All-in-All." This allows you to love Śhrī Kṛiṣhṇa with whichever sentiment you desire, whenever you desire. You have complete freedom in your choice of devotional sentiment, *bhāva* and there are no restrictions or rules governing the relationship. This highest emotion, combined with the selfless ideal of the *Gopīs*, should be incorporated into our *sādhanā* from the very beginning.

राधे राधे गोविंद गोविंद राधे। राधे राधे गोविंद गोविंद राधे॥

Practical Sādhanā

The meaning of *karma yoga* can be understood through the *Gītā*. Lord Kṛishṇa instructs Arjuna,

tasmāt sarveṣhu kāleṣhu māmanusmara yuddhya cha

(Gītā 8.7)

"Remember Me every moment while performing your duty."

In other words, your mind should be constantly absorbed in loving remembrance of Śhrī Kṛishṇa, while performing other necessary duties. How should we practically follow this discipline of *karma yoga*? This appears to be a serious problem because seeing with the eyes, or hearing with the ears and so on, is not possible without the involvement of the mind. Everyone experiences that if the mind is absorbed elsewhere, the senses are incapable of performing actions. How then can anyone engage in any action requiring total concentration, such as war, without the involvement of the mind and intellect, and at the same time remember God at every moment?

"yo māṁ smarati nityaśhaḥ "; " teśhāṁ nityābhiyuktānām "
"evaṁ satatayuktā ye "; " teṣhām satatayuktānām "

(Gītā)

All these verses in the *Gītā* insist that remembrance of God must be constant. Once the above question is resolved, the *karma yoga* of the *Gītā* can be performed practically.

Let us reflect on this. There are two types of actions. First there are those actions in which the mind and intellect are involved and second there are those actions in which the mind and intellect are not only involved, but also attached. If the difference between these two types of actions could be understood, then the secret behind practical *karma yoga* would immediately become clear. Actually, what I will explain here is not something new or unusual, but something you already understand. I will simply point it out to you.

Let us take an example of a faithful wife who is very attached to her husband. The husband returned to India from England after an absence of four years. The wife prepared various dishes for him and served him with great love when he arrived. When she asked him how he liked the food, he replied that it was very delicious. In the evening, she was unable to cook for some reason. So she instructed the cook to prepare the meal. He cooked and served the food, and asked his master, "How is the meal?" The cook received the same praise, as the wife.

Observe, even though the actions performed by the cook and the wife were the same, and the food prepared by both was equally tasty, nevertheless, there was a difference. The wife's action not only involved the mind and intellect but included attachment to her husband, whereas the cook's action involved the mind and intellect but was free from attachment to his master. How do we know this? After her husband had eaten, the wife went to her friend's home dancing with joy and embraced her saying, "Today my husband came home." But the cook said to his wife, "God alone knows, where he suddenly came from. It took me a full four hours to cook the food. I am completely exhausted. A cook's job is the worst job in the world." Now, because the wife was attached to her husband, she was also attached to the work she did for him. However, the cook was unattached to the master. He did the same work, but experienced no pleasure from it, because his attachment was elsewhere. It was to his own wife and family. Just as the cook was attached to his wife and children, and prepared the meal in a detached manner, you too have to lovingly attach your mind to God and, perform your worldly duties, without experiencing any pleasure from them.

A nurse and doctor are involved in the delivery of hundreds of babies in the hospital, but they experience no pleasure because they are emotionally unattached to all of them. The proof of this is seen when a baby dies. Then the nurse says to the parents, "I am sorry, I tried my best, but God willed otherwise. Please take the child now." The mother is in a terrible state and is crying loudly. This was her only child and it was stillborn. However, the nurse remains unaffected since she has no personal attachment. Handing the child over, she resumes her duties again. We have to perform our duties in this world like that nurse, without experiencing happiness or distress anywhere.

A cashier in a bank gives away millions of rupees everyday without experiencing any distress. But, if he accidentally loses a single note from his own salary, he becomes disturbed. He desperately tries to find it, cursing his own carelessness for losing it. However, he is not worried about the millions of rupees that go out of the bank everyday that he personally disburses, because the money does not belong to him. It is public money, therefore he has no attachment to it.

Let us take another example. Your neighbour's son has died. The neighbour is crying, but you are sitting relaxed in your house, sipping your tea. You say to your wife, "Get me another cup. I will have to go to the funeral. Who knows how long it will take" You calmly finish breakfast, leave your house and put on an appropriate expression of sympathy on reaching your neighbour's home. There you say, "How did such a terrible thing happen?" You go to the funeral and return tired and grumpy, "Of all days he chose to die today when I had planned to do so many things." This is how you must perform work in the world without receiving pleasure from them. Use the mind and intellect, but remain detached.

Actually, all the activities that we perform indifferently, that we receive no pleasure from but we perform out of compulsion, involve the mind and intellect, but not attachment. Duties performed on a daily basis with this detachment constitute the larger portion of our activities. Who wants to remain subordinate to a boss all day at work? But, you have to do it!

Suppose a guest knocks at your door at midnight. You get out of bed to open the door, muttering angrily to your wife. It happens to be an old neighbour of yours, who now lives in another town. Concealing your annoyance, you say, "Oh, it is you. Please come in. We were eagerly waiting for you for many days and in fact we were talking about you last night. If you had just informed us, we would have received you at the station." Acting in this way, you carry his luggage to a room and tell your wife, "Prepare some food for him." Now, even though your guest is famished, he says, "Please don't take all this trouble. This is no hour to eat." You say, "How could you say such a thing in your own house?" Anyway, food is prepared and everyone finally retires after the guest has eaten. In the morning when your guest is ready to leave, you say, "I really don't understand this. First of all you never visit us, and now you have hardly stayed with us for a few hours." You make a great show of trying to stop him by grabbing his luggage to prevent him from leaving. When he finally leaves, you say to your wife, "Doesn't he have any common sense, coming at such an unearthly hour? We had to make food for him, we were up all night and I have to go to office today. How strange people are in this world?" This is an example of actions performed without attachment. You do this all the time. This is referred to as 'etiquette' in the world where there is no love, just appropriate external behaviour. These actions involve the mind and intellect, there is no attachment.

When a Prime Minister or a special dignitary visits a city, there are great preparations for his arrival. He is greeted with elaborate pomp and ceremony. Various security arrangements are made for his safety. Day and night the local authorities remain worried. When the dignitary finally leaves that place, everyone heaves a sigh of relief, saying, "Thank God! It's over without any untoward incident."

Take another example. A father rushes to the doctor to save his son, who is seriously ill. He drives his motorcycle through heavy traffic. Anyone who has experienced driving a motor cycle knows how much concentration is required to drive properly. The father observes the vehicles that are coming towards him and the others that are coming from behind. He manages to avoid all of them and arrives safely at the doctor's house. He calls out anxiously, "Doctor! Doctor!" Every second that passes without a response from the doctor makes him feel restless. The doctor comes out of his house and asks, "What is it?" The man says, "Doctor! Come quickly! My son's condition is very bad." The doctor tells the father about his fees and they both quickly leave. The doctor sees the boy, writes a prescription and the father goes to the store to buy the medicine.

All these activities - going to the doctor, getting the medicine, and so on, involve the mind and the intellect, but the attachment of the father's mind is only to his son, not to the doctor or anything else. Similarly, we have to lovingly attach our mind to God and perform worldly actions, without experiencing happiness or sorrow from their consequences.

Some people might say that it is not possible to perform one's duties properly without attachment to one's children, parents, or spouse, and without attachment it would amount to forced labour. Actually such a plea is naive. The fact is that duties cannot be performed properly where there is attachment. For example, a baby has a stomach ache due to drinking too much milk. Hearing him cry, the mother is unable to bear it, so she gives him more milk and that makes his condition worse. Because the mother is attached, she cannot perform her duty towards the child properly as a nurse would be capable of doing. The nurse would give the right quantity of milk, at the right time, no matter how much the child cries or makes a fuss. In other words, attachment results in harm to the child, and it is only a person who is free from attachment who can properly perform his duty.

A judge presiding over a court case can only give an impartial judgement if he is perfectly detached from both the concerned parties. However, if he happens to love either of them, he will be partial. If he happens to hate either of them, he will be unjust. Action is performed best when the mind is free of both love and hate.

It is everyone's experience that wherever there is attachment, there is definitely some kind of discrepancy in the work performed. When we love a person, we experience happiness when we see, hear or touch that person. The result is that the mind does not remain in a balanced state, and the work becomes irregular. The same happens when the mind is affected by anger, jealousy, greed and so on. Work is bound to suffer. It is only when one is free of love and hate, that work can be performed perfectly.

If we centre our love in God alone, and limit ourselves to the performance of duties in the world, then both our goals will be accomplished easily. Duties of the material world will be performed properly, and we will also achieve our goal of attaining God. Look at the *Gopīs,*

yā dohane' vahanane mathanopalepa
preṅkheṅkhanārbharuditokṣhaṇamārjanādau
gāyanti chainamanuraktadhiyo' śhrukaṇṭhyo
dhanyā brajastriya urukramachittayānāḥ

(Bhāg. 10.44.15)

They loved Lord Kṛiṣhṇa and constantly thought of Him while performing all their household chores. We have many examples of devotees working in the world with the mind attached to God. King Janaka, Dhruva and Prahlāda ruled kingdoms, and Arjuna fought a war. We too have to work in the same way.

All these examples prove that everyone is well-practised in performing detached action. Your attachment is centred only in a handful of people, such as your spouse, children, parents, etc. and you limit yourself to the mere performance of duty towards others. Now all you have to do is restrict yourself to the level of duty-performance, even towards the handful you are attached to. It is the nature of the mind to love. If this love is directed to God, then both your material duties and spiritual goal can be pursued simultaneously. This is the intelligent course of action prescribed in the *Gītā*,

yogaḥ karmasu kauśhalam

(Gītā)

Fix the mind on God and continue to work with your senses and body, just as an axle remains fixed while a wheel continues to move.

Some say that work is hampered when love for God increases. This does not happen in the beginning, but it does happen in an advanced stage of spiritual practice. However, there is no need to be concerned about it. Even if you are eventually unable to perform your duties, there is nothing to worry about, because you will be freed of responsibility. But if you deliberately disregard your duties, and do not love God, then you will be punished for your negligence.

Thus, the practical form of *karma yoga* is to fulfil your duties in the world and lovingly attach your mind to God. At first you will have to practise this, but later on it will happen naturally. When a person first learns to ride a bicycle, he experiences great difficulty. After some practice, his hands continue to guide the handlebars, his feet keep on pedalling, and he even carries on a conversation with his friend. In the same way, after a little practice, *karma yoga* will become natural.

The three most important and indispensable requirements for practical *sādhanā* are,

1. *Nişhkāmatā* - Abandonment of selfish desires
2. *Ananyatā* - Undivided or exclusive devotion
3. *Rūpadhyāna* - Meditation on the Personal Form of God.

The first requirement has been dealt with extensively in the chapter of *Bhakti yoga*. Let us now deal with the other two.

Ananyatā

Devotion should be exclusive. One of the most important requirements in devotional practice which we tend to ignore, is exclusiveness. It is the lack of understanding of this condition that stops the spiritual progress of a devotee. The word *'ananya'* in simple term means 'no other'. 'Loving only Lord Kṛiṣhṇa' is what *ananyatā* means. If anything other than the Beloved enters the mind of the spiritual aspirant, it becomes an obstacle to his exclusiveness and prevents him from attaining his Beloved.

Let us understand the secret behind Śhrī Kṛiṣhṇa's rescue of Draupadi, described in the Mahābhārata. When Duḥśhāsana dragged Draupadi into the assembly hall to strip her off her clothing in the presence of all, she was in a dreadful predicament. Such an act would have been the most terrible insult for an Indian woman of her status and respectability. She thought, "My five powerful husbands will protect me. What reason do I have to fear?" But, when they did not respond because of circumstances, (they lost her in the game of dice) and remained silent, she gave up all hopes of being protected by them. Then she turned to the great preceptors of religious principles - Bhīṣhma, Droṇāchārya, etc. When they too remained silent, she gave up hope in their strength too. Now she had no hope of any help from any power in the universe, but she still relied on her own strength to protect herself by clenching her *sārī* between her teeth. But how could a helpless woman hope to protect herself against Duḥśhāsana, who had the strength of ten thousand elephants? At this time, Lord Kṛiṣhṇa was eating His meal in Dvārikā. Sensing His devotee's predicament, His hand stopped midway, neither putting the morsel of food in His mouth, nor on the plate. He sat motionless with His eyes unblinking, unable to even swallow what was in His mouth. Seeing this unusual pose of her Husband, Rukmiṇī asked Him what the matter was. He replied, "One of My devotees is in trouble." Rukmiṇī said, "Why don't you go to save her?" Śhrī Kṛiṣhṇa replied, "I have repeatedly said that I am bound by My Law,

ananyāśhchintayanto māṁ ye janāḥ paryupāsate
teṣhāṁ nityābhiyuktānāṁ yogakṣhemaṁ vahāmyahaṁ

(*Gītā* 9.22)

'I take complete responsibility only of one who is exclusively surrendered to Me.' She is still relying on her own strength, so I cannot help her."

When Duḥśhāsana pulled Draupadi's *sārī* with a jerk, she lost hold of it completely. Now, she gave up relying on her own strength and became totally dependent on Śhrī Kṛiṣhṇa. This was the moment of exclusive surrender. Immediately, the Lord took the form of an endless *sārī*, which Duḥśhāsana kept pulling until he gave up in complete exhaustion. The point to be noted here is that exclusiveness in devotional practice is extremely important, but most often people do not pay much attention to it.

Some people worship God, but in addition also worship celestial gods or worldly beings, and therefore never attain Him. We have only one mind and that should remain focused on divine subject matter related to Śhrī Kṛiṣhṇa alone. There should be no place for anything or anyone related to the *māyika* modes of *sattva, rājasa* or *tāmasa*. Most people today combine devotion to God with the worship of celestial gods and goddesses. Some even worship ghosts and spirits! All this is a deception. When God is the source of all material and non-material powers, why bother to worship so many deities? It should be remembered that worship of all powers will not amount to devotion to God, but worship of God alone, will amount to worship of all powers.

yenārchito haris tena tarpitāni jagantyapi
rajyante jantavas tatra sthāvarā jaṅgamā api.

(Bhakti Rasāmṛita Sindhu)

"One who worships God satisfies all, as He has automatically worshipped everyone." Veda Vyāsa clearly states,

yathā tarormūlaniṣhechanena
tṛipyanti tatskandhabhujopaśhākhāḥ
prāṇopahārāchcha yathendriyāṇāṁ
tathaiva sarvārhaṇamachyutejyā

(Bhāg. 4.31.14)

"Just as watering the root of a tree nourishes the trunk, branches, flowers and fruits, worship of Lord Kṛiṣhṇa amounts to worship of all deities and of the whole universe." There is no need for any separate worship. On the other hand, if we water the flowers, fruits and branches of a tree, the water will not reach the roots. In fact, even the flowers and fruits will not be nourished. In the same way, worship of all the celestial gods, men and demons does not satisfy them, nor does it amount to worship of God. Therefore, we must worship only the Supreme, Ultimate, Divine Personality, God and restrict ourselves to having only feelings of respect towards others, like a devoted wife who loves only her husband, but at the same time respects her in-laws and other relations. The *Gītā* clearly states,

yo yo yāṁ yāṁ tanuṁ bhaktaḥ śhraddhayārchitumichchhati
tasya tasyāchalāṁ śhraddhāṁ tāmeva vidadhāmyaham

(Gītā 7.21)

"Whatever form a devotee sincerely worships, I establish his faith in that form accordingly." The devotee acquires all the powers of his object of worship. Lord Kṛiṣhṇa states in the *Gītā*,

yānti devavratā devān pitṛin yānti pitṛivratāḥ
bhūtāni yānti bhūtejyā yānti madyājino' pi mām

(*Gītā* 9.25)

"Those who worship the celestial gods attain the celestial gods, those who worship their ancestors, attain them, those who worship men, spirits and so on, attain them, and those who worship Me alone, attain Me." What could be clearer? Śhrī Kṛiṣhṇa advises Arjuna again and again to surrender to Him alone.

māmeva ye prapadyante māyāmetāṁ taranti te

(*Gītā* 7.14)

tameva śharaṇaṁ gachchha sarvabhāvena bhārata
tatprasādātparāṁ śhāntiṁ sthānaṁ prāpsyasi śhāśhvatam

(*Gītā* 18.62)

sarvadharmān parityajya māmekaṁ śharaṇaṁ vraja
ahaṁ tvāṁ sarvapāpebhyo mokṣhayiṣhyāmi mā śhuchaḥ

(*Gītā* 18.66)

In these verses, the importance of undivided, single-minded devotion has been emphasized.

There are some who declare that they worship the Supreme Lord in order to attain liberation, and worship the other limited forms such as celestial gods in order to attain material things. This obviously implies that these people still desire temporary limited material possessions. This also proves that they do not know for a fact that God alone is the true and only source of Bliss. Even if one accepts the existence of some 'happiness' in this world, why not worship God, Who is the sole Master of this world? Worldly things will automatically be attained by such worship. Naive people give these arguments just to hide their material desires of uncountable lifetimes in the garb of worship. Besides, the very first condition of preparatory devotion is to abandon all desires right up to the desire for *mukti* or liberation. Exclusive devotion to God should be our only aim.

Along with the worship of Śhrī Kṛiṣhṇa, we are free to worship any other descension of God. This will not be a breach of exclusiveness in devotion. Some naive people go to the extent of considering different descensions of God as separate personalities and say, "I am a devotee of Lord Rāma, how can I practise devotion to Lord Kṛiṣhṇa? If chosen deity changes my exclusiveness will be hampered." Such thinking is ignorance and is actually the greatest spiritual offence, called *nāmāpurādha*. All the forms of God are one.

Rūpadhyāna

Rūpadhyāna is absolutely indispensable in devotional practice. By *rūpadhyāna* we mean the absorption of the mind in the loving remembrance of God's form. This condition is the most important, and requires deep reflection. It has already been said that the mind alone is the cause of bondage and liberation. Whether it is worship of God or of the world, it is the mind that has to be involved. If the mind is not meditating on God, it is bound to go to the world, because it is the nature of the mind that it cannot remain inactive even for a fraction of a second. Since the world and the mind have a common origin, *Māyā,* the mind is habituated to run towards the material world, as it has been doing since time immemorial. Therefore, it is absolutely imperative to absorb the mind in *rūpadhyāna*.

Now some people raise a question. "We have never seen God, so how can we possibly meditate upon Him? What should we do? In the world, we can meditate only upon a person who we have seen. Therefore, if we are blessed with a vision of God's divine form once, then *rūpadhyāna* will be easier."

Those who hold such a view are naive. To ask to see God first and then meditate, is like asking for perfection first, and practising devotion afterwards; or wanting to attain the reward first and then making the effort. Does this ever happen in the world? We never ask for a degree first and then appear for the examination or expect our thirst to be quenched before drinking water. Obviously, this does not happen in worldly activities. It is totally impossible to receive the fruits before planting the tree. It is the same in the spiritual realm, too. We have to practise *rūpadhyāna* first, and then we will see God.

Let us suppose for a moment that we are shown God before we begin to meditate on Him. The result of this will be more harmful than beneficial. We could even become atheists. This might seem highly improbable to you, but it is true. Once I reveal the reason, you too will accept it.

We all imagine that the beauty of God is greater than the beauty of innumerable *kāmadevas,* the most beautiful of all celestial gods combined. So we presume that, when limited beauty in the world captivates our heart, we are bound to be enraptured by that unlimited divine beauty of God if we get a chance to see Him. History is witness to great *paramahaṁsas* like the four Sanatakumāras, Janaka, etc. who were irresistibly attracted by His unlimited beauty. A mere glimpse of this made these realized souls forget the Bliss of *Brahman*. How then can we, who have experienced only insignificant temporary material joys, resist that irresistible unlimited beauty of God? The inner secret behind this is that, all these *paramahaṁsas* saw the actual divine form of God.

chidānandamaya deha tumhārī vigata vikāra jāna adhikārī

(Rāmāyaṇa)

The form of God is divine and blissful. That divine form can never be seen with material eyes. We require divine vision to see it. We cannot attain this divine vision as yet, because we are not eligible. Therefore, the infinitely beautiful divine form of God cannot be seen by us. Instead, we will see only a material form with our material eyes.

Right now, we have very elevated sentiments about the divine form of God and His extraordinary beauty, a mere glimpse of Whose toe-nails, can make great personalities like Brahmā and Śhaṅkara, give up their blissful absorption in the Impersonal Absolute. However, if we were to see Him during His descension with our material eyes and perceive a material form, then this faith of ours will vanish! We will say, "I have personally seen God. Whatever the scriptures have described, is just nonsense and mere imagination." And not only that,

āpu jāhiṁ aru ānahu ghālahiṁ

Along with our own downfall we will also be responsible for shaking the faith of others. During the descension of Lord Rāma, when He stood in Janaka's assembly to break the bow of Lord Śhaṅkara to win Sītā Jī's hand, all those present there saw Him differently, according to their various spiritual levels, although His body was divine, blissful and all-attractive.

jākī rahī bhāvanā jaisī,
prabhu mūrati dekhī tina taisī
dekhahiṁ rūpa mahā raṇadhīrā,
manahuṁ vīrarasa dhare sarīrā
ḍare kuṭila nṛipa prabhuhiṁ nihārī,
manahuṁ bhayānaka mūrati bhārī
rahe asura chhala chhonipa veṣhā,
tina prabhu prakaṭa kāla sama dekhā
viduṣhaṇa prabhu virāṭamaya dīsā,
bahumukha kara paga lochana sīsā
joginha parama tattvamaya bhāsā,
sānta suddha sama sahaja prakāsā
haribhaktana dekhe dou bhrātā,
iṣhṭadeva iva saba sukha dātā
rāmahiṁ chitava bhāyaṁ jehi sīyā,
so saneha sukha nahiṁ kathanīyā
ura anuḅhavati na kahi saka soū,
kavana prakāra kahahi kavi koū

(Rāmāyaṇa)

"Everybody saw Śhrī Rāma according to their respective sentiments. The warriors saw Him as the embodiment of strength and heroism. The wicked kings trembled in fear, as they saw a fearsome form. The demonic princes saw Him as death in personified form. The wise saw His universal form with innumerable eyes, hands, feet and heads. The *yogīs* saw Him as the Absolute Truth, effulgent, and the essence of purity and peace. The devotees saw their Beloved Lord as the Fountainhead of Bliss. The emotions of Sītā Jī cannot be put in words."

Therefore, with our defective material vision we will not be able to see the actual divine form of God, but will see only a material form, just as a person suffering from jaundice perceives white objects to be yellow. An ant with a grain of salt in its mouth experiences only the taste of salt, though moving around a pile of sugar. Similarly, we will not be able to perceive the divine blissful form of God as long as we are under the control of *Māyā*. In addition, further delusion will arise as we feel that we have personally seen God and now know the actual truth. We will claim, "Whatever is said in the scriptures is just deception and merely the imagination of poetic minds" and so on. This is exactly what happened during the descension of Śhrī Kṛiṣhṇa, too. Veda Vyāsa describes this vividly,

mallānāmaśhanirṇṛiṇāṁ naravaraḥ strīṇāṁ smaro mūrtimān
gopānāṁ svajano' satāṁ kṣhitibhujāṁ śhāstā svapitroḥ śhiśhuḥ
mṛityurbhojapater virāḍaviduṣhāṁ tattvaṁ paraṁ yogināṁ
vṛiṣhṇīnāṁ paradevateti vidito raṅga gataḥ sāgrajaḥ

(Bhāg. 10.43.17)

"When Śhrī Kṛiṣhṇa, arrived in the assembly of Kaṁsa, He was perceived differently by different people according to their purity of heart. To the wrestlers, His body appeared not to be of flesh and blood, but to be as hard as a thunderbolt. The average person saw Him as having the most super excellent qualities among men. The young ladies saw Him as the God of Love, supreme in tenderness and beauty. The cowherd boys saw Him as their dear-most friend. The wicked kings saw Him as the One who would overthrow them. His parents saw Him as their delicate little child. And His enemy Kaṁsa saw Him as Time, the ultimate destroyer even of Yamarāja, the god of death. The wicked trembled in fear seeing a fearsome gigantic form with thousands of faces, eyes, ears, etc. with flames equivalent to thousands of suns emanating from each of His mouths. The *yogīs* saw Him as the Ultimate Truth. The *Yādavas,* His clan members, saw Him as their worshipable deity." Now which of these viewers would you classify yourself as? It is only if you were a *yogī* or a devotee, that you would have seen Him as the Ultimate Truth or your Beloved Lord. Had you seen Him in any other way, whatever little sentiment you might have entertained of His being God, would have come to an end.

Therefore, never entertain this thought that you will begin meditation on God's form after seeing Him. First, practise devotion in order to become eligible to attain divine vision. Then you can see His divine form and experience the beauty and sweetness of His form described by the Saints and scriptures.

There is another point to note here. The claim that we first see something in the world, and then love it, has no basis. Imagine, if you want to become a District Commissioner, the highest post in the Indian Administrative Service. You have to appear in the I.A.S. examination to qualify for this post. You are restless to pass the examination and try for years, and finally achieve it. You may say that you had first seen the pleasure experienced by a D.C. and then made efforts to attain that position. But this statement is totally wrong, because the happiness of a person in a particular post is not seen by others, it is experienced by the person himself. This can be practically experienced by others only several years after passing the examination and attaining the post. The intoxicating effect of alcohol cannot be experienced before drinking it. You cannot experience the sweetness of a candy just by seeing it. The class, kind, and amount of pleasure or happiness of an object cannot be seen. It can only be guessed to some extent. For example: if you have tasted rock candy and heard the praises of Swiss candy, you would become eager to taste it. You would think, "When rock candy is so sweet and tasty, how many times more delicious must Swiss candy be?"

When a person reflects upon the prestige or respect that a D.C. enjoys, he becomes eager to attain that position and thinks, "Everyone in that district will pay their respects to me. I can make lots of money. Everyone will be subservient to me," and so on. To fulfil that aim, he works hard day and night.

Now, why can't we make an effort and practise devotion to attain something that guarantees a pleasure that is infinite times superior to anything we have attained in this material world? When you attain God, all the celestial gods, Indra, Varuna, Yamarāja and others will offer you respect, *Māyā* will not come near you, the three afflictions, the three effects of sins, the three imperfections, the three types of bodies binding you, etc. will not plague you anymore. You will attain never-ending Divine Bliss, and in addition, a divine body. This *sādhanā* is really easy when we give it a thought. So we have to engage ourselves in *rūpadhyāna*.

The next problem in *rūpadhyāna* is that, our meditation is bound to be material. How can we possibly practise divine meditation when we don't have the slightest idea of what the 'divine' is? The *Rāmāyaṇa* states,

go gochara jahaṁ lagi mana jāī so saba māyā jānehu bhāī

(*Rāmāyaṇa*)

That Supreme Divine Being is beyond the grasp of the senses, mind and intellect. The *Vedas* emphasize the same fact,

yato vācho nivartante aprāpya manasā saha
ānandaṁ brahmaṇo vidvān na bibheti kutaśhchaneti

(*Taitti. Up.* 2.9)

The mind is a product of *Māyā*. It is made of matter. Even the loftiest thoughts of this mind are material. God, on the other hand, is divine. He is totally beyond the senses, mind and intellect. Therefore, any form of God we visualize, will only be material. How then can we attain a divine result for our material meditation?

This subject needs deep reflection. Once the answer to this question is fully grasped by the spiritual aspirant, he will progress in *sādhanā* with great speed. Let us understand four important principles in this regard.

First principle - Seeing divinity in the divine gives a divine result.

Those deserving souls who actually saw the divine form of God were rewarded with the Bliss of Divine Love. This is universally accepted. The great souls such as Janaka, Uddhava, etc., who saw and loved the Lord as the Supreme Being, were rewarded with Divine Love.

Second principle - Loving the divine without awareness of His divinity also gives a divine result.

Those souls who loved God during His descension as Śhrī Rāma or Śhrī Kṛiṣhṇa without knowing and seeing His divine form attained a divine reward. For example,

tameva paramātmānaṁ jārabhuddyāpi saṅgatāḥ
jahur guṇamayaṁ dehaṁ sadyaḥ prakṣhīṇabandhanāḥ

(Bhāg. 10.29.11)

Some *Gopīs* were not aware that Śhrī Kṛiṣhṇa was the Supreme Personality God. They loved Him exclusively, simply as their Beloved and were rewarded with Divine Love. The reason is stated here,

dadāmi buddhiyogaṁ taṁ yena māmupayānti te

(Gītā 10.10)

"To those whose minds are totally absorbed in Me, I give divine intelligence and the divine power by which they attain Me." The *Gopīs* did this, and the Lord blessed them eternally with divine power. Even Kaṁsa received this Grace, because he had completely absorbed his mind in Lord Kṛiṣhṇa, through fear.

We can understand this through the example of fire. Whether you deliberately jump into fire, or you are caught unaware, the fire will burn you. Again, whether poison is taken deliberately or unknowingly, the result is death. In the same way, if you unite the mind with God, whether you know God to be God or you do not, the result will be the same; the attainment of Divine Bliss. However, you may say that this rule is applicable only during the descension period of God. What do we do today? Had we been there during the descension of God, we would certainly have benefited by seeing Him. Actually you were there during all the descensions of Lord Rāma and Lord Kṛiṣhṇa. The *Vedas* declare that the individual souls are eternal. Hence, you were always present whenever God descended on this earth. There have been countless descensions since beginningless time. But unfortunately, you were deluded by their external actions. You commented at that time, "This man Rāma, is even worse than I am. He is so infatuated with His wife! Such infatuation cannot be found even in the materialistic age of *Kali Yuga*." When the demon Rāvaṇa abducted Sītā Jī from the forest, Lord Rāma was drowned in such intense grief, that He even lost sense of His own self and whereabouts. He wandered about like a madman and questioned His brother Lakṣhmaṇa about His own identity. According to the *Vālmīki Rāmāyaṇa*,

ko'haṁ brūhi sakhe svaṁ sa bhagavānaāryaḥ sa ko rāghavaḥ
ke yūyaṁ vata nātha nātha kimidaṁ dāso'smi te lakṣhmaṇaḥ
kāntāre kimihāsmahe vada sakhe devyā gatirmṛigyate
kā devī janakādhirājatanayā hā jānaki kvāsi hā

Lord Rāma asked Lakṣhmaṇa, "Who am I?" Lakṣhmaṇa said, "You are an *āryana*." "Which *āryana* am I?" Lakṣhmaṇa replied, "You are Rāghava." Rāma then asked, "Who are you?" Lakṣhmaṇa said, "I am your servant, Lakṣhmaṇa." Again Rāma asked, "What are we doing here in the forest?" Lakṣhmaṇa replied, "We are searching for Devī Jī." Then Rāma asked, "Which Devī Jī?" Lakṣhmaṇa replied, "We are searching for Sītā Jī, the daughter of King Janaka".

Lord Rāma fainted at the mere mention of Sītā Jī's name. This kind of external behaviour would certainly make one think that He wasn't even a man of character, let alone a Saint or God! Now with an opinion like that, how would you be able to love Him and take advantage of His appearance on earth?

According to the *Rāmāyaṇa*,

he khaga mṛiga he madhukara śhreṇī tuma dekhī sītā mṛiganainī
yehi vidhi khojata bilapata svāmī manahuṁ mahā birahī ati kāmī

(Rāmāyaṇa)

In the anguish of separation from Sītā Jī, Lord Rāma called out to the trees, creepers, birds and rivers, asking them whether anyone had seen His doe-eyed Sītā? Even in today's age, who could be so madly in love with his wife, that separation from her drives him completely out of his mind? He does not even realize that trees won't tell him her whereabouts, and that he should be asking a person! There are many cases of men losing their wives, mothers and their children, but they do not become so oblivious to reality that they go around asking trees the whereabouts of their lost ones. The *Rāmāyaṇa* clearly declares,

rāma dekhi suni charita tumhāre
jaṛa mohahiṁ budha hohiṁ sukhāre

(Rāmāyaṇa)

"Even the greatest intellectuals are totally bewildered on seeing the actions of God." So it is a total misconception for ordinary material beings to assume that they would love God and attain Him during His descension.

Third principle - Loving material things with a divine sentiment gives a divine result.

We have just discussed that the reward of loving God knowingly or unknowingly is Divine Bliss, but the third principle is even more astonishing. The result of loving material things with a divine sentiment towards them is also the attainment of Divine Bliss. This may be rather difficult to accept, because we never get the reward of our sentiments towards an object in the material world. A person who eats a ball made of cow dung, thinking it to be a sweet, does not experience the taste of a sweet. He only experiences the taste of cow-dung. Again, one who does not know that there is poison in his milk, and also drinks it with the feeling that it is only milk will obviously die, even though he drank it with the feeling that it was milk. How then can a person attain a divine result for his sentiments if he loves a stone or any other material object with the feeling that it is God? According to these practical examples, the reward should be according to the object, not the feelings.

In this context, the subject of worship of deities made of stone, brass or other materials needs to be discussed. Let us understand the science behind it. Material objects are of two kinds: animate and inanimate. Both are under the control of *Māyā*. Consider the example of the ball made of cow dung and the person who thinks it to be a sweet. In this example, both the ball made of cow dung, as well as the imagined sweet are inanimate. Therefore he does not get the benefit of his imagination, but of the inanimate object, in this case, the dung ball. Let us take up the next possibility: the reward for the feelings of a living being in a lifeless object. Even if we imagine a living person in a lifeless object, such as a photograph, our feelings still won't be reciprocated because the person we are thinking about is not all-pervading or all-knowing. He does not know that we are thinking about him.

On the other hand, there is a divine result when we project feelings of divinity in an animate or inanimate material objects. For example, when a person worships a deity of stone with the feelings of divinity in that deity he attains a divine reward. The reason is that God is omnipresent. The ball made of cow dung or the living person pictured in the photograph are not all-pervading, so the feelings in these cases are not rewarded. God on the other hand, is present in each and every particle of the universe, and is omniscient. He knows our every thought. Residing in our hearts, He takes note of each and every idea, and rewards us according to our intentions. Now if someone were to ask, "Will we get a divine reward, if we drink milk containing poison and believe God is present in it?" The answer is that the reward depends upon the degree of our faith in the omnipresence of God. If there is complete faith, the reward will be divine. On the other hand, if the faith is incomplete, the result will be death. Our faith must be firm and unwavering, like that of Mīrābāī, who drank poison given to her with the feeling that her Beloved Śhri Kṛiṣhṇa was present in it. The poison had no effect. In the same way, the devotee Prahlāda believed that God was omnipresent, even in the fire he was made to sit in. Therefore, instead of burning him the fire protected him. But if we perform the same action without absolute faith, God will not alter the course of cause and effect. From this, it is obvious that God is different from material beings, both animate and inanimate. The first difference is that, He is omnipresent.

To derive spiritual benefit, the mind must be exclusively united with that omnipresent God. The second important difference is that even if God were not omnipresent, He is all-knowing. He knows our every thought and knows that, although we cannot visualize the divine, our desire is for the divine. Therefore, according to His divine law and compassionate nature, He will give us a divine reward. On the other hand, material living beings and non-living objects are not all-knowing.

Let us take a simple example to understand this principle. If you call out to a chocolate, it will not respond because it is a lifeless object. It does not have senses, mind, intellect, or consciousness. Now, if you call a person, he may come if he has heard you because he possesses a conscious mind, intellect and senses. However, if this person is too far away from you, or does not want to come, then he will not. God, on the other hand is not far. He is omnipresent and at the same time omniscient. He takes note of our every thought, and when we call out to Him, He will come, because it is His nature and His law to respond to our call.

Thus, we can meditate upon God using a material object such as a photo or an image and attain our divine goal. It is on the basis of this principle that innumerable souls have attained God, and are attaining Him through *rūpadhyāna*. It is a divine law that we will be blessed with God's Grace according to our sentiments when we sincerely practise devotion, even though our *rūpadhyāna* is material. Had God judged our meditation according to the standard set for Saints, no material being would have ever attained Him as it is impossible for anyone to visualize the divine form of God with a material mind.

The fourth principle - Loving worldly things with worldly sentiments gives a material result.

This is of no use in devotion. Like the first principle, it is known to all. If one attaches the mind to living being or non-living material objects with material feelings, the reward will be material, which is suffering in the endless cycle of birth and death. Attachment towards one's house, car, husband, wife, etc. with the corresponding material feelings gives a material result.

These, in short, are the four principles regarding material meditation and their corresponding rewards. There is one point to be noted here. It is easy to have divine feelings for a non-living thing, but if we centre the same feelings in a material living person, then this devotion will not be steady. For one person to constantly accept another as God is extremely difficult, because he sees imperfections in him. Various theistic sects emphasize *rūpadhyāna* of the Guru only. We can attain divine benefit from a Guru or Master, but if we frequently have material feelings towards him, it is bound to affect our devotion adversely. Only that devotion to the Guru is fruitful, in which we always retain a feeling of divinity towards him. Otherwise, to maintain steady divine feelings towards material beings is almost impossible. Therefore, the system of *mūrti*-worship or devoting oneself to an inanimate object with divine feelings is more prevalent in the world. Thus, one can take the help of an image or picture of one's choice in *rūpadhyāna*. However, worship through external images is not a must; it can alternately be practised with a form of your own imagination. But the important fact is that, *rūpadhyāna* is necessary. To practise devotion without absorbing the mind in the form of God, is fruitless effort. The greatest advantage of *rūpadhyāna* upon the divine form, is that the mind becomes easily focused. The reward of this meditational practice will be divine because God is all-pervading and all-knowing. The mind will not only turn away from the world, but will also attain eternal divine benefit.

Some people control the mind by concentrating it upon a point, flame, word or image. There are two drawbacks to this kind of meditation. Firstly, the mind can never concentrate continuously without getting a little taste of Divine Bliss. Secondly, whatever little concentration we achieve will be temporary, as our ignorance and *saṁskāras* of past innumerable lives quickly pull us back into the material world. Therefore, we must focus our mind on God alone so that we can be free from the world forever and attain eternal divine benefit. Besides this, it is extremely difficult to concentrate the mind on a dot or point, whereas it is natural and easy to attach the mind to supremely enchanting Lord Kṛiṣhṇa's all-attractive divine form, attributes, pastimes and so on.

Thus, *rūpadhyāna* is a must in our devotional practice. You should constantly practise *rūpadhyāna* remembering that the form you are visualizing is divine. You should constantly think, "God and the Guru are my All-in-All, and are always with me everywhere as my eternal protectors."

Generally, those who practise meditation, feel the presence of God with them, only while they are engaged in devotional practice, but they totally forget Him thereafter. This kind of devotional practice is not correct, because there is no point in earning ten rupees and losing it within a few minutes. Just as we are always conscious of the 'I', we should become conscious that God is with us, always and everywhere. Now, the question arises which descension of God should we meditate upon?

Most followers of Hinduism are generally followers of one of the two descensions, Lord Rāma and Lord Kṛiṣhṇa. This does not mean that these descensions are superior to the others. The question of greater or lesser is totally wrong. The main reason is that in these descensions there are far more divine pastimes than in other descensions. These pastimes help devotees to easily become attached to God. It is only from the point of view of providing the greatest facility for absorbing the mind in God, that these descensions have been given special importance. In reality, there is no imperfection in any descension. You may have seen sweets made of sugar. On certain festival occasions, sweets in various shapes, such as horses, elephants, dogs, deer and so on, are made especially for children. Being innocent at heart, children always quarrel among themselves. One says, "I want the horse" and the other says, "I want the dog," but their parents know that, whether one eats the horse, the dog or the doll, the sweetness will be the same. The difference lies merely in the external appearance. In the same way, every descension of God possesses infinite qualities and powers. There is no difference in their divinity at all, no matter which descension we love.

Someone might say, "The scriptures have mentioned up to twenty-four prominent descensions. What do I do if I like a twenty-fifth form of God apart from these?" Well, you are free to accept any form that pleases you, because innumerable descensions are manifesting at every moment in innumerable universes. Veda Vyāsa clearly states this in the *Bhāgavatam,*

avatārā hyasaṁkhyeyā hareḥ sattvanidherdvijāḥ

(Bhāg. 1.3.26)

There have been countless descensions. If you desire to worship God in a form that has not been referred to in the scriptures, you are free to do so. God will have to assume the form of your choice. He can effortlessly assume any form. You are completely free to visualize Him in any form or complexion or dress of your choice. He is so merciful that He has not made any strict rules or restrictions that could limit the devotional practice of any individual soul. This is the reason why God has been referred to as *One who has unlimited names and forms,* ***"ananta nāma rūpāya."*** It is our ignorance that binds God, Who has countless powers, within limits. We have been given complete freedom of choice in our devotional practice.

There are no limitations in the choice of a name. No matter where you live or what language you speak, you are free to chant whatever name you like. God has no objection whatsoever. Besides, no name is superior to another. To differentiate between them is an unpardonable spiritual transgression. Observe, Lord Kṛishṇa's playmates used to call him 'Kanhaiyā', Mother Yaśhodā called Kṛishṇa and Balarāma, 'Kanuā' and 'Baluā', or just 'Lālā'. The *Gopīs* went to the extent of calling Him a flirt and thief. Instead of being offended by these insulting names, Lord Kṛishṇa would long to hear them. In Dvārikā, the name 'Raṇachhora' is very popular, which means, 'the coward who runs away from battlefield'. Lord Kṛishṇa had fled to Dvārikā out of fear of His enemy, Jarāsandha, hence His devotees affectionately gave Him the name 'Raṇachhora'. Both the devotees and God derive great pleasure from these names, provided there is an intimate loving relationship. Without love, all the names and forms are virtually of no use. Thus, there should not be any doubt about the different names of God being equal. No name is inferior or superior, nor will one name take us to God more quickly than another. Actually, a devotee does not love the awe-inspiring names, forms or pastimes of the Lord. Arjuna saw the Universal form of Lord Kṛishṇa and requested the Lord to come back to His loving form as a friend. The names that reveal human-like qualities are dear to the devotees, because they reveal how kind and affectionate the Lord is towards His loved ones. Although the illiterate *Gopīs* of Braja rebuked the Lord by calling Him a thief and a flirt, He was overwhelmed by their rebukes. In short, there is no dispute concerning the names of God.

The same rule applies to the divine pastimes of Lord Rāma and Lord Kṛiṣhṇa. Whatever *līlās* of Śhrī Rāma, Śhrī Kṛiṣhṇa and other forms of God are written in the scriptures, are like a drop of water in a boundless ocean. The pastimes of Śhrī Rāma and Śhrī Kṛiṣhṇa have been going on since eternity, and every second, ever-new pastimes are being revealed. It is naive to bind the divine pastimes within limits.

hari ananta hari kathā anantā

(Rāmāyaṇa)

"There are countless descensions and countless pastimes."

rāmāyaṇa śhatakoṭi apārā

(Rāmāyaṇa)

This line too means the same. If someone says that he would like Lord Rāma and Lord Kṛiṣhṇa to perform new pastimes that have never been performed before, he is naive. There is no new pastime which you can imagine, that has not taken place since beginningless time. Nevertheless, you can meditate on whatever pastime you choose. The gist of all this is God can do anything under the control of your love. However, there is no question of His performing any pastime based merely on your imagination but not accompanied by your loving emotions.

God is also the abode of infinite divine qualities, each of which is unlimited. You can focus on any quality you like in your devotion. You are not restricted to choose a specific quality. Each person has different impressions in his mind due to innumerable past lifetimes, hence different devotees are attracted to different qualities. But you should not make any distinction between these various qualities. You can accept those that you are spontaneously attracted to.

In the same way, all the divine abodes are one and the same. You can choose whichever abode you like. In fact God can even meet you in hell, if you so desire! There is no place which is not an abode of God. However, like the form of God, one should always remember that the names, qualities, pastimes and abodes are also divine.

The *Rāmāyaṇa* declares,

prabhu vyāpaka sarvatra samānā
prema te prakaṭa hohiṁ maiṁ jānā

(Rāmāyaṇa)

"The Lord pervades everything equally. If someone desires to see God in a special personal form, He can be omnipresent in that form too." Nevertheless, we have been given the freedom to choose whichever abode we love the most, without harbouring any distinction between different abodes.

In the same way we must remember that all the Saints are equal. We should surrender to that Saint who benefits us, without having ill feelings towards others Saints..

The main point we have to remember is that, God has infinite names, infinite forms, infinite attributes, infinite pastimes, infinite abodes and infinite associates, that are all one. They all reside within each other. So, we can accept any of these and attain our Supreme Goal. Any kind of differentiation between Them is a grave offence, *nāmāparādha*. We can devote ourselves to whatever attracts us in the divine realm but we should take care not to use our intellect unnecessarily in that which does not concern us.

In the world, we often see that worshippers of a certain form of God with a certain name and qualities criticize worshippers of other forms, with other, names, qualities and so on. This is the greatest spiritual transgression, *nāmāparādha* one can commit. The apparent contradiction that appears to be in the writings of Saints, is their own special style of humour and their own specific intention to increase love towards their own worshipable Deity. There is no actual animosity. The scriptures declare,

na hi nindā nindyaṁ ninditum

Whatever so called criticism we find is only to glorify one's own particular style of devotion or particular deity. Once Sūradāsa, a great devotee of Lord Kṛiṣhṇa, said to Tulasīdāsa, a devotee of Lord Rāma, in the unique twisted language of *Rasika* Saints, "Your Beloved Rāma, is a descension who possesses only twelve divine arts, whereas my Lord Kṛiṣhṇa is endowed with sixteen; why then do you worship Lord Rāma?" Tulasīdāsa could have given a right answer, but he also replied in the same style, "Until today, I only knew and loved Rāma as a mere prince, but now that you have told me He is a descension of God who possesses twelve divine arts, my devotion to Him will multiply accordingly." This is the unique language of *Rasika* Saints who are internally one, but outwardly joke with each other sometimes, just as we do with each other in the world.

Our scriptures refer to different kinds of descensions, such as *aṁśhāvatāra, kalāvatāra, āveśhāvatāra, pūrṇāvatāra* and so on. The distinction in these lies only in the manifestation of specific powers necessitated by the specific purpose of the descension. Accordingly, they are classified as partial descensions, *aṁśhāvatāra* and so on. This manifestation of powers can be understood through a simple example. A university professor, teaching his little son the alphabets, has to come down to the child's level of intelligence. However, this does not mean that his ability is restricted to that level. His ability varies differently according to the need. He prattles to his child, speaks to his servant in the servant's native dialect and to his wife in his mother tongue. But when he delivers a lecture in the university, he reveals his full intellectual ability. The difference in the manifestation of powers in the various descensions of God is similar to this.

Taking this into consideration, the descensions of Śhrī Rāma and Śhrī Kṛiṣhṇa become the obvious choice for easiest meditation. Other descensions like Varāhā in which God descended as a Divine Boar, would be difficult to be attracted to because the mind will only be able to conceive of a material pig, which is not a very pleasing subject for meditation!

When we compare the two descensions of Śhrī Rāma and Śhrī Kṛiṣhṇa, we find that the pastimes of Śhrī Kṛiṣhṇa are numerous and far sweeter and intimate. In the beginning, the aspiring devotee will not be able to attain stability in meditation on just a form to absorb his mind. He will have to take the help of the pastimes as well.

The pastimes of Śhrī Kṛiṣhṇa are so irresistibly charming, that a devotee's mind is magnetically attracted to them. So, meditation upon the pastimes becomes easy for him. In the descension of Lord Kṛiṣhṇa we have pastimes of all the five loving sentiments, *śhanta, dāsya, sakhya, vātsalya* and *mādhurya*. The devotee can meditate upon any pastime that pleases him, and can even change them whenever he desires. In this way, devotional practice becomes easy.

The divine pastimes were revealed in their sweetest form during the descension of Śhrī Kṛiṣhṇa, whereas these remained obscured during the descension of Śhrī Rāma. This is the reason why even Saints who were present during the descension of Śhrī Rāma chose to return as *Gopīs* to experience the unique sweetness of Divine Love bestowed in the descension of Śhrī Kṛiṣhṇa.

Therefore, both from the point of view of experiencing the highest and sweetest nectar of Divine Love, and because of the ease provided in the practice of devotion, meditating upon Lord Kṛiṣhṇa is most appropriate. He is an infinitely beautiful and charming Ocean of Nectarine Bliss, the Stealer of the hearts of surrendered souls, the Crest-Jewel of the *Rasikas* and the Darling of Braja.

That Supreme Divine Personality, Śhrī Kṛiṣhṇa, becomes Śhrī Rādhā-Kṛiṣhṇa in Their divine pastimes. The *Upaniṣhad* states,

yeyaṁ rādhā yaśh cha kṛiṣhṇo rasābdhir
dehenaikaḥ krīḍanārthaṁ dvidhā' bhūt

(Rādhātāpanī Upaniṣhad)

"Both Śhrī Rādhā and Śhrī Kṛiṣhṇa are in fact one. But this Divine Personality has assumed two forms for the performance of loving pastimes."

However, since these pastimes are eternal, the forms of Śhrī Rādhā and Śhrī Kṛiṣhṇa are also eternal. Veda Vyāsa declares,

āttmā tu rādhikā tasya

(Veda Vyāsa)

"Śhrī Rādhā is the soul of Śhrī Kṛiṣhṇa." Even the Upaniṣhad refers to Śhrī Rādhā as the *Svāminī*, Divine Mistress of Lord Kṛiṣhṇa.

The *Upaniṣhads* also describe Śhrī Rādhā as "***hareḥ sarveśhvarī,***" the Governor and Controller of Śhrī Kṛiṣhṇa and "***kṛiṣhṇa-prāṇādhidevī,***" the Divine Personality Who rules Śhrī Kṛiṣhṇa's heart.

Therefore, you can choose to meditate on both Śhrī Rādhā and Śhrī Kṛiṣhṇa together, or separately, according to your desire and inclination.

An indispensable part of practical devotion is to set aside a regular time every day to devote yourself to chanting the names, attributes and pastimes of Śhrī Radha Kṛiṣhṇa, along with *rupadhyāna*, shedding tears of intense longing for Them. The rest of the day can be spent in all the essential duties of the world, with the constant awareness that Lord Kṛiṣhṇa is watching your every action. All your actions should be dedicated to Him. In this way your actions will be performed properly, and you will never feel tired. In addition, your practice of constant remembrance will be reinforced by this. Try it. The benefit you receive will speak for itself.

In this way, when you shed tears of longing in the remembrance of Śhrī Kṛiṣhṇa your heart will be purified and according to the divine law, the Guru will then grace you with Divine Love. Thus, you will attain God and will reach your ultimate goal of Supreme Bliss.

Along with our devotional practice, we need to know about and avoid the impediments that block our spiritual progress. These are collectively referred to as '*kusaṅga*[1]', bad association. Once, a blind man was making a rope. After twining a length of fifty feet, he found on rewinding the rope, that only one foot was left. Unknown to him, a buffalo was standing behind

[1] *Kusaṅga* or bad association consists of all the obstacles that impede spiritual progress.

him and was eating the rope as he was twining. Like this, bad association can make us lose more than what we gain through devotional practice. Thus it is essential to thoroughly understand what bad association is and how to cautiously avoid it?

राधे राधे गोविंद गोविंद राधे। राधे राधे गोविंद गोविंद राधे॥

Kusaṅga

There are only two areas in the world. One is divine, *satya* and the other is material, *asatya*. God and His Saints who are beyond *Māyā* alone are *satya*. Association with them through the complete involvement of the mind and intellect is referred to as *'satsaṅga'*, divine association. Anything or anyone else apart from this naturally comes under the three modes of *Māyā - tāmasa, rājasa* and *sattva*. Therefore, association with this area is referred to as *kusaṅga*, material association. In short, whatever leads to the attachment of the mind and intellect to the divine is *satsaṅga*, apart from this, everything else is *kusaṅga* or wrong association.

Kusaṅga is of many kinds. Once a person falls into wrong association, the decision of the intellect changes accordingly. Therefore, the spiritual aspirant is unable to judge with his own intellect that he has fallen into wrong association. Just as a drunkard's intellect is effected according to the quantity of alcohol he has consumed, in the same way, the intellect loses its power of discrimination according to the degree of wrong association.

An alcoholic who was very drunk fell into a ditch. Somebody asked him, "How did you fall in there? Why don't you go home?" Under the influence of alcohol he said, "O brother! I am at home." Is he just putting on an act? No, he is so drunk and his intellect is so overpowered by the effect of the drink that this is what he genuinely feels. He is fully applying his intellect, but his power of reasoning is lost, so what can he do? Similarly, when we are influenced by wrong association, our intellect loses its discriminating power and we cannot actually determine that we have fallen into wrong association.

The second point is that, as long as a person falsely identifies the body as the 'self', he can never easily consider himself to be fallen. Therefore, there is need of a Saint, who repeatedly makes the spiritual aspirant conscious of his mistakes and brings him to a state of awareness. Had this not been so, no individual would have progressed on the spiritual path, because it is the nature of every person to think that he is right. Even the greatest fool does not like to be told that he is a fool. Therefore, the intellect which is influenced by the three *guṇas* and is constantly fluctuating, definitely requires a controller who is beyond these *guṇas*. Only a Saint can act in this way.

The seed of wrong association is always present in the mind of everyone who identifies the 'self' with the body. This seed grows speedily when it comes into contact with external subjects which are influenced by the three *guṇas*. You must have experienced that your mental tendencies constantly change several times a day according to your environment. Sometimes you have the thought, "Who knows when I will have to leave this world. I must practise devotion as soon as possible. Besides, it is not the world that is holding onto me, I am wilfully attaching myself to it and getting trapped in the process." Sometimes you think otherwise, "What's the hurry? I'll think of God sometimes later. There is still plenty of time. I will devote myself later tonight, tomorrow or after a few years" and so on. Sometimes you even think, "Life is short. Who knows what will happen after death? So the best thing to do is eat, drink and be merry. There is no such thing as God. He is just a fabrication of deluded minds." The problem is that you do not actually understand the meaning of the word 'merry'. Unlimited, eternal merriment, Divine Bliss is what the Saint also desires.

All these daily fluctuations in our life are experienced due to the constant change in the *guṇas*. Everyone experiences these changes. Observe how your mental state constantly fluctuates. Suppose at a certain moment your mind is inclined towards the practice of *sādhanā*, but the next minute you are exposed to a *rajoguṇa* or *tamoguṇa* environment. For example, your wife or son embraces you or does something that increases your attachment to them. Your mental state does not take long to change when exposed to such situations. The change is immediate, and you deviate from your devotional practice. All this is due to the great impact of the three *guṇas* within and the material environment outside.

Now think, how can an individual possibly progress spiritually? Firstly, the mind is influenced by the three *guṇas*. Secondly, 99% of the external world provides wrong association, and thirdly his own *saṁskāras* of innumerable past lives of material attachments, create disturbance. Tulasīdāsa has given a realistic picture of this pathetic state of conditioned souls,

graha gṛihīta puni vāta vasa, tā puni bīchhī māra
tāhi piyāiya vāruṇī, kahiya kahā upachāra

(*Rāmāyaṇa*)

A monkey is mischievous by nature. Now imagine if it suffered from hysteria, were stung by a scorpion and made to drink alcohol, what would its condition be? This is exactly the condition of all souls under *Māyā*.

Firstly, each individual has sinned since beginningless time. Secondly, he has evil tendencies owing to past *saṁskāras*. Thirdly, he is in an environment adverse to spirituality. Fourthly, the intellect being under the sway of the three *guṇas*, is in a perpetual state of intoxication. Only God can help the individual in this deplorable condition!

However, there is no need to be discouraged. Constant devotional practice will rectify everything. Even a wild animal like a lion can be disciplined by a trainer's whip. The first thing that a spiritual aspirant must do, is set his intellect right. It is clearly stated in the *Gītā*,

'buddhināśhāt praṇaśhyati',

"The individual soul suffers downfall owing to the perversion of the intellect." When a disciple has surrendered his intellect to God and the Guru, then he should use his intellect only according to the instructions of the Guru. For example, an ignorant villager is properly tutored by his lawyer before a court hearing. Because he retains this knowledge in his mind, he does not falter even when being cross-examined by an intelligent prosecutor. Similarly, one whose intellect is surrendered to the instructions of the Guru, will not falter or fall in the face of the onslaughts of *Māyā*.

Some people might say that this is an extremely simple thing to do. If a devotee were to keep his mind and intellect absorbed in divine thoughts, then he would not be influenced by both internal and external bad association. But, in the initial stage it is not easy to keep the mind continuously absorbed in divine subjects. This only happens gradually through regular devotional practice. Tulasīdāsa has supported this fact,

kahata sugama karanī apāra, jāne soī jehi bani āī

(Rāmāyaṇa)

Kusaṅga is of many kinds. The first is reading of non-spiritual subjects that are adverse to spiritual growth, the second is listening to talks about such subjects, the third is seeing things that distract one from the spiritual path, the fourth is thinking about them and so on. Amongst all these, the worst is thinking. All the others, that is, reading, seeing, hearing and so on, eventually come to the stage of thinking, which accordingly changes the mentality of a person and overpowers his intellect. The disastrous result is that the mind becomes totally inclined towards those adverse subjects. The *Gītā* reveals this truth very clearly, particularly in this verse,

dhyāyato viṣhayān puṁsaḥ sagas teṣhūpajāyate

(Gītā 2.62)

Whenever we constantly think about any object, we become attached to it. However, it must be noted that this thinking process comes later. *Kusaṅga* begins with seeing, reading and hearing about subjects that are adverse to spirituality. So, if you save yourself from the first cause, then freedom from bad association can be achieved very easily. If a fire is not given fuel, how will it grow? If water, in the form of saintly association, is poured on the internal fire of bad association, then this fire will gradually be extinguished. Normally, we are aware of all the dangers of bad association, yet we pretend to be strong enough to combat them. In the very first stage we arrogantly claim. "No wrong association can influence me, I am aware of everything." But it is not wise to challenge the effect of bad association. It is like a foolish doctor who knows that a certain poison is deadly, yet carelessly drinks a little of it. The poison will definitely do its work of killing, irrespective of the fact that the doctor possesses knowledge of its nature.

Therefore, one should not carelessly indulge in even the most ordinary kind of *kusaṅga*. In fact, you should consider it as your greatest enemy and stay as far away from it as you possibly can, until you attain God. Tulasīdāsa states this as follows,

aba maiṁ tohi jānyo saṁsāra
bāndhi na sakai mohi hari ke bala, prakaṭa kapaṭa āgāra
sahita sahāya tahāṁ basu śhaṭha jehi, hṛidaya na nandakumāra

(Tulasīdāsa)

"O world! I have thoroughly understood you now. You can never bind me because Lord Kṛishṇa is my strength. O *Māyā*! You can take all your accomplices and settle in those hearts where Lord Kṛishṇa does not reside." Thus no one has the power to challenge the influence of wrong association before he attains God. Only the Saints who have attained perfection cannot be influenced by any kind of association. A couplet from Rahīma says,

chandana vişha vyāpai nahım, lipaṭe rahalu bhujaṅga

"A Saint is like a sandalwood tree which remains unaffected by the poison of snakes in the form of *kusaṅga*."

There is a special kind of wrong association which does not seem to be bad, but can lead to the same kind of downfall. Reading the various *Vedas, Purāṇas* and scriptural texts independently is also *kusaṅga*. This statement seems shocking, but it needs to be properly understood. All the scriptural texts are written by Saints and are therefore inspired by God. Only a genuine Saint understands the truth of these texts. When you read them on your own, there will be countless doubts and questions in your mind, which cannot be solved without direct experience. If it is possible to understand them at all, that understanding comes only with the help of a Saint. Therefore, we find all these divine texts themselves stating emphatically that their correct understanding can only be attained from the Saints,

tadviddhi praṇipātena paripraśhnena sevayā
upadekṣhyanti te jñānaṁ jñāninas tattvadarśhinaḥ

(Gītā 4.34)

"To learn the truth contained in the scriptures, one must approach a Spiritual Master."

If you desire to read the *Vedas, Purāṇas* and scriptural texts yourself and decide upon the Truth, then first read the advice given by the Saints,

śhruti purāṇa bahu kaheū upāī
chhūṭai na adhika adhika arujhāī

(Rāmāyaṇa)

If you attempt to understand the scriptural truths without guidance from Saints, then instead of freeing yourself from ignorance, you will get more and more confused and entangled. When you attempt to find the answer to one question from the scriptures on your own, you will end up tormented by a thousand other questions. This is because you are unable to grasp the secret of these divine texts. The reason for this has been given by Tulasīdāsa,

muni bahu, mata bahu, pantha purānani,
jahāṁ tahāṁ jhagaro so

(Vinaya Patrikā)

"There have been innumerable paths and means propounded by innumerable sages and Saints since time immemorial. Even the *Purāṇas* contain a lot of apparent controversies and contradictions." Your power of reasoning is material. Hence your interpretation of these texts will also be faulty.

Next, being critical of other people's faults is the worst and most serious form of *kusaṅga*. It has two repercussions. Firstly, it leads to an increase of vanity, which becomes the immediate reason for a devotee's downfall. Secondly, frequent contemplation of others' faults gradually contaminates one's own intellect, and inclines one towards those very faults! As a result, our actions too are affected by these faults. Besides this, the entire world is full of imperfections. How far can we go on thinking about them?

It is acceptable for a wise man to call an ignorant person a fool. But what authority does a fool have to call someone else a fool? If it is your habit to constantly pick on others' faults, then the best thing to do is to continue to find fault, not with others, but with yourself. Your faults are no less than theirs. Once you become aware of your own faults, it will not only put an end to your habit of fault finding, but will also greatly benefit you. Tulasīdāsa states,

jāne te chhījahiṅ kachhu pāpī

"When a person recognizes his own faults, he definitely makes some attempt to get rid of them."

In my opinion, finding faults in others is a positive proof of one's own faults. Take the example of the father, who goes straight to the doctor to get medicine for his son who is seriously ill. He does not stop anywhere on the way, even if anyone tries to talk to him. If someone forcibly stops him, he bluntly says, "I am in a hurry, I will see you some other time", and rushes straight to the doctor. In the same way, the spiritual aspirant should strictly follow the path advised by his Guru in order to get rid of his mental ailments and attain his Supreme Goal. He should be so busy taking his medicine in the form of devotional practice that there is no idle time left to find faults in others. The spiritual aspirant must be extremely vigilant to avoid this dangerous, unwholesome habit of contemplating others' faults.

Arguing or debating with faithless or unqualified people regarding our spiritual path or devotion is also *kusaṅga*. When even the all-capable Saints are unable to grace an ineligible person with proper understanding, then who do you think you are, if you try to do so? Even if your attempt is based on a genuine desire to benefit the other person, it will have the opposite result because of his faithlessness. In addition, his opposition or disbelief will affect and disturb your mind.

According to the scriptures, one who practises devotion and continues to engage in arguments and disputes, commits a grievous sin. Bharata, the brother of Śhrī Rāma makes a statement in this regard,

bhaktyā vivadamāneṣhu mārgam āśhritya paśhyataḥ
tena pāpena yujyeta yasyāryo'numate gataḥ

(Vālmīki Rāmāyaṇa)

"If I had anything to do with Śhrī Rāma's exile, may I be guilty of the grievous sin like getting into arguments and disputes about the path of devotion."

You should neither listen to nor take part in fruitless discussions and arguments. If an undeserving soul does not understand these subjects, it should not surprise or upset you, because there was a time when you yourself did not understand. The supreme good fortune of understanding the spiritual science and becoming inclined towards it, is attained only through the Grace of God and the Saints.

The intimate secrets of the divine realm should not be revealed to an unqualified person. In his present state, he cannot comprehend those incomprehensible subjects as he is devoid of spiritual experience. He will only transgress, losing whatever little faith he has. In addition, his faithlessness will disturb the mind of the person revealing those divine secrets.

Making a big show of one's devotion in order to attract people, is also *kusaṅga*. Often a devotee who has understood or gained a little experience on the spiritual path, goes around telling others about it. The direct result is growth of subtle pride. Due to this pride, his inclination to entertain and influence people becomes stronger and he loses his true wealth of humility. It is also seen that a spiritual aspirant who happens to shed a tear or two of repentance, pretends to be a great devotee before people. Owing to his self-pride, he makes a deliberate false show of being engrossed in the highest state of longing like that of the *Gopīs*. This person suffers in two ways. Firstly, this outward show multiplies his self-pride and secondly, the desire to boast before others deprives him of genuine tears of repentance. Therefore, a *sādhaka* should carefully avoid the dangerous disease of showing off, for worldly appreciation. He should in fact conceal his devotional practice and spiritual experiences from everyone, except his Guru. He should reflect upon the experience himself, but should be careful to acknowledge it as being a result of his Guru's Grace, and not his own doing.

Self-pride is the greatest impediment in devotion. One should not become a victim to pride in one's spiritual progress, by comparing oneself with an ignorant disbeliever. There are innumerable examples of those who were disbelievers one day, but suddenly turned into such great devotees overnight, that they went far ahead of those practising spiritual discipline for years! All this specially happens due to *saṁskāras* of past lives. What do we know about anyone's *saṁskāras.* Thus, we should not look upon anyone with contempt, keeping in mind the fact that God graces everyone directly or indirectly. However, we must associate only with those whose company intensifies our devotion.

If a spiritual aspirant is unable to understand the divine secrets of higher states of devotion, he should not make an unauthorised attempt to understand them. These states are comprehended only through experience, not merely by reading or hearing about them. Tulasīdāsa has clearly stated,

khaga jāne khaga hī kī bhāṣhā

(Rāmāyaṇa)

Only a Saint can understand the language of another Saint.

bhagavad-rasika rasika kī bāteṁ
rasika binā kou samujhi sakai nā

A Saint of Vṛindāvaṇa, Bhagavat Rasika, says that the language of a *Rasika* Saint can only be understood by another *Rasika* Saint. Everywhere in the scriptures, there are references to qualifications even for the mere reading of the texts. The *Rāmāyaṇa*, mentions the qualities of the person who is eligible to read it,

je śhraddhā sambala rahita, nahiṁ santana kara sātha
tina kahaṁ mānasa agama ati, jinahiṁ na priya raghunātha

(Rāmāyaṇa)

"A person, who has neither complete faith, nor the association of Saints, nor love for Lord Rāma, is not qualified to study the *Rāmāyaṇa*. Such a person cannot understand the *Rāmāyaṇa*." This criteria of eligibility is extremely important. Later, the *Rāmāyaṇa* forbids even the relating of this scripture to such undeserving people. For example, the government permits only certain people to own revolvers. If a revolver were given to a thief or a madman, it could result in great harm. Listen to the condition of eligibility specified in the *Gītā*, in this context,

idaṁ te nātapaskāya nābhaktāya kadāchana

(*Gītā 18.67*)

"The *Gītā* should not be related to anyone who is not a devotee." The *Bhāgavatam* mentions the following condition,

muhuraho rasikā bhuvi bhāvukāḥ
pibata bhāgavataṁ rasamālayam

(*Bhāgavat Māhātmya 6-80*)

"Only the *Rasika* devotees should drink the nectar contained in the *Bhāgavatam*." It is a universal principle that those who are unqualified, cannot through their own efforts, attain understanding or experience of anything beyond their level of eligibility.

To listen to, or read about any path apart from the one taught by one's Guru, is also *kusaṅga*, even though that path is being propagated by another Saint. There is a reason behind this. When a seeker hears of different paths, he will wander from one to another, and not make any tangible progress.

ito bhraṣhṭostato bhraṣhṭaḥ

Suppose for instance, you are following the path of devotion and you listen to a Saint recommending the path of *jñāna*. You will be confused. "Well, this Saint seems to be saying something totally different from what I have been told." Your limited intellect is not capable of grasping the actual truth. Besides differences in paths, there are also different methods of practice in one's own path, depending upon the faith and tendency of a spiritual aspirant. You hear about another's devotional practice and wonder, "That method seems to be better than mine. Perhaps, I will be able to attain my goal faster through that method." On the other hand, if you happen to bear ill-feelings towards another aspirant's devotional practice, the result is worse, because it will be considered a spiritual offence. Hence, one should constantly think, meditate upon and follow only the method of devotion which has been advised by one's own Guru, without any adverse feelings towards the other paths. You should not be critical even of the aspirants who are practising devotion under the guidance of your own Guru, but with different methods than yours. You should understand that all kinds of devotional practices are correct. Everyone follows the method which is suitable for his progress. What do we have to do with all this?

Insulting a Saint or even a *sādhaka* is also very serious *kusaṅga*. Most often, aspirants consider only their Guru and themselves as genuine. They bear ill-feeling towards other Saints and spiritual seekers. This is one of the greatest offences a person can commit. This offence will lead to your earning the displeasure of both your Guru and God. Remember, all the Saints and forms of God are one. If you happen to feel that your devotion is progressing better in the association of another Saint, then you should definitely follow him. But one should be very careful here. If you happen to bear a grudge against the previous Saint you were in contact with, then it will be a case of earning a penny and losing a pound!

All the names, attributes, abodes and associates of God, are identical. To bear any ill-feelings towards even one, amounts to ill-feeling towards all. All the associates and descensions of God are one. This truth should always be firmly fixed in your mind. It is generally observed that people fall into sectarianism, and condemn each other's worship. For example, worshippers of Lord Rāma criticize the worshippers of Lord Kṛiṣhṇa, *vaiṣhṇavas* criticize *śhaivites* and so on. This is also a very grave spiritual transgression. You must only concern yourself with the form, names, qualities, pastimes and abodes of the descension for which you have faith and love. At the same time, accept all others as manifestations of the same one God, so that there are no ill-feelings.

There is something important that needs to be understood here. Let us take for example, Lord Rāma and Lord Kṛiṣhṇa. They are both complete descensions and are in fact one personality,

asmatprasādasumukhaḥ kalayā kaleśha

(Bhāg. 2.7.23)

kleśhavyayāya kalayā sitakṛiṣhṇakeśhaḥ

(Bhāg. 2.7.26)

It is stated that Lord Rāma is the abode of all virtues and He manifested them fully in His descension. In the same way, Lord Kṛiṣhṇa is also stated to be a perfect descension endowed with all divine virtues.

Some people quote the *Bhāgavatam*,

kṛiṣhṇastu bhagavān svayam

They say that this verse clearly establishes Śhrī Kṛiṣhṇa alone as a complete descension and all other descensions as partial manifestations. They probably have not read of the glories of Lord Rāma described in the very same *Bhāgavatam*! In addition, just as the *Bhāgavatam* glorifies Śhrī Kṛiṣhṇa, the *Rāmāyaṇa* too states,

rāmastu bhagavān svayaṁ

"Lord Rāma is the Supreme Personality."

The *Brahmavaivarta Purāṇa* states,

tvaṁ sītā mithilāyāṁ cha tvachchhāyā draupadī satī
rāvaṇena hṛitā tvaṁ cha tvaṁ cha rāmasya kāminī

"O Rādhā! You were Sītā at Janakapurī, and Draupadi, Satī, etc. are Your expansions. It was You whom Rāvaṇa kidnapped, and You were the Consort of Lord Rāma." The *Padma Purāṇa* states,

purā maharṣhayaḥ sarve daṇḍakāraṇyavāsinaḥ
te sarve strītvam āpannāḥ samudbhūtāśhcha gokule

(*Padma Purāṇa*)

It was Śhrī Rāma, who granted a boon to the sages in the Daṇḍaka forest saying that He would come as Śhrī Kṛiṣhṇa to bless them with the nectar of Divine Love. These very sages descended as *Gopīs* in Gokula during the descension of Lord Kṛiṣhṇa.

Many people relate the story of Tulasīdāsa, a great devotee of Śhrī Rāma who visited Vṛindāvana and saw Śhrī Kṛiṣhṇa in person. He told Śhrī Kṛiṣhṇa to take up a bow and arrow in place of His flute or else he would not bow to Him.

kahā kahouṁ chhavi āja kī, bhale bane ho nātha
tulasī mastaka taba nave, dhanuṣha bāṇa lo hātha

(Tulasīdāsa)

Using this example, they argue that if Tulasīdāsa refused to bow to Śhrī Kṛiṣhṇa, it implies that Śhrī Rāma and Śhrī Kṛiṣhṇa must be different Personalities. But the secret behind this needs to be understood. First of all, Tulasīdāsa addressed Śhrī Kṛiṣhṇa as his Master, *Nātha* and then requested Him to take the bow and arrow in his hands i.e. appear in the form of Śhrī Rāma. What efforts does the Supreme Personality need to appear in the form of Śhrī Rāma or Śhrī Kṛiṣhṇa? The only difference between the two forms is that Śhrī Rāma holds the bow and arrow, the emblem of maintaining law and order while, Śhrī Kṛiṣhṇa holds the flute, the emblem of Divine Love. Further, if Tulasīdāsa requested Śhrī Kṛiṣhṇa to appear as Śhrī Rāma, Who he considered the Supreme Personality and complete manifestation of God, Śhrī Kṛiṣhṇa must also be the same

Personality. After all, Who else could become Śhrī Rāma? Therefore, the apparent difference in Śhrī Rāma and Śhrī Kṛiṣhṇa is only in Their pastimes. My understanding of what Tulasīdāsa meant is, "I worship you with the feelings of servitude, not amorous love. Vṛindāvana is reserved for those devotees who love You intimately as their Beloved. A devotee with the feelings of servitude, such as myself has no place here. Therefore, please respect my position and appear before me as my Master, holding a bow and arrow." Besides, who else, but Śhrī Rāma could fulfil the desire of someone like Tulasīdāsa? And why would he beg from anyone other than his own Beloved Lord? By this prayer, Tulasīdāsa actually proved that Śhrī Kṛiṣhṇa was his own Beloved Lord, Who fulfilled his desire. This is obvious from the following verses in the *Vinaya Patrikā,* verse 199.

virada gariba nivāja rāma ko
dhruva, prahlāda, vibhīṣhaṇa, kapipuli, jaṛa,
pataṅga, pāṇḍava, sudāma ko

Here, Tulasīdāsa gives Śhrī Rāma the credit of delivering the Yamala and Arjuna trees, protecting the Pāṇḍavas, and honouring Sudāmā. All of these are actually Śhrī Kṛiṣhṇa's pastimes. Similarly, he says, Rāma purified Kubjā, when in fact, she only appeared in Śhrī Kṛiṣhṇa's descension.

pāṇḍu suta, gopikā, vidura, kubarī, sabīra,
suddha kiye suddhatā lesa kaiso
aisī kauna prabhu kī rīti,
gayī mārana pūtanā kucha kālakūṭa lagāya

Why is he crediting Śhrī Rāma with the deliverence of Putanā in this verse, which is something actually done by Śhrī Kṛiṣhṇa? In addition, read verses 83, 178, 217, 240 and so on. Therefore, it is clear that Tulasīdāsa considers Śhrī Rāma and Śhrī Kṛiṣhṇa to be one and the same Divine Personality.

In the *Garga Saṁhitā,* Lord Rāma Himself declares,

dvāparānte kariṣhyāmi bhavatīnāṁ manoratham

(Garga Saṁhitā)

"I will descend as Lord Kṛiṣhṇa in the age of *Dvāpara* to fulfil your desires." The scriptures state that the complete descension of God has four manifestations who came in Śhrī Rāma's descension as Śhrī Rāma, Bharata, Lakṣhmaṇa, and Śhatrughna. In Śhrī Kṛiṣhṇa's descension they came as Śhrī Kṛiṣhṇa, Balarāma, Pradyumna and Aniruddha. This is clearly stated in the scriptures.

It is a grave offence to think that a Saint of the stature of Tulasīdāsa, distinguised between Lord Rāma and Lord Kṛiṣhṇa.

Even an ordinary scholar understands this philosophical truth about the oneness of the various forms of God. Therefore, all descensions should be regarded as one, but devotion should be for that descension whose pastimes you find most appealing.

There are some who worship Lord Rāma, but later feel more attracted to the divine pastimes of Lord Kṛiṣhṇa, and desire to worship Lord Kṛiṣhṇa instead. However, they fear that it would be a sin to change their deity. It is unfortunate that such people do not even understand the simple fact that for a woman to see her husband dressed in different styles, is neither a sin, nor is it adultery. Who can be a greater devotee of Lord Rāma than Lord Śhaṅkara? The scriptures state that he came to have a glimpse of the divine child, Kṛiṣhṇa, the moment He was born. He also took part in the *Mahārāsa* dance of Śhrī Kṛiṣhṇa. Not only that, all the associates of Lord Rāma came again in the descension of Lord Kṛiṣhṇa. For example, the three brothers of Lord Rāma, Lakṣhmaṇa, Bharata and Śhatrughna, appeared as, Balarāma, Pradyumna and Aniruddha respectively; Devī Sītā appeared as Śhrī Rādhā; Hanumāna Jī was present on the flag of Arjuna's chariot; Jāmavanta personally fought Śhrī Kṛiṣhṇa; Śhūrpanakhā came as Kubjā; the women of Janakapurī came as the *Gopīs*; Rāvaṇa came as Śhiśhupāla and so on. However, one point is certain and that is, the sweetness of the loving divine pastimes of Śhrī Kṛiṣhṇa is far superior to that of Śhrī Rāma. That is why the Saints during the descension of Lord Rāma begged Him to bless them with this special Bliss. So philosophically speaking, the pastimes of Śhrī Kṛiṣhṇa are the pastimes of Śhrī Rāma in a different form.

Nevertheless, the spiritual aspirant is free to choose the pastimes of Śhrī Rāma in *Tretā Yuga* or the pastimes of Śhrī Kṛiṣhṇa in *Dvāpara Yuga* for his devotional practice. The dilemma of 'changing one's deity' will automatically be resolved as one practises devotion. However, if one wants to experience the highest Bliss of Divine Love, one will have to take recourse to the remembrance of the captivating pastimes of Śhrī Kṛiṣhṇa.

The conclusion is that one should be extremely cautious about avoiding all kinds of *kusaṅga*. Factually, anything which hinders one's remembrance of God, is *kusaṅga*. However, one has to avoid ill-feelings even towards an atheist. Externally, the words of great Saints and atheists can sound very similar. The greatest *Rasika* Saints, the *Gopīs,* in their state of separation from Śhrī Kṛiṣhṇa, say that they do not want to even hear the name of that cruel one. Similarly, an atheist also says that he doesn't want to hear the name of God. Externally, the words are the same, but there is a vast difference in their feelings. The language of *Rasika* Saints is often very misleading. Therefore, one has no authority to dismiss someone as an atheist merely on the basis of his words. And, even if one does have the authority, what is the benefit of criticizing someone? Rather, there is only harm. Even a moment's *kusaṅga* is powerful enough to bring about an aspirant's spiritual downfall. He can only be permanently saved from the effect of *kusaṅga* when God personally takes full responsibility for his well-being, which happens only at the stage of complete surrender.

I believe the greatest enemy that keeps a seeker away from God is *kusaṅga*. Otherwise, how could it be that he is still bound by *Māyā,* inspite of meeting innumerable descensions of God and countless Saints? Therefore, the effort to avoid all forms of *kusaṅga* is even more important than the practice of devotion. In the words of Saint Tulasīdāsa,

baru bhala vāsa naraka kara tātā
duṣhṭa saṅga jani dei vidhātā

(Rāmāyaṇa)

"O Lord! you may send me to hell if you like, but never give me the association of a person averse to You."

To conclude, the ultimate goal of the individual soul and the path to its attainment have been briefly explained here. The truth is that until we practise spiritual discipline under the guidance of a genuine Guru, it is impossible to attain that Supreme Goal! A genuine Guru is one who has attained Divine Love and has complete mastery over the scriptures. Nevertheless, till you are fortunate enough to meet such a Guru, this book of divine philosophy will definitely be beneficial in guiding you on your path to God. Once you meet a true Master, everything will fall into place.

राधे राधे गोविंद गोविंद राधे। राधे राधे गोविंद गोविंद राधे॥

Glossary

Advaita	Non-Dualism, Monism
Ajñāna	Ignorance
Ānanda	Bliss
Aṇimā	One of the eight yogic supernatural powers (*siddhis* of *yoga*) by which one can become as small as an atom
Aṁśhāvatāra	Partially empowered descension of God who appears for a particular purpose
Artha	Worldly prosperity
Ārya	A civilized follower of Vedic culture; one whose goal is spiritual advancement
Ātmā	Individual soul
Banamālā	The divine flower garland worn by the Supreme God Kṛishṇa and Vishṇu only. It falls to the knee and has five kinds of flowers: *tulasī, kunda, mandāra* (native plant and flower of Braja), lotus and *parijata* (a celestial flower)
Bhagavān	God
Bhakti	The path of intense love for a Personal Form of God, leading to the attainment of *Prema* or Divine Love
Bhāva(s)	Loving sentiments related to specific relationships
Bhūta	Evil spirit or ghost
Bhukti	Material enjoyments
Brahman	Impersonal Aspect of God
Brahmabhūta	Established in identity with *Brahman*
Brahmacharya (chāri)	Celibate student
Brahmānanda	Infinite Bliss of formless *Brahman* which is experienced as an ocean of absolute serenity by a *jñānī* Saint

Brahmāṇḍa	A single universe governed by a Brahmā, Viṣhṇu and a Śhaṅkara and consisting of fourteen planetary systems
Braja	The holy land where Śhrī Kṛiṣhṇa performed his most intimate pastimes
Chātaka	The name of a bird which lives only on those rain-drops that shower when the constellation *Svāti* is in the ascendant
Dvāpara Yuga	The third of the four cyclical ages of cosmic time consisting of 864,000 years
Garimā	One of the eight yogic supernatural powers by which one can make oneself extremely heavy at will
Gopī (s)	The maidens of Braja exalted in the scriptures for their selfless amorous love for Śhrī Kṛiṣhṇa
Guṇas (s)	The three constituent modes of *Māyā* consisting of *sattva* (mode of goodness), *rājasa* (mode of passion) and *tāmasa* (mode of ignorance)
Guṇāvatāra	Those manifestations of God in the material world, who govern the universe and preside over the three *guṇas*
Guru	The Spiritual Master
Hlādinī Śhakti	The most intimate power of God which imparts Bliss to both God and the devotee and the essence of which is *Prema* or Divine Love
Jagata	Universe, world
Jagadīśha	Lord of the universe
Jñānayoga	When practice of *jñāna* is accompanied by devotion to a Personal God
Jīvanmukta	One who has attained realization of the self but is not completely liberated from the bondage from *Māyā*. He is only liberated from *avidyāmāyā* i.e the modes of *tamoguṇa* or *rajoguṇa*. But the bondage *vidyāmāyā* i.e *sattvaguṇa* remains
Jñāna	The path of attainment of Impersonal *Brahman*. The person who follows this path is called a *jñānī*
Kājala	Collyrium

Kāla	Time
Kali Yuga	The last of the four ages of progressive decline which the world goes through in each consisting of 432,000 of which roughly 5000 years have passed
Kāma	Sensuous gratification
Karma	Also known as *dharma* refers to the strict performance of duties as prescribed in the *Vedas* according to one's caste or stages in life. A person who follows this path is called *karmī*
Karma Yoga	The practice of keeping the mind absorbed in God while engaging in duties prescribed by the scriptures
Kaustubha	A ruby like large divine jewel with marvellous facets which is worn by the Supreme God (Śhrī Kṛiṣhṇa, Rāma and Viṣhṇu) in His necklace
Kunda	A kind of flower, like jasmine
Kriyamāṇa Karma	Actions that are being newly performed and added to the store of actions (*sañchita karma*)
Kuṇḍa	Pond, pool
Lughimā	One of the eight yogic perfections of assuming excessive lightness at will.
Līlā	Divine pastimes of God and His eternal associates, performed solely for the purpose of gracing humanity.
Mahābhāva	The highest stage of *Gopī-prema*
Manana	Contemplation
Mandāra	Native plant of flower of Braja
Mantra	The evocative sentence, verse, or stanza related to: (a) The propitiation of the celestial gods to be used in the fire ceremonies (*yagña*), or (b) for general prayer to Supreme God
Māyā	The external inert power of God. It consists of three *guṇas* or modes
Māyāvāda	Doctrine of illusion
Māyika	That which is related to *Māyā*
Mokṣha / Mukti	Liberation from *Māyā* or material bondage

Mūrti	Deity, duly consecrated form of God (of stone, brass, etc.) meant to assist devotees in worship and remembrance
Nāmāparādha	These are the most serious spiritual transgressions, which are the greatest impediments in one's devotional practice such as offences against God, the Saints, the scriptures and the divine names
Nātha	Lord, Master
Nididhyāsana	Profound and repeated meditation
Nirguṇa Nirākāra	The formless and nonperceivable existence of Absolute
Brahman	Divinity
Nirvikalpa Samādhi	*Nirvikalpa* means a total thoughtless state of mind, and *Samādhi* means to be fully absorbed in the *sāttvika* state of the mind or in the Divine state. Thus, this term is used for both, a *jñānī* or a *yogī* Saint
Nitya Siddha	A Saint who is a Saint from eternity (an eternal associate of God)
Pañchakoṣha	Five sheaths or vestures of *Māyā* which enshrines the soul - *annamaya koṣha* , *prāṇamaya koṣha* , *manomaya koṣha*, *vijñānamaya koṣha* and *ānandmaya koṣha*
Para Dharma	This is superior *dharma* or duty of every soul, also called *Bhāgavat dharma,* which brings God realization. This is direct devotion to God in His Personal Form. It is called *Bhakti.* It differs from *apara dharma* or lower duties which are based upon the body
Parama Puruṣha	The Supreme Lord
Paramātmā	The Supersoul; the localized aspect of the Supreme Lord; the indwelling witness and guide who accompanies every conditioned soul.
Paramahaṁsa	A person who has attained the final stage of *jñāna* or *yoga* and is completely absorbed in the Bliss of the Impersonal *Brahman*.
Pārasa	Touchstone. A very rare and presently nonexistent gem that could convert ferrum into pure gold simply by touching

Pārijāta	A celestial flower (tree) of god Indra's garden having yellowish pure white flowers with very special fragrance
Prakṛiti	Original material energy
Pralaya	Dissolution
Prānāyāma	Breathing exercises as a means of advancement in *yoga*.
Prapatti	This term was used by Jagadguru Rāmānujāchārya to express the feelings of a devotee who very humbly surrenders his heart, mind and soul at the lotus feet of his loving God and earnestly desires for His divine vision
Prārabdha	The fate or luck of a person in the present life decided by those actions of psst lives which have already begun to bear fruits
Prema	Pure spontaneous devotional love for God
Puruṣha	'The enjoyer;' the individual soul or the Sureme Lord
Puṣhṭi	The path of devotion to Śhrī Kṛiṣhṇa as described by Vallabhāchārya, where a devotee, depending upon the Grace of Śhrī Kṛiṣhṇa, humbly surrenders and dedicates his whole being for the service of Śhrī Kṛiṣhṇa and Śhrī Kṛiṣhṇa takes his full responsibility
Rājasa	mode of passion; (adj. rajasika)
Rajoguṇa	It is one of the qualities of *Māyā* (normal or selfish or a mixture of good and bad qualities)
Rasika (s)	The highest of Saints who are ever absorbed in drinking the nectar of the most intimate loving pastimes of Śhrī Rādhā Kṛiṣhṇa
Ṛiṣhi (s)	A saint, an ascetic
Rūpadhyāna	Practice of absorbing the mind in the remembrance of the form of God usually accompanied by chanting of His names, qualities, divine pastimes and so on.
Sachchidānanda	Existence, Knowledge and Bliss - the three attributes of God; the Supreme God qualified by these attributes
Sādhaka	Spiritual aspirant
Sādhanā	Prescribed spiritual discipline

Samādhi	Complete absorption of mind into the object of meditation, i.e the Supreme Spirit (the eighth and last stage of *yoga*)
Sañchita karma	Accumulated actions of the past which have yet to bear the fruit
Saṅkīrtana	Congregational chanting of the names, qualities and so on, of God
Saṁnyāsa	The renounced order of life for the service of God and God realization. The one who takes this order is called *saṁnyāsī*
Saṁskāras	Inclinations or tendencies in the present life caused by one's actions in past lives
Sarvajña	All knowing, omnipresent
Satya Yuga	The first of the four cyclical ages of cosmic time comprising of 1,728,000 years
Seva	Service consisting of complete submission of one's body mind and words in pleasing the Supreme Lord
Sharat Pūrṇima	It is an extremely auspicious day for the devotees of Lord Kriṣhṇa because five thousand years ago, it was on this full moon night, that their Beloved Lord *Kṛiṣhṇa* had revealed the glory of selfless Divine Love to the world by performing the divine dance, *Mahārāsa*, with the *Gopīs*
Suṣhupti	Profound sleep
Swāminī	The Supreme Goddess, Queen of Vṛindāvana - Śhrī Rādhā
Svarga	There are seven celestial or heavenly regions that are attained by the performance of virtuous deeds as prescribed in the *Vedas*. All these abodes are within the *māyika* realm
Svāti	The star Arcturus, considered as forming the fifteenth lunar asterism
Tāmasa	Mode of ignorance; (adj. *tāmasika*)
Tamoguṇa	It is one of the qualities of *Māyā* - evil quality
Tretā Yuga	The second of the four cyclical ages of cosmic time comprising of 1,296,000 years

Vaishṇava	The selfless worshipper of Bhagavān Vishṇu, Rāma or Kṛishṇa
Vānaprastha	A man who has retired from householder life to cultivate greater renunciation, according to the Vedic social system
Varṇa	The prescribed religious practices (according to the *Vedas* and scriptures) for the purification of the mind for the people of the four orders of life and for the four caste systems of the society. The four orders of life are: religious student, family man, partly renounced man and fully renounced man respectively, called *brahmachārya, gṛihastha, vāṇaprastha* and *saṁnyāsa*.
Yajña	Sacrifice
Yoga	Spiritual discipline as formulated by Patañjali and based on the *Saṁkhya* system of philosophy to link oneself with the Supreme
Yogamāya	The divine personal power of God by which He and His associates can do anything and everything
Yuga	An age as described in the *Vedas*

Jagadguru Shri Kripalu Ji Maharaj

Jagadguru Shri Kripalu Ji Maharaj is the only Saint of this age who has been honoured with the title of 'Jagadguru' the highest authority among all Hindu Vedic Saints and scholars. This title is given only to that Saint who brings about a spiritual revolution in the world through his divine teachings. Jagadguru Shri Kripalu Ji Maharaj is the supreme exponent of Sanatan Dharm, the eternal Vedic religion, and his reconciliation of all the philosophies and faiths is unparalleled.

He was born in 1922 on the auspicious night of Sharat Purnima into a highly respectable Brahmin family in Mangarh, a village of district Pratapgarh in the State of Uttar Pradesh, India.

He completed his early education in Mangarh and Kunda. Later he studied Sanskrit grammar, literature and Ayurveda at Indore, Chitrakoot and Varanasi.

At the tender age of sixteen, he retreated to the dense forests near the Sharbhang ashram in Chitrakoot and then to the forests near Vanshivat in Vrindavan. During that period he was deeply engrossed in the divine love of Shri Krishna and whosoever saw him in that state of trance, was astonished and felt that he was an embodiment of love and bliss. Nobody at that time could have thought that he had unfathomable and immeasurably vast ocean of *jnan* (knowledge and wisdom) hidden within him. Immersed completely in the ecstatic bliss of love he forgot to pay attention to his physical state and the world around him and remained unconscious for hours on end. He would sometimes burst into unrestrained laughter and sometimes break into a roaring cry. Unmindful, he would go without food and water for days. Tears flowed from his eyes unchecked. While he was wandering around in this state of trance, sometimes his clothes got caught up in thorny bushes; sometimes he would trip over a rock and fall. Gradually, he concealed this bliss of divine love and started propagating the *bhakti* of Shri Krishna. Soon, along with his inspiring messages of divine love, he started revealing his divine wisdom and knowledge of the scriptures to the people.

In the year 1955 he organized a huge conference at Chitrakoot, which was attended by all Jagadgurus and many eminent scholars from Kashi and various other places of India. Another religious conference of similar scale was organized by him in 1956 at Kanpur. The most learned scholars of Kashi attending that conference were amazed by his scriptural omniscience. On that occasion the eminent scholar of Kashi, a leading luminary in the field of scriptural debate, the universally recognized and the foremost philosopher of India and *Pradhanmantri* (General Secretary) of Kashi Vidvat Parishat, Acharya Shri Rajnarayan Ji Shukla *'Shatshastri'* made a public proclamation at Kanpur on 19.10.1956, part of which is quoted in the following lines:-

"The scholars of Kashi do not easily accept a person as a scholar having knowledge of all the scriptures. As a first step we challenge the claimant to have a debate on the scriptures. We evaluate him by testing his knowledge in all possible ways and only after he is found to have met our standards, we accept him as one who is well-versed in the shastras. Today we from this forum want to inform this huge congregation of eminent scholars that we have recognized the leading Saint Shri Kripalu Ji Maharaj and his God-given genius. We advise you too to recognize him and take advantage of his knowledge.

It is a great privilege for all of you that a Saint is in your midst who can present before you the entire gamut of divine literature. Kashi is the Gurukul of the whole world. We the residents of Kashi are present here. Yesterday when we heard the brilliant speech made by Shri Kripalu Ji, we had to bow our heads in respect. We want that people in general too should recognize Shri Kripalu Ji Maharaj and listen to his easy to understand, delightful, self-experienced and extraordinary teachings and follow them in their lives practically and derive benefits from them."

Thereafter, the Kashi Vidvat Parishat (a body of 500 top-ranking scriptural scholars) invited him to visit Kashi. Some emotionally charged devotees were intrigued to find a thirty four year-old youth amongst the elderly scholars and articulated their feeling in the following words:

udita udaya giri mañcha para raghuvara bala pataṅga

- *As the rising sun shines so did Ram in the assembly of great kings.*

The extra-ordinary discourses delivered in classical Sanskrit by Shri Maharaj Ji and his out of this world personality soaked in the bliss of divine love left the learned gathering completely spellbound. They unanimously admitted that he was not only a great scholar of the *Vedas* and all other scriptures, but also an embodiment of divine love. They then unanimously honoured him with the title of *'Jagadguru'*. They also declared that Shri Maharaj Ji is *'Jagadguruttam,'* supreme amongst all Jagadgurus.

...dhanyo mānya jagadgurūttama padaiḥ so'yaṁ samabhyarchyate

This historic event happened on January 14, 1957. At that time Shri Maharaj Ji was all of 34 years. It is worth knowing that Shri Maharaj Ji is more than just a successor to the earlier Jagadgurus. Kashi Vidvat Parishat honoured him with the title of the fifth "original Jagadguru" of the world. Prior to him only four Saints were honoured with the original title of Jagadguru. They are Jagadguru Shri Shankaracharya, Jagadguru Shri Ramanujacharya, Jagadguru Shri Nimbarkacharya and Jagadguru Shri Madhvacharya.

Thus in the present times Jagadguru Swami Shri Kripalu Ji Maharaj is the fifth Jagadguru in the world's history. He

॥ श्रीविश्वनाथो विजयते ॥

श्रीमतां यमनियमाद्यखिलयोगाङ्गानुष्ठाननिष्ठानां, भक्तियोगवशीभूतभग-
वद्भावानां, धार्मिकभूमण्डलमण्डनायमानानां, विविधविद्याम्भो-
निधीनां, जगदुद्धारमहाध्वरप्रवर्त्तकानां वास्तवधर्माचार्याणाम्

श्री १००८ स्वामिकृपालुमहाराजानां

समर्हणायां श्रद्धोपनिबद्धः

पद्यप्रसूनोपहारः

यद्भूषणत्वमहनीयपदोपलब्धि-
प्रादुर्भवत्पदविवेचनचातुरीकः ।
शेषाहिरापमहिमानमशेषमान्यं
विश्वेश्वरो विजयतां स दयापयोधिः ॥ १ ॥

वैराग्यार्कमरीचिशोषितजगद्व्यामोहपङ्कः क्षितौ,
नूत्नःकोऽपि सविग्रहःकृतधियामानन्दपुञ्जोदयः
स्वामिश्रीलकृपालुनाममहितः सद्भक्तिपुष्पावली-
प्रोल्लासाय वसन्ततामुपगतःख्यातःसमुद्योतते ॥ २ ॥

यद्व्याख्याननवीनमेघपटलध्वानेन चित्ताटवी
नास्तिक्योपहतात्मनामपि मुदा सूते विवेकाङ्कुरम् ।
स्फूर्जत्तर्कविचारमन्त्रनिवहव्याक्षिप्तदुर्भावना-
भूतावेशविषविषरं विजयतामेकोऽयमीड्यो नृणाम् ॥ ३ ॥

नानावर्णनसंविमर्शनकलाकौतूहलैः कोविदान्
धिन्वन् व्याकुलितान् नरान् नयपथं प्रीत्या मुहुः प्रापयन् ।
तृष्णार्त्तान् भगवत्कथाऽमृतरसैः सिञ्चन्नसौ धीमतां
वाक्पुष्पाञ्जलिपूजितोऽमितगुणाम्भोधिः समुज्जृम्भते ॥ ४ ॥

येनाऽस्मिन्निखिलेऽपि भारतमहादेशे विशेषोल्लस-
त्प्रज्ञेनोज्ज्वलभक्तियोगकलितं संस्थापितं मण्डलम् ।
धर्मोद्धारधुरीणभावमनिशं कीर्त्या समं वर्द्धयन्
धन्यो मान्य जगद्गुरूत्तमपदैः सोऽयं समभ्यर्च्यते ॥ ५ ॥

तदीये लोकानामुपकृतिकरेऽस्मिन्नुपगमे
पुरे शम्भोरुयत्कतिपयपदाम्भोरुहभरैः ।
श्रुतिस्मृत्युक्तार्थप्रवचनगुरोः संयमिमणेः
कृपालोस्तस्यैषा विलसतु सपर्या बुधगणे ॥ ६ ॥

काशीस्थपण्डितश्रेणी प्रशस्या कुसुमार्चनात् ।
कृपालुस्वामियोगीन्द्रस्वागतं शुभमेधताम् ॥ ७ ॥

मकरसङ्क्रान्तिः
२०१३ वि.

राजनारायणशुक्लः
न्यायाचार्यः (मन्त्री)

नारायणशास्त्री खिस्ते
महामहोपाध्यायः
साहित्यवाचस्पतिः
(अध्यक्षः)

भवदीयोदयैषिणीः—
काशीविद्वत्परिषत्

Certificate awarded to Jagadguru Shri Kripalu Ji Maharaj by Kashi Vidvat Parishat, Varanasi on 14th January 1957.

propounds the philosophy of reconciliation while he has proved the philosophical doctrines of all the four previous Jagadgurus to be true. Shri Kripalu Ji Maharaj is of the view that there are many paths that lead us to God realization and yet the path of *bhakti* is the best and easily accessible to all.

Shri Maharaj Ji makes no distinction of caste, creed, colour, or race. With his infinite love and compassion he gathers all into the purity of his divine embrace and his divine effulgence shines through all he says, all he does and all he is. Every seeker is amazed to see how approachable he is, and enjoys the special privilege of individual attention from him. Thus, he makes each one feel that they belong to him. His tall, stately regal yet childlike personality have an indefinable attraction that draws all to him, whether young or old, men or women or of any country or language. The all-satisfying love that emanates from him, makes each one feel the affection of a parent, friend and teacher, all in one. It is very easy to become a recipient, because there is no giver like Shri Maharaj Ji. True to His name 'Kripalu', He is the very 'Ocean of Grace.'